Upon This Rock

White Rock Baptist Church's Dynamic People
and Their Influence in the Durham, North
Carolina, Community, 1866-2016

Volume 1: 1866-1932

Joyce Blackwell, Ph.D.

ISBN: 978-1631030376

DEDICATION

Dedicated with love to the

former and current White Rock Baptist Church Family

as well as Dr. Reginald Van Stephens to whom God

gave this vision

and

in memory of all deceased pastors and members.

CONTENTS

ACKNOWLEDGMENTS

This has been a journey. And although the scholarly pursuit appears to be a one-person flight, it is anything but. Instead, it has been a collaborative effort. First and foremost, thank God for giving Reverend Dr. Reginald Van Stephens the vision for this book, and for providing me with the wisdom, guidance and perseverance to complete this important project.

I also thank the members of White Rock Baptist Church who generously provided their stories, photographs and other relevant documents. This could not have been done without you.

Many thanks to the editors of this work, namely Reverend Dr. Reginald Van Stephens, Deborah Taylor, Eloise Jordan, Deacon and Trustee Derek Hunter, and Rebecca Redd-Jolly. A very special thanks to Pastor Stephens, Deborah and Eloise. They provided detailed and penetrating criticism. Their many comments improved not only the substance of this book but its style and grammar. Hence, my debt to Pastor Stephens, Deborah and Eloise is overwhelming, and it is more than perfunctory to remark that the errors that remain are literally my own.

A very special thanks to Pastor Stephens for reading and reading and reading some more every draft of this work. His provocative questions forced me to rethink more than once my approach or analysis of a particular topic. The insight, perspective, and rigor he brought to the work are appreciated. What a blessing!

Many thanks to Deacon Ernest Jenkins, chair of the Diaconate Ministry, for providing the means that enabled us to have the resources necessary for the research and writing of this book. It is his generosity as well as that of White Rock Baptist Church that made it possible for this book to be published.

I am greatly obliged to the following institutions and their librarians or archivists for giving me access to their archives and permission to use their manuscript collections: Duke University Special Collections; North Carolina Central University Archival

Collections; University of North Carolina Special Collection, Oral History Program Collection, and Southern Historical Collection; North Carolina Mutual Life Insurance Company Archives; Shaw University Archival Collection; North Carolina State Archives; and the Library of Congress Archive Collection. I am especially grateful to Maria Estorino and her staff at the University of North Carolina's Special Collections Office.

This work owes much to Danah Starns, Publishing Consultant, at CaryPress International. I will always be grateful for her support and patience. Thank you.

Many thanks to the team that began this journey with me almost two years ago, and is still with me today: Deaconess Martha Lester-Harris; Deaconess Saundra Hartsfield; Minnie Forte-Brown; Dr. Linda Hubbard-Curtis; Deaconess Shirley Jenkins; Eloise Jordan; Deborah Taylor; Deacon Derek Hunter; Eloise Jordan; Deacon Ernest Jenkins; Sherron Williams; Carolyn Thornton; Deborah Taylor; Cynthia Thomas Traynham; Dr. Shirley Arrington; Beverly Evans; Rebecca Redd-Jolly; Deaconess Vivian Crump; and Sue Jarmon. A special thanks to Minnie Forte-Brown and her team for developing an extraordinary mini-documentary about White Rock Baptist Church, and Deaconesses Martha Lester-Harris and Saundra Hartsfield who always agreed to assist whenever asked.

I am also thankful to all interviewees: Lou Suitt Barnes; Minerva Fields; Elizabeth Frazier; Dr. Paula Harrell; Sue Jarmon; Deacon Emeritus Dr. John Lucas; Raymond McAllister; Mildred Page; Deaconess Vivian Samuels; Dr. James Schooler; Deaconess Mary Thomas; Carolyn Walker; Minnie Forte-Brown; Mary Hester-Smith; Joyce Campbell; Margo Garrett; Valerie Bibby; Paula Singletary; Nathan Garrett; and Irwin Holmes. Most of the information received from these interviews will appear in Volume II of this two-volume work.

And what would I have done without Sue Jarmon, LaVerne Davis, and Leon Carter? They were always there downloading documents and assisting with the collection of photos and whatever else was needed. Not once did they complain. Each of you is amazing.

At the heart of this journey was Jesus Christ. None of this would have been possible without our Lord and Savior. Hallelujah and praise God!

Finally, thanks to everyone who understood this major undertaking and gave me the space and time I needed to complete the first volume.

ABBREVIATIONS

ABHMS	American Baptist Home Mission Society
ABPS	American Baptist Publication Society
BEMC	Baptist Educational and Missionary Society
BSSSC	Baptist State Sunday School Convention
CAC	Child Advocacy Commission
DCABP	Durham Committee on the Affairs of Black People
DCNA	Durham Committee on Negro Affairs
LCFM	Lott Carey Foreign Mission
NAACP	National Association for the Advancement of Colored People
NACW	National Association of Colored Women
NBC	National Baptist Convention
NNBL	National Negro Baptist League
SWW	Shepard, Womack, Williams Missionary Circle
WBC	Woman's Baptist Convention
WBHMC	Woman's Baptist Home and Missionary Convention
WBO	Woman's Baptist Organization
WRBC	White Rock Baptist Church

Upon This Rock

Introduction

"And you will know the truth, and the truth will set you free . . ."
- John 8:32 (ESV)

Nearly two years ago, while beginning the archival research for this book, I listened to countless numbers of current and former White Rock Baptist Church members eagerly share their memories about either growing up in the church or the Hayti community. They often spoke proudly of their relatives who worked in several ministries in the church and were responsible for organizing Black-owned businesses. I not only welcomed but encouraged the captivating stories.

All of these amazing accounts given by such wonderful people would have been great for inclusion in the book. Unfortunately, in some instances, the powerful, haunting and fascinating stories could not withstand archival scrutiny and, therefore, were not included in *Upon This Rock*. The stories that could be corroborated by the existing evidence, however, were incorporated. My extensive research of papers that some church members donated to local university libraries, meeting minutes of church ministries and African-American-owned businesses and organizations in the community, newspaper articles, interviews and countless other documents yielded a considerable amount of information. A detailed analysis of those same documents revealed a compelling story that had never been told and one that could not be recounted in one volume.

Upon This Rock: White Rock Baptist Church's Dynamic People and Their Influence in the Durham, North Carolina, Community, 1866-2016, therefore, is a two-volume book, that tells the story of how the church, inspired through prayer and built primarily around the Word of God, was made significant through its members who interpreted their Christian faith by serving the African-American community's needs. The church, organized in 1866 in Durham, served as a context in which its members made plans to rebuild their lives as free men and women, interpreted their relationship to the African-American community both in Durham and across the State, and charted a vision that helped them to effectively address the problems that they confronted on almost a daily basis. For these and other reasons, White Rock Baptist Church became a significant arena for spiritual support, educational opportunity, economic development, political activism, and racial uplift.

Volume 1 focuses on the years between 1866 and 1932. Although the period is broad, it represents a distinctive time in African-American history, an era when the definition of African Americans' status in America was repeatedly and actively contested. Time and time again it tested their faith in Jesus Christ and, oftentimes, White Rock's members responded in a manner appropriate for those who understood and embraced God's Word. This study reflects the shifting scale of the challenges and how the church and its members dealt with them. White Rock's members initially responded to their status by trying to adjust to a new life—one in which they were, for the first time, on their own. They found refuge working in White Rock's various ministries and, when possible, helping African Americans in Durham and across the state adjust to their new environment. They worked primarily through religious institutions, organizations, associations and committees. By the late 1880s, they responded to their status with a more defined interpretation of their Christian faith. The church's members began to advance programs of self-help and race improvement—some originating through ministries in the church. The money that they earned from African-American-owned businesses was often invested in programs in White Rock and in the African-American community. An African-American elite class began to emerge who adopted middle-class standards and values. As they made progress, the so-called "Black elite" realized that it would be beneficial to the entire race if they also helped poorer African Americans to advance. They also believed that it was what Jesus Christ wanted them to do.

Upon This Rock is not designed to be a comprehensive history of White Rock Baptist Church through all these years. At best, this book represents a discovery of the church's past that has until now been either neglected or misrepresented. Therefore, I offer it as an historical account of exemplary lives within the church and the movement for African-American community and cultural development.

The activities of White Rock's members cannot be viewed simply on a religious level. The intensity of their activism renders it also a social phenomenon whose roots penetrate deeply into the fabric of Durham's society. The factor that empowered the struggle of the church's members came directly from both religious and social contexts and was intimately related to their relationship with Jesus Christ, own definition of themselves, and what they considered as their rightful place in society. The challenge, then, was to reconstruct both the religious and social aspects of the history of activism by White Rock's members in the Durham community.

This book attempts to move forward to show change and continuity. However, the multitude of issues, both non-secular and secular, forced me to examine the topic thematically as well. For example, when a handful of African-American male preachers organized the first Baptist Educational and Missionary Convention (BEMC) in 1867, they also invited women to attend but as a part of BEMC's recently formed Woman's Convention. Since the two groups worked on different issues at the same convention, their work is examined in separate chapters. Yet, I attempt to show how the two organizations simultaneously grappled with the development and evolution of Black Baptist churches and missionary societies.

Some chapters begin with a personal scenario to give the reader a better idea of the significance or the importance of the topic for Black religious leaders and White Rock Church members. In order to avoid confusion, the scenario is separated from the narrative by a symbol.

In both volumes of this story, the human protagonists consist of pastors like Reverends Zuck Horton, Dr. T. W. H. Woodward, Dr. Augustus Shepard, Dr. Reginald Van Stephens, Dr. Miles Mark Fisher, and Dr. Lorenzo Lynch as well as numerous members including, among others, Margaret Faucette, Dr. Aaron Moore, Charles C. Spaulding, James Rufus Evans, Allen Goodloe, William Daniel Hill, Elna Spaulding, Reverend Dr. James Shepard, William Jessie Kennedy, Jr., Minerva Womack, Margaret Goodwin, Susie V. G. Norfleet, Tempie Whitted, J. M. Schooler, Dr. James Hubbard, J. A. Whitted, Annie Day Shepard, Nancy Cooper, James Taylor, and Dr. John Lucas. Arrayed against them are de jure segregationists and White local politicians serving on the Durham City Council, Durham County Board of Commissioners, and in the mayor's office. The actions of both groups mobilize a supporting cast that is state and national in scope. It includes African-American race leaders Frederick Douglass, Booker T. Washington, Mary McLeod Bethune, Harriet Tubman, Dr. W.E.B. DuBois and Reverend Dr. Martin Luther King, Jr., as well as presidents Theodore Roosevelt and William McKinley; a group of White entrepreneurs and philanthropists such as Julian Carr, Brodie Duke, Washington Duke, William Thomas Blackwell, Margaret Olivia Slocum Sage, Julius Rosenwald, John Slater and Anna Jeanes along with Reverend Dr. Henry Tupper, founder and CEO of Shaw University; sectors of the African-American middle class in Durham, many who owned businesses, such as Richard Fitzgerald, founder of Durham's first African-American-owned brickmaking company and John Merrick, founder of several African-American-owned businesses in Durham; and Whites who supported education for African Americans such as Nathan Carter Newbold, North Carolina's agent for rural schools. Some notable African-American religious and business leaders make cameo appearances. Among them are one of North Carolina's former representatives in the United States Congress, Henry Cheatham Plummer; Reverend Dr. James E. Shepard, founder of a college to train ministers; and entrepreneur, Dr. Stanford L. Warren.

The many men and women examined in this book exemplify God's vision and purpose for humankind, and how many members of White Rock Baptist Church applied the principals of the Kingdom of God in their daily lives. At its heart, however, this story is about Christians who believed that they had been commissioned by Jesus Christ to take specific action on earth — that their Christian faith required that they serve the African-American community's needs.

Organizers, pastors and members of White Rock Baptist Church are descendants of a race that has a long relationship with Christianity. In other words, contrary to popular belief in the African-American community, devotion to Jesus Christ has been a large part of the Black experience. For example, in his book, *The Early Church of Africa*, Dr. John Mbiti outlines the fact that the message of Jesus penetrated Africa before it ever reached Europe. He asserts, "Christianity in Africa is so old that it can be rightly described as an indigenous, traditional and African religion."[1]

Likewise, the conversion of the Ethiopian eunuch described in the Book of Acts predates the Apostle Paul's first missionary journey into Europe by several years. There is clear, historical documentation of the Christian church in Africa by the third century, or between 201 A.D. and 300 A.D. During this period, Christianity was the dominant religion in North Africa and most notably Egypt. By the year 300 A.D., Egypt had more than a million Christians.

Two hundred years later, Christianity spread to the Nubian Kingdoms and, in large part, because of widespread trading and traveling over the next five centuries, Christianity spread to Southern and Western Africa, the homelands of most American slaves. There is also growing evidence that the long-standing

---

[1]Dr. John S. Mbiti, *African Religions and Philosophy* (London, United Kingdom of Great Britain: Heinemann Publishers, 1969), 229, as cited in *The Early Church and Africa*, John Kealy and David Shenk, Oxford University Press, 1975, 1.

presence of Christianity in Egypt and in present-day Ethiopia provided a base for the introduction of Christianity in Southern and Western Africa. Since it was another 400 to 500 years before people of African descent began arriving in America, some Africans had either already been converted to Christianity or were familiar with its basic tenets.[2] Therefore, regardless of how Whites interpreted Scripture when providing Christian instruction to slaves, some slaves had their own interpretation of the same Biblical verse because of their prior Christian teachings. For example, while the Bible did teach, "Slaves, obey your earthly masters with respect and fear," some slaves also recalled the additional passage, "And masters, treat your slaves in the same way. Do not threaten them, since you know that he who is both your Master and theirs is in heaven and there is no favoritism with him."[3]

Some slaves also discovered that the slavery alluded to in the Bible was substantially different from what they were experiencing. Too many masters wanted their slaves to submit to the commands of Scripture but were unwilling to live by those commands themselves. The slaves realized this contradiction but did not allow that to interfere with receiving the transcendent truth of the Bible. In its pages, they found hope, courage, strength and comfort. For that reason, these same slaves chose to follow the Jesus they read about in the Bible. Jesus Christ provided the hope and power they needed to survive slavery.

Some slaves' belief and faith in Jesus Christ enabled them to endure trials and hardships that one can only imagine. This same faith also inspired African-American leaders of the antebellum period as well as in post-emancipation America to respond courageously to the many problems that people of African descent experienced. *Upon This Rock* recounts how African-American Christians of the White Rock Baptist Church believed that it was their relationship with Jesus that fueled their struggle, energized their activism, and gave them hope for a better future for their

---

[2]Ibid., 290-295.

[3]Ephesians 6: 5, 9, New International Version of the *Bible*.

race. They further believed that their Christian faith required that they were active agents of change in the African-American community.

From the antebellum period until now, numerous African-American Christians who fought against racial oppression attempted to do so in the context of their belief in God. In other words, African-Americans' profound Christian faith usually dictated their response or responses to White racism. This is very evident when exploring how White Rock's members and leaders, whether enslaved or free, tackled racial oppression. Like most Christian African Americans, they reacted in one of three ways when addressing racial oppression and/or injustices that were common occurrences in their lives. They responded with either: (1) resignation; (2) accommodation; or (3) liberation.

White Rock members who responded to racial oppression with resignation gave up on ever having a good life while on earth and, instead, placed all hope on a life beyond. In other words, they believed that they would only have happiness in eternal life. As a consequence, they faithfully read and studied God's Word, and lived as they believed God wanted them to so that they would one day go to heaven and live happily ever after. This response made it easier for them to endure the daily abuses, insults and humiliation because they knew that the suffering was only temporary. These members quietly studied the Bible and discreetly engaged in ministry work. Some of these members are highlighted in one of the last chapters in each volume titled, "Other Unsung Heroes and Heroines."

Conversely, some of White Rock's members chose the second option or response, accommodation, when addressing oppression. They believed that their status in life was preordained by God and, therefore, it must be accepted without any attempt to alter their human condition. Pastors and members who responded in this manner believed that they were better Christians if they accepted their condition. God knew what was best for them. Because of their alleged inaction, it is difficult to trace their work both in the church and the African-American community.

For those White Rock members who adopted the third response, liberation, they were determined to break the shackles of oppression. They believed that God was concerned about those under the bondage of oppression and, therefore, gave them the strength to struggle against this type of persecution, confident that God would help them to be successful.[4] The vast majority of the church's members highlighted in Volume 1 and Volume 2 of this book fall into this category.

Sometimes, White Rock's members adopted one or both of the first two options when addressing racial oppression. This is often reflected in some of the religious music and worship during the antebellum and immediate post-Civil War eras. The music usually imparted Christian values while also describing the hardships of slavery and life in the first three decades after slavery ended.[5] Worship services were often characterized by call and response and extreme emotionalism. Both the music and worship are best illustrated in *Upon This Rock* during the tenures of White Rocks pastors, from Reverend Zuck Horton to Reverend Allen Eaton. During Reverend Augustus Shepard's tenure as pastor, worship service and music began to change, becoming more formal and less emotional. This change is due, in part, to a noticeable shift in the church's demographics as more middle- and upper- class African Americans began to join worship services. This new group also began to perceive differently the role of the church in the struggle against racial oppression. Therefore, they embraced the concept of liberation. With this option, when Whites would not allow them access to their businesses and organizations, various White Rock members sought to break the shackles of oppression within society by creating their own institutions.

---

[4]John W. Fleming, "Black Theology," *The Black Christian Experience,* ed. Emmanuel L. McCall (Nashville, Tennessee: Broadman Press, 1972), 85; Gayraud S. Wilmore and James H. Cone, *Black Theology: A Documentary History, 1966-1979* (New York, New York: Orbis Press, 1979), 100-102; and James H. Cone, *For My People* (New York, New York: Orbis Press, 1984), 5-30.

[5] See Dr. Miles Mark Fisher, *Negro Slave Songs in the United States* (Ithaca, New York: Cornell University Press, 1953).

This historical account of White Rock Baptist Church reveals that those members that employed options one and three were active agents of change in the both the church and African-American community. Their faith in Jesus Christ, and interpretation of that Christian faith, would not allow them to be passive or feel as if they were powerless. Interestingly, pastors and members who followed Jesus Christ were arguably some of the most effective leaders and the community's most impressive achievers to respond to the realities of their time. Despite their humble beginnings, many White Rock pastors and members helped shape the city of Durham and the African-American community in several key areas: religion, education, politics, economics, and philanthropy and/or self-help.

This book is divided into two volumes with several parts, each volume addressing different phases in the evolution of the church's history. The picture that emerges in both volumes provides an interesting and revealing look at a unique group of African-American Christians, whose activism was not only shaped by their faith in the teachings of Jesus Christ but the multidimensional pressures of living in a racially-conscious society.

Volume 1 is divided into four parts. **Part One** focuses on the lives of White Rock's earliest members during slavery and their earliest days as free men and women. *Chapter 1* provides a detailed account of the experiences of White Rock Baptist Church's organizers and charter members during slavery and its immediate aftermath. This approach is important in helping the reader to understand the climate in the country and the brutal impact of slavery on people who would soon be free in a White-dominated society that had a difficult time with emancipation. It is equally important to understand the environment in which White Rock Baptist Church was formed. Understanding slavery, in general, and the related legislation is important for readers to view the founding of White Rock in the proper context. The inhumanity of slavery made the church's founders and charter members stronger Christians and it is their boundless faith in Jesus Christ that helped them to overcome the cruelties of forced bondage. During slavery, many African Americans, including Margaret and William Faucette, Reverend Zuck Horton, Gos Lee, Melissa Lee, and Sally Husband concluded that God did not, and would not, turn a blind eye to the sufferings of the slaves.[6] Furthermore, as far as they were concerned, nor would God wink at the conduct of those who oppressed African people in America. This continued to be the prevailing thought of many of these same slaves once they gained their long-awaited freedom. Therefore, *Chapter 2* describes how White Rock Baptist Church was first organized, highlighting challenges and how its earliest founders successfully addressed those difficult encounters.

Part Two concentrates on White Rock Baptist Church's earliest connections to various religious institutions in North Carolina. *Chapter 3* discusses the ministries of White Rock's full-time pastors between 1866 and 1932, which included Reverend Zuck Horton (1866-1869), Reverend Samuel Hunt (1869-1879), Reverend Frederick Wilkins (1879-1881), Reverend T.W.H. Woodward (1881-1884), Reverend B. K. Butler (1884-1885), Reverend Allen P. Eaton (1886-1898), Reverend Dr. Augustus Shepard (1901-1911), Reverend Dr. E. M. Brawley (1913-1919), Reverend Dr. James Kirkland (1920-1924), Reverend Dr. S. L. McDowell (1924-1930), and Reverend Dr. William Ransome (1931-1932). *Chapters 4* and *5* describe efforts by the leadership of White Rock Baptist Church and its members to work with others in the Durham community in organizing African-American Baptists across the State after the Civil War. Their devotion to Jesus Christ had been a large part of their experience as slaves and free African Americans, and it did not end after the Civil War and emancipation. It is, in part, their devotion and faith that led many of them to establish White Rock and to assist other African

---

[6]Please read the following works for a more detailed account of how African slaves in America explained their ability to endure the horrendous institution of slavery: Dr. Cain Hope Felder, *Troubling Biblical Waters: Race, Class, and Family* (Maryknoll, New York: Orbis Books, 1990) is a comprehensive and challenging examination of the significance of the Bible for African Americans; and Dr. Cain Hope Felder, *Stony the Road We Trod: African American Biblical Interpretation* (Minneapolis, Minnesota: Fortress Press, 1991) examines how the Bible was used in American African-American religion to create a community that resisted oppression and fomented social change.

Americans in building churches that ultimately became powerful forces in their respective communities. While *Chapter 4* specifically focuses on the efforts of White Rock's members in organizing the first African-American Baptist Convention in North Carolina, *Chapter 5* concentrates on the earliest work of some of White Rock's women in the state's Black Baptist Convention.

Part Three expounds on the role that White Rock Baptist Church and some of its members played in the development of Durham's African-American community, beginning as early as 1866. *Chapter 6* traces the development of the Colored Orphan Asylum of North Carolina and its impact on African-American society. While *Chapter 7* discusses White Rock Baptist Church's affiliation with educational institutions like North Carolina Central University, Stanford L. Warren Library and Hillside High School, *Chapter 8* continues the discussion that began in earlier chapters by examining various African-American-owned businesses either founded by members of White Rock or those who had a special affiliation with the church. These institutions include North Carolina Mutual Life Insurance Company, Mechanics and Farmers Bank, and Lincoln Hospital. *Chapter 9* briefly chronicles significant local political institutions found by members of White Rock and why the city's African Americans were late becoming involved in politics. *Chapter 10* focuses on the role of some White Rock members in the cultural development of Durham's early African-American community. Durham's Black elite, many who were members of White Rock Baptist Church, created their own social and cultural institutions. Moreover, they engaged in racial uplift activities, fully embracing the notion that in order for the entire race to make progress, the African-American middle- and upper- classes had to teach and instill in the Black masses middle-class morals and manners. This would be one of the last, and important, steps to racial progress and for White Rock's members who believed that helping their race was fulfilling God's purpose for their lives.

Part Four highlights some of White Rock Baptist Church's unsung heroes and heroines that were not mentioned in earlier chapters. *Chapter 11* explores the church and community work of several White Rock members who quietly served in their church and the African-American community. They are known as "unsung heroes and heroines" and include, among others, such long-time church members as Minerva Womack, Dr. James M. Hubbard, Susie Norfleet, Minerva Fields, William D. Hill, William J. Kennedy, Jr., Sylvia Williams, and James Rufus Evans.

In the **Conclusion**, the writer provides a summary of main points and draws conclusions that emphasize how the political, social, economic, educational, and cultural/social activities engaged in by members were always rooted in how they interpreted their faith and how they chose to respond to the realities of the time. The church, indeed, served as the rock upon which so much of the Durham community was built. In many ways, White Rock's contributions to the African-American community in Durham is unmatched by any similar institutions in the area.

PART 1

The Beginning

Chapter One

"For it is By Grace You Have Been Saved":
Transitioning from Slavery to Freedom

"Now the Lord is the Spirit, and where the Spirit of the Lord is, there is freedom." – 2 Corinthians 3:17 (NIV)

Margaret Ruffin Faucette, one of the well-known organizers of White Rock Baptist Church, was born a mulatto slave around 1822, in an Orange County town known as Hillsborough, North Carolina.[1] Her parents were Jesse Ruffin and Rebecca "Becky" Norwood Ruffin who lived on Attorney John W. Norwood's plantation, which is currently known as the Occaneechi Farm. Her ancestors were of the Occaneechi Indian tribe from the

Margaret Ruffin Faucette (in 1919), Courtesy of White Rock Baptist Church Archives, Durham, N.C.

---

[1] North Carolina State Board of Health, Bureau of Vital Statistics, Standard Certificate of Death, Faucette Family Reunion Program Booklet, July 11-13, 2008. In 1881, Durham officials sought to become an autonomous political subdivision and decided to separate from Orange County. Durham County was formed on April 17, 1881 from portions of land transferred into the county from Orange and Wake counties.

Indian Reservation in Orange County.

Margaret's husband, William Faucette, was born a year earlier on the plantation of David Faucette, also in Hillsborough. The plantations that William and Margaret lived on were within walking distance of each other.

Eventually, during the antebellum period, William, a field slave, and Margaret, a house slave, met each other, courted, "married" and became the parents of 13 children. William continued to work as a farm hand even after he married. Likewise, Margaret continued to work as a house slave, where she spent most of her time in the house of her owners. While living in the "big house," Margaret learned about some of the better things of life, such as the feel of fine silk and the use of crystal and china. It is also in her master's home that she taught herself to read. The Bible was her constant companion. Margaret was a "devout Christian and sought every opportunity to let everyone with whom she came in contact know about the God she served, and His goodness. She also constantly sang God's praises."[2]

***

The antebellum era was one of the most difficult periods in American history for African Americans. For slaves and free Blacks, it was characterized by decades of deep despair. During this tumultuous period, America's total population was 23.1 million, which included approximately 4 million slaves and ½ million free African Americans. The total population in North Carolina was 738,000 people; one-third of those were slaves. In other words, 1 out of 3 people in North Carolina during the antebellum period were slaves. There was also another group of people in the State known as free people of color who comprised approximately 20,000 of the overall population.

Slavery expanded greatly in America between 1800 and 1860 and, as it grew, servitude deepened its hold on Southern society.

---

[2]Mrs. Gazelle Poole Lipscomb and Mrs. Nannie James Cooper Greens, "Brief Biography of Margaret Ruffin Faucette," Family Reunion Program Booklet, 2008.

In North Carolina, for instance, the restrictions of the law gripped African Americans even more tightly than in some other states as slavery's final crisis—the Civil War—became imminent. For one, slaveholders were determined to remove all threats to slavery from society. One such threat, they believed, was the free African American. Whites feared that the mere presence of free African Americans would constantly remind slaves of their bondage` and, subsequently, create more unrest among the enslaved population.

Eventually, the North Carolina General Assembly passed laws designed to control free African Americans. In the process, state legislators reduced free Blacks to a status little different from slavery and made the institution of slavery even more difficult to escape. "Little by little," historian Guion Johnson wrote, "the Legislature stripped the free African American [in North Carolina] of his personal liberties."[3] For example, in 1826, legislators passed a law prohibiting any free African American from entering the state of North Carolina. Nine years later, in 1835, free African Americans lost the right to vote, no matter how much property they might own. Other laws that North Carolina legislators passed during the antebellum period denied their free African American population the right to preach in public, to possess a gun without a special license, to buy or sell alcoholic beverages, or to attend any public school. Finally, in 1861, the North Carolina General Assembly barred any free African American person from owning or controlling a slave, thus making it impossible for them, through hard work and thrift, to purchase freedom for their wives, husbands, or children, or even to earn money from owning slaves. Overall, free African Americans lost many of their rights during the antebellum period.

Just as it had done with free African Americans, the North Carolina General Assembly also passed laws to regulate the lives of slaves. For slaves, like the Faucettes, North Carolina's laws became more all-encompassing. For example, as time passed, members of the North Carolina General Assembly began to hear

---

[3]Guion Johnson, *Ante-Bellum North Carolina: A Social History* (Chapel Hill, NC: University of North Carolina Press, 1937), 49.

of an increasing number of instances in which Whites were secretly providing slaves with educational instruction. William and Margaret Faucette, as well as countless other slaves, were eager to be formally taught how to read and write, primarily so that they could read and better understand the Bible. In the spirit of the Second Great Awakening, or era of Religious Revivalism, some Whites believed that God wanted them to educate the poor, heathen and wretched slaves; therefore, they acted accordingly.

Members of the General Assembly opposed such instruction because they felt that a literate slave was much more difficult to control. Therefore, in 1830, they passed a law which prohibited anyone from teaching a slave to read or write. The law stated,

Whereas, the teaching of slaves to read and write has a tendency to incite dissatisfaction in their minds, and to produce insurrection and rebellion to the injury of the citizens of this state; therefore, it is hereby enacted, by the General Assembly, that any person who shall teach or even attempt to teach any slave to read and write shall be liable to indictment and, if convicted, if it is a white woman or man who is offending the law, he or she shall be fined not less than $100 and not more than $200; if it is a free person of color who is offending, that person shall be whipped, not exceeding 39 lashes nor less than 20 lashes; if a slave is teaching a slave to read and write, he shall be carried before any justice of the peace, and upon conviction, he shall receive a mandatory sentence of 39 lashes on his or her bare back.[4]

Camp Meeting of the Methodists in North America, Second Great Awakening, 1819, Courtesy of Public Domain.

Thus, as the Faucettes and other slaves grew up in antebellum North Carolina, it became a crime for them to learn how to read and write. Margaret Faucette, who was determined to read the Bible, risked a whipping each time that

[4]Joyce Blackwell, *The Control of Blacks in North Carolina, 1829-1840* (Thesis, North Carolina Central University, Durham, NC, 1977),38; North Carolina General Assembly Statutes, 1830, University of North Carolina, North Carolina Collection, Louis Round Wilson Library Special Collections, Chapel Hill, North Carolina.

she attempted to teach herself.

Another major movement began during the antebellum period that led to additional laws being passed by North Carolina legislators, around the same time as previous laws, to further restrict the activities and behavior of slaves. The Second Great Awakening, a movement led by preachers, was a Protestant religious revival that began around 1790 and gained momentum by the beginning of the antebellum period. By 1820, membership had rapidly increased among Baptist and Methodist congregations. The religious movement was characterized by enthusiasm, emotion, and an appeal to God.

The revivals enrolled millions of new members in Baptist and Methodist denominations and led to the formation of new denominations. The Second Great Awakening also stimulated the establishment of many reform movements designed to remedy the evils of society before the anticipated Second Coming of Jesus Christ.[5] Furthermore, many white slaveholders felt that it would be good for America if free African Americans and slaves, whom they regarded as heathens, were provided religious instruction. It is also, as previously stated, in the spirit of this movement that numerous Whites felt that they were morally obligated to teach slaves how to read and write, which eventually led opponents of the practice to pass legislation, in 1831, prohibiting such action. They also believed that they had a responsibility to "Christianize" the African slaves, further thinking that Christianity would make slaves better workers and more human.

"African American Harry" Hosier, African Preacher, Late 18th century evangelistic tour. Courtesy of Public Domain.

Across the South, Baptists and Methodists preached to slaveholders and slaves alike. During the movement, even African Americans could be authorized to preach — many as early as 1800. One illiterate

---

[5]Timothy L. Smith, *Revivalism and Social Reform: American Protestantism on the Eve of the Civil War* (Eugene, Oregon: WIPF and Stock Publishers, 2004), 42.

freedman, "Black Harry" Hosier, proved to be able to memorize large passages of the Bible verbatim. He became a cross-over success and was just as popular among White audiences as the African American ones to whom he was supposed to have ministered.[6]

Hosier's experience, however, was unique. African Americans who were authorized by White ministers to preach did not usually do so before White congregations. During the Second Great Awakening, slaves and free Blacks also began to form Baptist and Methodist congregations across the South. By the early 19th century, independent African-American congregations numbered in the several hundred in many cities. With the growth in congregations, African Americans began to form primarily Baptist associations in Virginia, Kentucky and other Southern states.

The revivals also inspired slaves to demand freedom, especially, it seems, as more of them worshipped with Whites and were allowed to preach to members of their own race. A growing number of Whites began to become concerned that evangelical Protestantism, which had been the catalyst for the conversion of both African Americans and Whites in the South, had inspired the races to pray, sing, shout and cry together during the Second Great Awakening. They were concerned that this had begun to loosen the slaves' bonds and lead to spiritual equality. In North Carolina, slaveholders became increasingly uneasy about the interracial revivals. They believed religious egalitarianism promoted slave unrest. Some slaveholders in the state grumbled that "Negroes had grown so much worse" from imbibing New Light Baptist teachings, further adding that some African American Baptists only "pretended to be very religious" and "Negro preachers did not know anything of religious matters" despite their claims.[7] Therefore, the same North Carolina

[6]Philip Morgan, *Slave Counterpoint: African American Culture in the Eighteenth-Century Chesapeake and Lowcountry* (Chapel Hill, NC: University of North Carolina Press, 1998), 655.

[7]Jeffrey Crow, Paul Escott and Flora Hatley, *A History of African Americans in North Carolina* (Raleigh, NC: North Carolina Department of Cultural Resources, 2002), 30.

legislature, which passed the law to prohibit African Americans from learning how to read and write, called an emergency session to address their fears that allowing slaves and free African Americans to be taught biblical scriptures and to preach would lead to calls for racial and social equality. Subsequently, in 1832, members of the North Carolina General Assembly passed the law, *An Act to Forbid Slaves or Free Negroes to Preach the Gospel, An Act for the Better Regulation of the Conduct of Free Persons of Color or Slaves,* which stated,

It shall not be lawful for any free person of color, or slave, to preach or exhort in public, or in any manner, to officiate as a preacher or teacher in any prayer meeting or in any other association for worship where slaves of different families are collected together. If any free person or slave shall be convicted before any court, having jurisdiction, he shall, for each offense, receive, but not exceed, 39 lashes on his bare back; wherein, a slave shall be guilty, he shall, upon conviction, receive not less than 39 lashes on his bare back.[8]

After this law was passed, it became illegal for slaves and free African Americans to preach in North Carolina. Likewise, White plantation owners began to more closely monitor any religious instruction received by free African Americans and slaves, further requiring that at least one white person was always present when such instruction was being provided.

White slave-owners and politicians failed to realize that when they provided religious instruction to enslaved men and women, the slaves discovered something. They learned, among other things, that while the Bible did teach, "Slaves, obey your earthly masters with respect and fear," it also said, "And masters, treat your slaves in the same way. Do not threaten them, since you know that he who is both your Master and theirs is in heaven and there is no favoritism with him."[9] They also learned that the slavery alluded to in the Bible was substantially different from

---

[8]Joyce Blackwell, *The Control of African Americans in North Carolina*, 38-39; North Carolina General Assembly Statutes, 1832, University of North Carolina, North Carolina Collection, Louis Round Wilson Library, Special Collection, Chapel Hill, N.C.

[9]Ephesians 6: 5, 9, New International Version, *Bible*.

what they were experiencing. Slaves felt that too many masters wanted them to submit to the commands of Scripture but were unwilling to live by those commands themselves. The slaves discovered this contradiction but did not allow that to interfere with receiving the divine truth of the Bible, which gave them hope, strength, comfort and courage. In the end, most slaves chose to follow the Jesus that they knew in the Bible. Jesus provided the hope and power that they needed to survive slavery.

The North Carolina General Assembly passed additional laws to further control or regulate the lives of free African Americans and slaves during the antebellum period. One cause for the increased restrictions was the intensifying sectional crisis between the North and South; however, a more direct cause was the resistance and rebelliousness of free and enslaved African Americans.

The peculiar nature of the enslavement of African Americans gave rise to thoughts of freedom. The African slaves knew intuitively that slavery was not God's final status for them. Listening to the Biblical stories of God's concern for His chosen people, they identified analogously with the oppression of "the chosen people." As far as they were concerned, God had created human beings with the spirit of freedom at the core of their being, and if God had not chosen African Americans to be slaves, nor should the White slaveowner. Furthermore, some slaves genuinely felt that slavery denied them their identity, dignity and freedom and was contrary to God's will. Therefore, scores of them fought for their freedom long before emancipation in 1865.

Nat Turner's Rebellion, Southampton County, Virginia, 1831. Courtesy of Public Domain.

One legendary example of slave opposition to bondage was the bloody uprising in 1831, led by Nat Turner, an African American preacher, and his followers, in Southampton County, Virginia. A short, coal-Black man, Turner was fearless, honest, temperate, religious, and extremely intelligent. A White lawyer, Thomas R. Gray who recorded Turner's confessions once he was captured, asserted that Turner "for natural intelligence and quickness of apprehension, [was] surpassed by few men [he had] ever seen." He further added, "Nat Turner knew a great deal about military tactics, and had a mind capable of attaining anything. . . ."[10] Feeling no remorse for killing almost sixty whites during the rebellion, Turner calmly contemplated his execution. Gray provided the best characterization of him when he wrote:

He is a complete fanatic, or plays his part most admirably. . . The calm, deliberate composure with which he spoke of his late deeds and intentions, the expression of his fiendlike face when excited by enthusiasm, still bearing the stains of blood of helpless innocence about him; clothed with rages and covered with chains; yet daring to raise his manacled hands to heaven, with a spirit soaring above the attributes of man; I looked on him and my blood curdled in my veins.[11]

David Walker, around 1829.
Courtesy of Public Domain.

The African-American rebels "curdled" the blood of many Southern whites. The ubiquitous rebel was the bogey man for young Whites, worrisome property for his master, and a hero in the slave quarters. Symbolic of African American resistance to slavery, the rebel indicated quite clearly that the African American slave was often ungovernable. Slave insurrections were frequent. Christian slaves interpreted insurrections as interventions by God on behalf of their freedom, "thus setting a pattern of interpreting the hand of God in acts which promised the liberation of slaves."[12]

Frankly, before Nat Turner's infamous rebellion, North Carolina Whites and Southern slaveholders were already on edge

---

[10]F. Roy Johnson, *The Nat Turner Slave Insurrection* (Murfreesboro, NC.: Johnson Publishing Company, 1966), 244.

[11]Ibid., 244-245.

[12]Olin P. Moyd, *Redemption in Black Theology* (Valley Forge, Pennsylvania: Judson Press, 1979, 58-59; and Vincent Harding, *The Other American Revolution* (Los Angeles, California: University of California Press, 1980), 19-36.

and fearful because of a vehement and powerful protest against American slavery by David Walker, a native North Carolinian. Walker, born in 1785, was a free African American because his mother was free. Under the laws of slavery, the status of children followed that of the mother. His father, however, was a slave. Described as "being six feet in height, slender and well-proportioned" with "loose" hair" and "dark" complexion, David Walker could not endure life in a slaveholding state like North Carolina. Therefore, impelled by his hatred of slavery, Walker left North Carolina and, by 1827, he had become established as a clothier in Boston, Massachusetts.

It is in Boston, in 1829, that Walker penned a thundering attack on slavery known as David Walker's *Appeal.* In this essay, Walker articulated the relationship between the slave's quest for freedom and religious belief. Writing with the fire and authority of an Old Testament prophet, Walker denounced American slavery and all African Americans and Whites who supported or tolerated it. Walker drew upon biblical and historical comparisons in the *Appeal.* He maintained that God would not suffer human bondage to continue much longer. Furthermore, he called on all African Americans to aspire to full freedom and to give their support to God's plan of deliverance. After he finished writing the document, Walker had it distributed throughout the South.

Walker's *Appeal* resulted in additional "restrictive" legislation by the North Carolina General Assembly. For instance, in addition to the laws mentioned above, slaves and free African Americans could not write, publish or distribute seditious publications. Additional legislation prohibited slaves from gathering in groups of more than three without a White person present, speaking in their native tongues, owning property, selling any goods, beating drums, consuming alcoholic beverages, carrying firearms, and testifying in court against a White person. Even more surprising, slaves and free African Americans could not marry or socialize with each other. Violation of any of these laws carried a penalty that ranged from a small fee to a maximum 100 lashes on the bare back.

Enslaved and free Black North Carolinians learned to live

under a system they hated but could not remove. Bereft of power, they had to accommodate themselves to the reality of slavery. Free African Americans and slaves were constantly under White surveillance and, if or when they resisted, the organized power of patrols, the state militia, and the federal army were close at hand to suppress uprisings or protests. Yet, their faith in God remained strong; as a result, they refused to submit to racial oppression and bondage. Christian slaves sensed that God's all-caring love and omnipotent power were the source of their right and would help them to remain strong until the chains of bondage were completely severed.

Hence, the inescapable task of most African American North Carolinians, like the Faucettes, Hortons, Husbands, and even Augustus Shepard (born a slave in 1846), was to endure bondage and live with oppression. In a hostile environment that became more constraining with each passing day, a growing population of enslaved African-American men and women struggled and persevered. They shouldered slavery's burden and refused to be broken. They resisted innumerable daily wrongs, maintained their self-respect and resentment of injustice, and fashioned lives that encompassed as much as possible the joys of family, love, and hope. These were not small accomplishments. For people in slavery, they were essential, hard-won victories.

Nonetheless, while experiencing some successes, enslaved North Carolinians continued to perform the hard labor that built wealth for their White masters. The type of work that they performed depended on where they lived. For example, in Washington and Bertie counties, in the eastern part of the State, slave owners made a profit by sending timber, fish, and grains to the sugar plantations of the West Indies. Therefore, many slaves in these two counties grew the grain, felled the timber, and caught the fish that produced these profits. In the state's southeastern counties, such as Brunswick and New Hanover, many slaves worked on rice plantations. In the Piedmont counties like Durham, Orange, Person and Granville, many slaves worked in tobacco. These crops ensured that the slaves' work would be hard. Indeed, it was. Slaves worked year-round-from sun up to sun down since their masters wanted to get as much work as possible out of them.

After slaves worked all day, they had other tasks to perform at night before they could go to sleep. Men had to feed, water, and tend to the livestock on the plantation or repair farming tools. The women usually had assignments related to the making of clothes.

On far too many plantations work continued with little regard for the weather. Sarah Gudger, who as a slave had lived near Asheville, North Carolina, recalled that her owner would "send us niggers out in any kind of weather, rain or snow, it never matter [sic]. . . . Many the time we come with our clothes stuck to our poor old cold bodies, but 'twarn't no use to try to get 'em dry. If the Old Boss or de Old Missie see us they yell: 'Get on out of here you Black thing, and get your work out of the way.'" Sarah Gudger added, "We knowed to get," for the penalty of disobedience was "the lash."[13]

Field Slaves on Plantation in Johnson County, Courtesy of Public Domain.

Slave women, like many of Margaret Faucette's adult daughters, labored in the fields beside men, for their gender brought them no exemption from heavy work. Slave women in North Carolina would have children one day and return to the fields the next day, if not the same day, with their baby in tow. Women, whether pregnant or not, were expected to pick cotton, hoe rows of corn or pick tobacco. The labor was heavy. One former slave, Susan High of Wake County, reported that for her owner women had to "clear

[13]*Federal Writers' Project: Slave Narrative Project, Volume 11, North Carolina, Part 1, Adams-Hunter*, 1936. Manuscript/Mixed Material. Retrieved from the Library of Congress, Washington, D.C. (Accessed August 01, 2017).

land by rollin' logs into piles and pilin' brush in the new grounds."[14]

Work conditions were not any better for house slaves. While their physical labors were lighter, they were always on call. At any time of day or night they might be ordered to perform some task, from fanning the master and his wife all night during the hot summer months so that they would not perspire, to serving as wet nurses for their mistresses' newborn babies to being subjected to rape or other physical abuse by the White master or mistress. Furthermore, the house slaves had little privacy or time away from Whites and were virtually prevented from interacting or communicating with other African Americans on the plantation. Trying to avoid these types of conditions must have been extremely difficult for Margaret Faucette who spent more time with her owners than her family. House slaves paid a substantial price in their so-called "prized" roles.

Slave Cabin, Orange County, N.C., 1834. Courtesy of Public Domain.

Slaves in North Carolina lived in log cabins with dirt floors and window openings covered with shutters. The logs were poorly chinked and, therefore, the wind blew through the cracks in the walls on cold winter days. Slaves' cabins were dark, smoky, and crowded, and the chimneys were a fire hazard. If the sticks in the chimney caught on fire, someone had to push the structure away from the house quickly before it too was in flames.

The slaves' food was monotonous and nutritionally deficient. Slaves on North Carolina plantations, regardless of the size,[15]

---

[14]Ibid.

[15]The typical slave owner in North Carolina in 1860, when Margaret and William Faucette were adults, owned only one slave. Fifty-three percent of the state's slave owners held only five or fewer slaves, and in the total population of slaves a modest 2.6 percent lived on plantations with fifty or more slaves. Many house servants on small plantations in North Carolina also worked in fields at busy times such as during the harvest season.

usually received cornmeal and fat pork, along with molasses and small amounts of coffee, that were rationed weekly to each slave family. Lindsey Faucette, one of William's and Margaret's children, born in 1853 on the Norwood Plantation, recalled how little food that slaves had, which made him and other ex-slaves more appreciative of the food that they did get once free. He stated, "My old boss at Occoneechie, Mr. Norwood, didn't have no cooking going on Sundays. He wouldn't allow a servant in the kitchen until Monday morning. 'Course he was a Presbyterian, but he was right. Hungry people should have come up when I did. A piece of cornbread tasted like cake then."[16] Of course, slaves could, if they desired, supplement and improve their diets. To make their diet more palatable, slaves would sometimes make kush, a spicy alternative to simple cornbread. Kush was cornmeal, onions, red pepper, salt and grease, if slaves had the ingredients.

Slaves also tried to improve their diets by hunting or fishing. "My old daddy partly raised his children on game," reported Louisa Adams. "He caught rabbits, coons, an' possums. He would work all day and hunt at night."[17] Some masters allowed their slaves to plant gardens. Vegetables from the gardens supplemented their diets. But not all slaves received adequate nutrition, and most were not all were well-fed.

Field and House Slaves on a Southern Plantation. Family Represents Several Generations, 1862. Courtesy of the Public Domain.

Slaves' clothes were rough and inadequate. Men usually had only two trousers and two or three shirts to last the year; women had a similar number of dresses in dull colors. These

---

Margaret's master fell in the 2.6% category while William's master fell in the 53% category.

[16]George Lougee, "Merchant Almost Reached his Goal—100th Birthday," *Durham Morning Herald*, Sunday, January 30, 1977, p. 5.

[17]*Federal Writers' Project: Slave Narrative Project, Volume 11, North Carolina, Part 1, Adams-Hunter*, 1936. Manuscript/Mixed Material. Retrieved from the Library of Congress, Washington, D.C. (Accessed August 01, 2017).

garments were often made from Rosenburg (commonly called "nigger cloth"), a heavy coarse cotton of the kind used in feed sacks or drapes. Children, both male and female, typically wore only a shirt until they were practically grown. "I went as naked as your hand," said Mattie Curtis of Orange County, "till I was fourteen years old. I was naked like that when my nature come to me. Marse Whitfield ain't carin', but after that mammy told him that I had to have clothes."[18]

Slaves' shoes were often of poor quality. According to former slave Louisa Adams, slaves "got one pair of shoes a year." She further added, "When they wore out we went barefooted [sic]. Sometimes we tied them up with strings, and they were so ragged the tracks looked like bird tracks, where we walked in the road."[19] Although the shoes were poorly made and obviously uncomfortable, the slaves felt that they were better than not having any shoes. Louisa Adams recalled, "My brother wore his shoes out and had none all through winter. His feet cracked open and bled so bad you could track him by the blood."[20]

Slaves were valuable to North Carolina slave owners. But, their value did not guarantee that they would receive good physical treatment. Their treatment reflected the fact that they were a despised and oppressed race. For most slaves, whipping and physical abuse were the worst parts of slavery. They regarded whippings as cruel and unjust. One former slave, Viney Baker of Durham County, recalled the whippings she received while a slave. "They used to tie me to a tree and beat me till the blood run down my back. I don't remember nothin' that I done, I just remember the whuppin's. Some of the rest was beat worser than I was too, and I

Runaway Slave and His Whipping Scars from Multiple Whippings, 1862. Courtesy of the Public Domain.

---

[18]Ibid.

[19]Ibid.

[20]Ibid.

use to scream that I was sure dyin'."[21]   Another former slave, Willis Cozart, who grew up in Person County, recalled seeing "niggers beat till the blood run, an' I've seen plenty more with big scars . . . A moderate whuppin' was thirty-nine or forty lashes an' a real whuppin' was an even hundred."   He added, "Most folks can't stand a real whuppin'."[22]

Moreover, no house or field slave was safe from whippings. Even pregnant women were beaten. For instance, former slave Lucy Brown's mother told her that "before the babies was born they tied the mammy down on her face if they had to whup her to keep from runnin' [sic] the baby."   At other times, "the massa or overseer dug a shallow hole in the groun'" to hold the pregnant woman's abdomen, and then he "whipped her back."[23]

Although beatings sometimes ended in death, they were not the only form of physical abuse that slaves, like William and Margaret Faucette, Reverend Dr. Augustus Shepard, and Reverend Zuck Horton, could endure. Sometimes slaves' ears were clipped or they had toes or feet removed. At other times, a member of a slave's family was sold to another slave owner in another county or state.   For many slaves, having a family member sold and never seen again was unbearably painful.

Whites, on the other hand, felt that the lash was essential to controlling slaves. Beatings strengthened authority and supported order on the plantation. The North Carolina slave lived in a very oppressive and often brutal environment.

The end of the antebellum period was marked by the election of Republican Abraham Lincoln as President of the United States. By the time he was elected, in 1860, the nation had become extremely divided over the question of slavery. The Northerners wanted to end slavery for two main reasons: (1) they resented how Southern elites had become so prosperous from the practice,

---

[21]Ibid.

[22]Ibid.

[23]Ibid.

thus becoming the wealthiest class of people in America at the time; and (2) they felt that it was time for America to transition from an agrarian society to a more industrialized nation. Conversely, Southerners were opposed to ending a practice that had not only proven to be profitable for them but also best for a people they considered to be innately inferior and uncivilized. Each side was supported by either antislavery or proslavery factions.

When Lincoln campaigned for office, he did so on the promise that although he would not disturb slavery in the Southern states, he was firmly opposed to the expansion of slavery to new territory. Southerners did not believe or trust Lincoln and, therefore, opposed him for president. Despite their opposition, Abraham Lincoln garnered enough votes[24] to become the President. Eleven Southern states immediately seceded from the United States of America and formed their own nation, the Confederate States of America. Overnight, the United States, overnight, became two nations—both with their own President, governing body, and capital city.

In April 1861, a month after his inauguration, President Lincoln ordered military troops to fire on Fort Sumter, South Carolina, beginning the bloodiest war in American history. The future of slavery and the Union depended on the outcome of the Civil War.

William and Margaret Faucette, like so many other slaves, knew why the war was being fought and felt that it was for good cause. To them and countless other slaves, the Civil War represented the unfolding of God's plan, a divine purpose to end the evil institution of slavery. Therefore, slaves patiently waited for the war, with its widespread carnage and destruction, to end.

---

[24]In the South, the laws in 1860 prohibited African Americans from voting. Only Whites could. In the North, where free African Americans had been forced, by Southern slave codes to live, were allowed to vote. Consequently, there were more Northerners voting than Southerners in the presidential election of 1860. Moreover, the Republican Party was the dominant party.

During the course of the war, President Lincoln was forced to issue the Emancipation Proclamation of 1863, freeing only the slaves in Southern states and territories that were fighting against the North at the time. Seventy-five percent of the 4 million slaves were thus freed by the Emancipation Proclamation; but, for the most part, real freedom was slow to come. The other 25% of the slaves were eventually freed after the Civil War when the U.S. Congress passed the 13th amendment, which was ratified by the required number of states in December 1865.

For North Carolina slaves, the end of the Civil War and the awarding of long awaited freedom brought great joy but also sorrow, momentous excitement but also suffering, and new opportunities but also dangerous risks. It was a watershed event

Emancipation Proclamation of 1863,
Courtesy of Public Domain.

in the history of African Americans, but it was more complex and threatening than one could ever imagine. A 260-year practice of human bondage, based primarily on the belief that the oppressed were innately inferior and ordained by God to serve whites, suddenly ended. Since most Black Americans had only known a life of bondage or captivity, they experienced mixed feelings about being free. For many African Americans, the master had taken care of them all of their lives. Who would take care of them now? Many of them turned to religion, drawing their strength from their faith in God. [25]

---

[25]Orange County, North Carolina, included portions of present-day Durham County, North Carolina, until 1881.

Chapter Two

Injecting Life into a Sacred Institution:
Organizing White Rock Baptist Church

"For which of you, intending to build a tower, sitteth not down first, and counteth the cost, whether he have sufficient to finish it?"
– Luke 14:28 (KJV)

Freedom! No more slavery! Those words and phrases meant different things to slaves and ex-slaveholders after the Civil War. African Americans, of whom the majority was illiterate, had to decide how to successfully navigate in a free society with no money, food, shelter or clothes. Freedom sounded great, but poverty and illiteracy made real freedom much more difficult to attain. This dire situation elicited different responses from ex-slaves and free Blacks, which is precisely what happened in Durham, North Carolina.[1]

Ex-slaves in Durham and other slaveholding cities and territories actively sought out ways to shed all of the vestiges of slavery. Many discarded the names their former masters had

---

[1]Orange County, North Carolina, included portions of present-day Durham County, North Carolina, until 1881.

chosen for them and adopted new names like "Freeman" and "Lincoln" that affirmed their new identities as free citizens. Other African Americans resettled far from the plantations they had labored on as slaves, hoping to eventually farm their own land or run their own businesses. By 1877, the desire for self-definition, economic independence, and racial pride coalesced in the founding of dozens of African-American towns across the South.

Perhaps the most well-known of these towns was Hayti, a self-contained all-Black community, established around 1870 by former slaves, in Durham.[2] As will be discussed in later chapters of this volume, residents of Hayti took pride in the fact that African Americans owned all of the property in town, including banks, insurance companies, shops and the surrounding land. Tight-knit communities like Hayti provided African Americans with spaces where they could live free from the indignities of segregation and the exploitation of working on White-owned farms and former plantations.

INFORMATION WANTED OF MY SON, Allen Jones. He left me before the war, in Mississippi. He wrote me a letter in 1853 in which letter he said that he was sold to the highest bidder, a gentleman in Charleston, S. C. Nancy Jones, his mother, would like to know the whereabouts of the above named person. Any information may be sent to Rev. J. W. Turner, pastor of A. M. E. Church, Ottawa, Kansas.

Newspaper Ad by an Ex-Slave in Search of a Family Member, 1866, Courtesy of Public Domain.

Another aspect of the pursuit of freedom was the reconstitution of families. While some ex-slaves refused to leave plantations and cried for the master, countless others immediately left plantations in search of family members who had been sold away. Newspaper ads sought information about long lost relatives. When not reconstituted, families were rebuilt as newly-freed people sought to gain control over their own children or other

---

[2]Arnold Shaw, *"Honkers and Shouters": The Golden Years of Rhythm and Blues* (New York, New York: Crowell-Collier Press, 1978), 382; Booker T. Washington, "Durham, North Carolina: A City of Negro Enterprises," In the *Booker T. Washington Papers*, Volume II (1911-1912), by Louis R. Harlan and Raymond W. Smock, eds. (Urban, Illinois: University of Illinois Press, 1981), 56-64; and Andre D. Vann and Beverly Washington Jones, *Durham's Hayti: An African American History* (Charleston, S.C.: Arcadia Press, 1998).

children who had been apprenticed to White masters either during the war or as a result of the Black Codes—laws passed to control the lives of African Americans once they became free men and women. Above all, ex-slaves wanted freedom to control their families.

Many ex-slaves also rushed to solemnize unions with formal wedding ceremonies. African Americans' desires to marry fit the government's goal to make free African-American men and women responsible for their own households and to prevent Black women and children from becoming dependent on the government.

Concord Missionary Baptist Church, Concord, N.C., 1880s. Courtesy of Public Domain.

Recently freed people also placed great emphasis on education for their children and themselves. The ability to finally read the Bible for themselves induced work-weary men and women to spend all evening or Sunday attending night school or Sunday school classes. It was not uncommon, as will be discussed in Part Three and Part Four of this volume, to find a one-room school with more than 50 students ranging in age from 3 to 80. Booker T. Washington famously described the situation when he said, "it was a whole race trying to go to school. Few were too young, and none too old, to make the attempt to learn."[3]

One of the more marked transformations that occurred after African-American emancipation was the proliferation of independent Black churches and church associations. Many of these independent churches were quickly organized into regional, state, and even national associations. Through associations like

---

[3]Booker T. Washington, *Up From Slavery: An Autobiography* (Garden City, New York: Doubleday and Company, Inc., 1901), 36.

the Baptist Educational and Missionary Convention (BEMC) of North Carolina, Baptists became the fastest growing post-emancipation denomination, building on their anti-slavery associational roots and carrying on the struggle for African-American rights.

Perhaps the most significant internal transformation in churches had to do with the role of women—a situation that eventually would lead to the development of independent women's conventions in the Baptist, Methodist and Penecostal churches. As will be examined in later chapters, women like Hattie Shepard, Sally A. Eaton and Tempie Whitted of White Rock Baptist Church and leaders of the Woman's Baptist Home Mission Convention (WBHMC) of North Carolina, worked to protect African-American women from sexual violence by White men—a major concern of the majority of African Americans at the time.

African-American churches provided centralized leadership and organization in post-emancipation communities. Moreover, the construction of Black churches symbolized freedom to many African Americans, which is one of the many reasons why a handful of ex-slaves organized White Rock Baptist Church (WRBC), in present-day Durham, North Carolina, in the fall of 1866.

Margaret Ruffin Faucette, Organizer of White Rock Baptist Church, Courtesy of White Rock Baptist Church Archives, Durham, N.C.

Ex-slave Margaret Faucette, a semi-illiterate devout Christian, from Hillsborough, North Carolina, believed that engaging in fervent and constant prayer was the best way for her people to cope with pervasive poverty, homelessness and illiteracy. She felt that it was time for African Americans to depend on their faith in Jesus Christ to help them successfully transition from slavery to freedom. Therefore, praying and worshipping God became her primary focus once slaves in her community became free.

Margaret Faucette, who had become a widow by 1866, moved from her former plantation in Hillsborough to what eventually became known as present-day Durham. For a while, she found lodging in the home of a friend, Mrs. Sally Husband. As a praying woman, Margaret could often be found wherever there was a prayer meeting. She and other ex-slaves met at any place that they could find, whether it was in a shed or beneath a brush arbor,[4] to praise God for His kindness, goodness, guidance and protection. The ex-slaves reveled in the truth that they were not mere beasts who did not deserve freedom. The Bible taught them that they were children of the Most High God, citizens of His heavenly kingdom, and that they had inherent value as humans. When Margaret Faucette and other members of the African-American community entered into prayer and worship, they must have experienced a fleeting but galvanizing foretaste of an eventual eternal reward. What else could they possibly need?

Well, Mrs. Faucette wanted much more and made certain that her family and friends knew it. She had a burning desire to have a definite place of worship. Therefore, not long after she rented the room from her friend, Sally Husband, Faucette invited Reverend Samuel "Daddy" Hunt, an early preacher of ex-slaves and free

Reverend Zuck Horton, First Pastor of White Rock Baptist Church, Courtesy of White Rock Baptist Church Archives, Durham, N.C.

African Americans in Durham, Reverend Zuck Horton and her friends Sally, Joshua Perry, Gos Lee, and Melissa Lee to come to her room to have a prayer meeting. These meetings eventually became services conducted by the church's first pastor, Reverend Horton, who had been preaching before various groups of recently freed slaves throughout the county. With this new appointment, Reverend Horton whose wife, Elizabeth, had recently died, could now settle down and preach to one group of people.

---

[4]Brush arbors were rough, open-sided shelters constructed of vertical poles driven into the ground with additional long poles laid across the top as support for a roof of brush, cut branches or hay. In the immediate aftermath of the Civil War, they were used by ex-slaves as a place to hold religious meetings or services until churches could be built.

First Baptist Church is Organized

Once Reverend Horton became the pastor, their place of worship became known as First Baptist Church. News spread quickly about the new church and, before long, more ex-slaves began to attend services. The room was soon too small for the growing membership. Three subsequent moves followed, first to a cotton gin on Elm Street and then to a warehouse on Peabody Street, and finally to a lot on the corner of Pettigrew and Coleman streets, in Durham. Just before the third move, Reverend Horton died. Less than a year later, Reverend Samuel "Daddy" Hunt was selected by the church's Trustees as its second pastor. The church's name was changed to Colored Missionary Baptist Church.[5]

First Baptist Church Becomes Colored Missionary Baptist Church

Land was ceded to the Colored Missionary Baptist Church on March 13, 1877 by Cornelius Jordan and his wife, Phyllis Jordan. Cornelius, a free mulatto born in 1825 in Orange County, was a farmer and landowner who knew Margaret Faucette. The deed executed by the Jordans was conveyed to the first Trustees and the second pastor of the church. The Trustees referred to in the deed included John W. Cheek, Henry A. Reams, Edward Dolby, Thomas Garwood, and Willis Moore; the pastor was

The First Brick Building of White Rock Baptist Church, 1886-1897, Courtesy of White Rock Baptist Church Archives, Durham, N.C.

Reverend Samuel Hunt. The church's leadership and members built a framed church on the property and it was Margaret Faucette who gave the first $1 towards the $75 that it cost to have the church built. Once the church was constructed, Gos Lee suggested that the

[5]Kelly Bryant, "A Historical Sketch of White Rock," September 7, 1999.

congregation change the name to White Rock Baptist Church because of the large white flint rock located on the property. Nine years later, the church was relocated to Fayetteville Road and Mobile Avenue where the first brick building was erected.[6]

Colored Missionary Baptist Church Moves to New Location and Becomes White Rock Baptist Church

Once the church was moved to a fixed structure, the pastors and members began to establish ministries. The church immediately became involved in helping the community and attracted to its membership several members who eventually became prolific African-American leaders in what was then the Durham Township of Orange County. Some of these members included Dr. Aaron McDuffie Moore who had recently moved to Durham, and Charles Clinton Spaulding and both his first wife, Fannie Jones, who soon died and then his second wife, Charlotte Beatrice Steven Garner.[7]

Margaret Faucette remained an active member of the church from the time that it was first organized until it found its more permanent home. In 1910, old and somewhat feeble, she moved in with her daughter, Nannie Cooper, and son-in-law, James Cooper. Years later, Nannie James Greene fondly recalled a story that her mother, Nannie Cooper, told her about her grandmother, Margaret Faucette. She said,

My mother, Mrs. Nannie B. Cooper, told me that as Dorcas in the Bible went around doing alms deeds, so it was with grandmother. When there was sickness in the neighborhood, she made soup and packed her basket, threw her shawl around her shoulders and away she would go to do her deeds of love and kindness. No grandchild, or young person, visited her without receiving her blessing. The blessing was a kiss, a piece of candy that she had saved for such an occasion, or bread and

---

[6]White Rock Baptist Church Records, 1880s-1990s, North Carolina Central University Archives, Records and History Center, Durham, NC.

[7]Spaulding Papers, Manuscript Division, Rare Book Room, Duke University, Durham, North Carolina.

butter with preserves, or a little cinnamon sprinkled on the bread and butter. . . . Grandma [Margaret] had a song in her heart at all times as she went about her work. Some of the songs that she sang included "Amazing Grace," "I am Bound for the Promised Land," "Soon I will be Done with the Troubles of this World," and "Go Down Moses, Tell Ole Pharaoh to Let My People Go.[8]

Conclusion

It is amazing that only a year after slavery ended, ex-slaves came together in North Carolina to start afresh by establishing a place of worship that provided its members and others with the peace, comfort and strength that they needed to be able to effectively and appropriately respond to the other issues that they faced. White Rock Baptist Church became that place of worship and refuge for members of the African-American community.

White Rock quickly grew in membership and gradually evolved into a place where its members made meaning of the experiences of long-awaited emancipation, interpreted their relationship to the African-American community both in Durham and across North Carolina, and charted a vision for a collective present and future. By 1932, ten different men had served as pastors of White Rock and many of them were instrumental in helping to organize African-Americans Baptists in the State. A more comprehensive discussion of these pastors and their involvement in the organization of ex-slaves who became Baptists is in Part Two of this book.

---

[8]Gazella Poole Lipscomb and Nannie James Cooper Greens, "Dedicated to Margaret Ruffin Faucette," Faucette Family Reunion Program Booklet, July 11-13, 2008.

PART 2

The Church's Earliest Connections to
Religious Institutions in
North Carolina

Chapter Three

A Brief Sketch of White Rock's Earliest Pastors: From Reverend Zuck Horton to Reverend Dr. William Ransome

"And he said to them, 'Go into all the world and proclaim the gospel to the whole creation.'" – Mark 16:15 (ESV)

The infamous Reverend Dr. Augustus Shepard drove his shiny, Black Ford Model T onto the parking lot of White Rock Baptist Church as deacons, members and curious bystanders watched with great anticipation. He parked the car and sat in it for a minute to reflect on the church that he was about to pastor. Just before he was called to the church, it had been torn asunder and in the midst of a major lawsuit. During the chaos and internal strife, many members left to worship at other area churches.[1] As a proviso in the settlement of the lawsuit, a decision of the court was that members of White Rock could not name a pastor for three years. In 1901, at the end of the three-year period,

---

[1]J.A. Whitted, *Biographical Sketch of the Life and Work of the Late Reverend Augustus Shepard, D.D.* (Raleigh, North Carolina: Edwards and Broughton Printing Company, 1912), 51.

the church's leadership chose him as the new pastor. Then one of the deacons lightly tapped the driver's side of the window, which brought Dr. Shepard back to reality.

Reverend Shepard exited the vehicle. As he did so, the growing crowd could not help but notice his well-pressed, white shirt, Black suit, and polished Black shoes. This was his first day as pastor of White Rock Baptist Church, and Reverend Shepard was more than ready to assume the role. He provided a different image for White Rock's leadership than previous pastors. He was well-educated, a world traveler, and both nationally and internationally known.

Reverend Shepard's tenure as pastor was the beginning of a major watershed in the church's history. During his ten-year tenure, not only did the church weather its internal strife but it also experienced changes in its demographics. Reverend Shepard's predecessors, however, had laid an important foundation upon which he was able to build. Without them, there may not have been a White Rock or a Dr. Shepard.

***

White Rock Baptist Church was the *first* African-American religious institution organized in Durham, North Carolina. For its organizers, all recently freed slaves, the church represented religion, community and home, and this continues to be the case today. Like most 19th century African-American churches, White Rock ministered to the needs of the soul and served a host of secular functions, which placed it squarely in the center of African-American social life. This was more evident beginning with Reverend Allen P. Eaton, the church's sixth pastor, and his successors. In the early years, White Rock doubled as a community meeting center and school until a permanent structure could be built, as well as a political hall—the latter especially during Reconstruction.

Reverend Zuck Horton (1866-1869)

Margaret Faucette and other recently freed slaves who gathered under brush arbors to pray and worship, in 1866, selected Zuck Horton as their first pastor because he had gained a reputation in the slave community as a "preacher to Negroes of Durham."[2] Later that same year, the praise services were moved from the "brush arbors" to a room that Faucette had rented on Pettigrew and Husband streets in Durham. Once they began meeting at Mrs. Faucette's home, the group officially became known as First Baptist Church.

Reverend Zuck Horton, Courtesy of White Rock Baptist Church Archives, Durham, N.C.

Little is known about Reverend Horton. Like many of his contemporaries who rose to prominence after the Civil War and emancipation, Reverend Horton and members of First Baptist Church developed a different kind of religious observance that combined elements of African ritual, slave emotionalism, southern suffering, and individual eloquence. In the early days of First Baptist Church, under the leadership of Reverend Horton, church services probably fused African and European forms of religious expression to produce a unique version of worship that reflected the anguish, pain, and occasional elation of nineteenth-century African-American life not only in Durham but across the South.

Reverend Horton served as the preacher of First Baptist Church for three years. He was also actively involved in organizing the first two Baptist Educational and Missionary Conventions. Having lived as a slave for most of his life, the harsh conditions of the institution eventually took its toll. Despite his illness, Reverend Horton continued to seek after God. A product of the Second Great Awakening, Reverend Horton's spiritual journey ended in 1869 when he quickly transitioned to be with his heavenly Father.

As a trailblazer for Durham men in ministry, he laid an arguably strong foundation upon which his successors would proudly build. White Rock Baptist Church was a church inspired

---

[2]Dr. Miles Mark Fisher, *Friends: Pictorial Report of Ten Years Pastorate, 1933-1943* (Durham, N.C.: Service Printing Company, 1943), 8.

through prayer, built primarily around the Word of God and, as described in later chapters, made significant through people who interpreted their Christian faith by serving community needs and African-American cultural development.

Reverend Samuel "Daddy" Hunt *(no photo available)* **(1869-1879)**

Reverend Samuel "Daddy" Hunt, a founding member of First Baptist Church, became its second pastor. When Reverend Hunt assumed leadership of First Baptist Church, its name was changed to the Colored Missionary Baptist Church.[3] Over the next several years, he served as the pastor and continued to convert ex-slaves to Christianity. Furthermore, he led praise and prayer services in the home of Margaret Ruffin Faucette. It is alleged (although not proven) that Reverend Hunt married Faucette, a widow.[4]

Eventually, in March 1877, Reverend Hunt and his rapidly growing congregation decided to build a church. However, they needed land on which they would construct the building. The group also had to demonstrate that once they identified a plot of land, they would find donors to help pay for it. Reverend Hunt and his members were able to acquire land when Cornelius Jordan, a free mulatto who had amassed a considerable amount of wealth during slavery, ceded land to them. Jordan, his wife Phyllis, and Margaret Faucette had known each other since their early days in nearby Orange County. Mrs. Faucette was responsible for persuading the Jordans to cede the land to the church. To further show her commitment to the effort, Ms. Faucette contributed the first $1.00 towards the $75 that it cost to have the church built. Once the modest frame building, located on Peterson and Coleman streets, was constructed, it underwent another name change. Prior to moving into the new building, Reverend Hunt and the congregation of the Colored Missionary Baptist Church decided to change the name to White Rock Baptist

---

[3]Kelly Bryant, "A Historical Sketch of White Rock," September 7, 1999.

[4]Leslie Brown, *Upbuilding Black Durham: Gender, Class, and Black Community Development in the Jim Crow South (Chapel Hill, N.C.: The University of North Carolina Press, 2008), 33.*

Church as suggested by another founding member and trustee, Gos Lee. Membership substantially increased after Reverend Hunt and his existing congregation moved into the new church.

During Reverend Hunt's tenure as pastor, the church services continued to involve a devotional prayer by a leading member of the church, singing by the congregation, and the pastor's sermon. Those who prayed requested a powerful God to ease the earthly burden of the congregation. The prayers were enhanced by the congregation's response, an expression of agreement with the words, "Yes, Lord," "Have mercy, Lord," and "Amen."[5] After the prayer, the congregation usually showed their devotion through song. Oftentimes, an individual would stand up and lead the church members and visitors in song.

Finally, after prayer and song, Reverend Hunt would deliver his sermon. Like many of his contemporaries, Pastor Hunt probably employed all the drama and poetry at his command, injecting vivid imagery and analogy into his biblical accounts conveying understanding of the rewards of righteousness and the wages of sin. One could imagine that Reverend Hunt's sermons stirred the congregation to strive for a more profound faith and a more righteous way of living in a society full of adversity. In doing so, he inarguably provided spiritual guidance for a people whose faith and capacity for forgiveness were tested almost daily. For White Rock's congregation during this period, the church was indeed "a rock in a weary land" and Jesus Christ was the head and in control.

In the meantime, the second pastor of White Rock, demonstrating unwavering faith in God, led his congregation through one of America's most challenging eras—Reconstruction. He never gave up and neither did his members. They continued to place their faith in God as they fought racism heaped upon them by former slaveholders and other racist *Whites* who

---

[5]White Rock Baptist Church Records, 1870s-1980s, Southern Historical Collection, Louis Round Wilson Library, University of North Carolina, Chapel Hill, N.C.; and White Rock Baptist Church Records, 1870s-1980s, African American Resources Collection, James E. Shepard Library, North Carolina Central University, Durham, N.C.

genuinely believed that the most appropriate place for Negroes was bondage. In the end, Reverend Hunt would become one of the longest serving pastors of White Rock Baptist Church.

Reverend Frederick Wilkins (1879-1881), Reverend W. T. Woodard (1881-1884) and Reverend B. K. Butler (1885-1887) *(no photo available)*

Reverend Frederick Wilkins, Third Pastor, Courtesy of White Rock Baptist Church Archives, Durham, N.C.

Reverend W. T. Woodard, Fourth Pastor, Courtesy of White Rock Baptist Church Archives, Durham, N.C.

Reverend Hunt eventually left the church. His next three successors — Reverend Frederick Wilkins, Reverend W.T. Woodard, and Reverend B. K. Butler *(no photo available)* — served as pastors of the church a combined total of seven years, at a time when race relations in Durham and across the nation was at its lowest. Renowned African-American historian Rayford Logan called the post-Reconstruction period in American history from 1877 to 1915 the "nadir in Black life" as lynchings of African-American men, women and children became prevalent and Supreme Court rulings supporting segregation defined African Americans' place in society. African Americans were regarded by the majority race as second-class citizens.[6] During this era, the role of Black churches in their local communities became even more important. It was no different for White Rock and the pastors that led the church during this turbulent time.

Whites believed that Black American churches symbolized African-American freedom and unbridled and dangerous autonomy; therefore, they were set on fire in record numbers or their members were subjected to verbal and physical threats.

---

[6]Rayford Logan, *The Betrayal of the Negro: From Rutherford B. Hayes to Woodrow Wilson* (originally published as *The Negro in American Life and Thought: The Nadir, 1877-1901* and subsequently expanded) (Cambridge, Massachusetts: DaCapo Press, 1997), 59.

While the historical records are virtually silent on how Pastors Wilkins, Woodard and Butler addressed racist attacks, which sometimes silenced its most vocal members, eyewitness accounts suggest that these three men "helped to make Reconstruction's aftermath easier."[7] Furthermore, it is obvious that Reverend Butler did not fear efforts to stop African Americans from building churches. After serving a year as pastor of White Rock, for example, he resigned and organized the Mount Vernon Baptist Church in Durham. Overall, as Christian believers, White Rock's members dealt with obstacles and challenges during this contentious era by praying more and maintaining their focus on Jesus Christ, who would guide them through this temporary crisis. The Holy Spirit was indeed at work in White Rock Baptist Church.

The life and work of the church's next two pastors—Reverend Allen P. Eaton and Reverend Dr. Augustus Shepard—best illustrate how White Rock successfully weathered the storm during the "nadir" of African-American life. Along with some of their more prominent members, Reverend Eaton and Reverend Shepard began to provide alternatives to African Americans living in Jim Crow, or a legally segregated society. Despite efforts by Whites to impede the progress of African Americans, many of them continued to earn a living, rear their children, pursue the benefits of education, and attempt to better themselves individually and collectively. White Rock provided the space many of its members needed to pursue, or actually realize, their goals and dreams during years of retrogression and disappointment as well as progression and satisfaction. Emboldened by the Holy Spirit, many of White Rock's members continued to follow a variety of paths, becoming businessmen as well as farmers, city dwellers as well as rural residents, and men and women of high culture as well as untutored simplicity.

One of the blessings of freedom for African Americans was the opportunity it afforded to come together as much as they

---

[7] Dr. Miles Mark Fisher, *Friends*, 8.

wanted.[8] They did so in clubs, lodges, fraternal organizations and societies, which had suddenly become commonplace. African-American community life also came together in churches. Many African-American churches, like White Rock, became involved in organizations such as the Woman's Baptist Home Mission Convention and the Baptist Educational and Missionary Convention. Several of White Rock's pastors and their wives, such as Reverend Zuck Horton, Reverend Samuel Hunt, Reverend W.T. Woodward, Reverend Allen P. Eaton and his wife, and Reverend Dr. Augustus Shepard and his wife, were actively involved in these conventions. They worked within these organizations and White Rock not only to strive towards achieving racial equality but also to continue to expand the church and its ministries.

Reverend Allen P. Eaton (1888-1898)

When Reverend Allen P. Eaton arrived at White Rock, in 1888, to serve as its sixth pastor, the church was outgrowing its physical structure. As the attack on African Americans' civil, political and economic rights heightened, many Durhamites found solace in the church. This resulted in a marked increase in membership. Therefore, as Reverend Eaton and the church's leadership were forced to look outward to address Durham's many inequalities, they also looked inward to determine how to best meet the needs of a church that was bursting at the seams. Consequently, Pastor Eaton began to engage members in discussions about expanding the church.

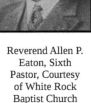

Reverend Allen P. Eaton, Sixth Pastor, Courtesy of White Rock Baptist Church Archives, Durham, N.C

Moreover, Reverend Eaton was one of the early pastors of White Rock who became extremely active in the Black Baptist conventions during his ten-year tenure. The initiatives that he supported at conventions provide some insight on the types of

---

[8]Jeffrey Crowe, Paul Escott and Flora Hatley, *A History of African Americans in North Carolina* (Raleigh, N.C.: North Carolina Office of Archives and History, 2002), 96.

sermons that he may have preached. During this period in American history, many members of his congregation were probably feeling somewhat discouraged about life as a former slave in the United States. As a leading African-American preacher in North Carolina, he may have used his sermons to encourage members of his congregation to take their just and rightful places in society. One could envision Reverend Eaton, especially during this time, juxtaposing the parallels of the Israelites and African Americans in some of his sermons, using the Scriptures to encourage his congregation to remain faithful in the Almighty God. After all, both Israelites and African Americans were once enslaved people who lived under brutal and harsh conditions but were able to prevail because God was in control. Moreover, one could surmise that never in Reverend Eaton's sermons was God depicted as anything other than the all-powerful and all-knowing God who acted mightily on behalf of the poor and oppressed. He knew that his people needed this type of message as they fought to forever remove the shackles of oppression.

The new White Rock Baptist Church Built during Reverend Eaton's Tenure, 1896, Courtesy of White Rock Baptist Church Archives, Durham, N.C.

Regardless of the topic of Reverend Eaton's sermons, the church experienced growth during this era. As a consequence, church expansion was a constant topic for discussion. After much prayer and planning, Reverend Eaton and his congregation laid the cornerstone for a new church structure in 1893, almost seven years into his tenure. The brick structure, located on the corner of Fayetteville Street and Mobile Avenue, had a seating capacity of between 250 and 350 people (accounts given by different historical sources vary). It was completed in 1896.

Despite his many efforts, Reverend Eaton had a difficult twelve-year tenure at White Rock—one filled with internal strife between the leadership and congregation. Reverend Dr. Miles

Mark Fisher, the church's thirteenth full-time permanent pastor, once described Reverend Eaton's tenure as one of "confusion, with no happy adjustment between the lay and the clerical leadership."[9] A year after the new church was built, Reverend Eaton decided to leave White Rock to form St. John's Baptist Church on Dunstan Street in Durham.

The infighting between White Rock's leadership and the congregation did not end with Reverend Eaton's resignation. Instead, it escalated to the point that the courts were called upon to intervene. According to eyewitness accounts, the disagreement that resulted in a court ruling had to do with who would replace Reverend Eaton. Church members who advocated for Reverend Eaton's dismissal wanted to play a greater role in deciding who would be the next pastor. There were at least two opposing factions at White Rock who felt that they should select the next pastor. Members of the congregation, which formed one faction, and the church leadership, which formed the second faction, protested strongly against each other's proposed list of potential pastors. Finally, both groups decided that it was an issue that would not be resolved within the church. Therefore, members of the congregation sued the church's leadership, thereby forcing the local courts to resolve the issue. The courts finally decided "that for the next three years the pastor of the church should not be one who had previously been mentioned as a successor to Pastor Eaton."[10] In other words, as a proviso in the settlement of the suit, the courts required that the "names of three ministers prominently mentioned before by either faction of the church [had to be] excluded from the list of those who would be considered for pastor for three years."[11] Reverend Dr. Augustus Shepard, who would eventually become the next full-time pastor, was among the three ministers that some church members had requested. As a consequence of the court's ruling, White Rock's leadership and

---

[9]Dr. Miles Mark Fisher, *Friends*, 8.

[10]Ibid, 8; J.A. Whitted, *Biographical Sketch of the Life and Work of the Late Reverend Augustus Shepard, D.D.* (Raleigh, North Carolina: Edwards and Broughton Printing Company, 1912), 25.

[11]J.A. Whitted, *Biographical Sketch*, 51.

members decided to appoint a pastor on a temporary basis. For the next three years, Reverend H. H. Henderson served as pastor of White Rock, with the understanding that, once the three-year moratorium of hiring a new permanent preacher ended, a search would begin. The historical records are silent about Reverend Henderson's tenure. Reverend Henderson spent the next three years trying to stabilize the church. No major changes were made during the time that he served as pastor.

Reverend Dr. Augustus Shepard (1901-1911)

After the three years expired, Dr. Shepard's oldest son, Dr. James E. Shepard, the founder of North Carolina Central University, nominated his father for the position. James Shepard was confident that his father could bring structure and calm out of chaos and peace out of confusion at White Rock. Dr. Augustus Shepard's nomination prevailed, thereby making him the eighth pastor of a church that was clearly in turmoil.

Reverend Dr. Augustus Shepard, Eighth Pastor, Courtesy of White Rock Baptist Church Archives, Durham, N.C.

Some people believed that Reverend Augustus Shepard arrived at White Rock at the right time in 1901. Strife and confusion had become commonplace in the church, and many of its longtime members, like Margaret Faucette, were not happy. During this time, White Rock was like the church in Corinth and Reverend Dr. Shepard was Apostle Paul.[12]

Trying to heal from internal dissension and declining membership, the church's members welcomed Dr. Shepard with open arms. He did not disappoint them. A very popular and nationally- and internationally- renowned preacher, it was not difficult to convince some of White Rock's members who had

---

[12]For a more detailed description of how Apostle Paul addressed the problems that plagued the church of Corinth, read 1 Corinthians 5 and 2 Corinthians, New International Version of the Bible; See also Wayne Jackson, "A Troubled Church," *Christian Courier* (November 11, 2011): 14.

opposed his nomination to embrace him.

During his first three years at White Rock, he managed to attract prominent members of the Episcopalian, Presbyterian, Methodist, and Congregational churches to White Rock. It was during this time that the church's demographics began to change from that of African Americans of all socioeconomic statuses to primarily those who were considered the elite of Black Durham. One member suggested that more of Durham's prominent African Americans changed their membership to join White Rock because of Dr. Shepard's "impressive academic credentials, unfailing sweetness of temper, custom to think no evil, even of his enemies, his unswerving employment of means of prayer" and reputation as "a Gospel preacher of the rarest type."[13]

What is clear is that the congregation seemed to have been searching for pastors who were well-educated when they selected Reverend Dr. Shepard. He was well-known but also was a college graduate who had connections with members of the local, state and national communities. Members also wanted a preacher who was an intellectual and scholar. The members of the congregation who wanted preachers to have these types of credentials and experiences were themselves, for the most part, college graduates, served on boards of businesses and organizations in the community, and had professional, white collar jobs. They were Durham's African-American elite. Therefore, when White Rock's congregation searched for its next pastor in 1901, they used themselves as examples of the ideal pastor.

White Rock was quickly becoming a church for middle- to upper- class African Americans and the pastor, the congregants believed, should reflect his congregation. According to Reverend Dr. Miles Mark Fisher, when he arrived at White Rock in 1933, he found a church of "advantaged members" who were "representatives of North Carolina College for Negroes," which included "President Shepard, Dean of Women Ruth Rush, Dean of Men J. T. Taylor, Dr. J. H. Taylor, Rev. Prof. Hughley, Prof. I. B.

---

[13]J.A. Whitted, *Biographical Sketch*, 45, 51-52.

Oglesby, Prof. C. T. Willis, "Little Coach" J. B. McLendon. Librarians Miss Parepa Watson, Miss Margarie Shepard, and Mr. Eric Moore, and Bursar Miss Sudie Holloway, and the Head of the Department of Biology of Shaw University, Dr. Roger Young." Fisher further added, "Three Principals of the Durham City Schools [were] trustees—Prof. William McElrath, Hillside Park High School, and Prof. J. M. Schooler, Lyon Park Elementary School." Reverend Fisher also mentioned that among the members of the congregation were several school teachers, one dentist, Dr. James Hubbard, Sr., one physician, Dr. Bruce, and several nurses. Finally, Dr. Fisher listed among notable members other middle-class African Americans who were "grocers, druggists, shoemakers, barbers and business owners."[14]

As more members of the Black elite joined White Rock, fewer blue collar African Americans sought membership; instead, they began to join other churches that had been organized such as Second Baptist Church (currently known as First Calvary Baptist Church), New Bethel Baptist Church, St. John's Baptist Church, and Mount Vernon Baptist Church.

Dr. Shepard was also extremely interested in rebuilding White Rock's Sunday School, and had the experience to be able to successfully do so. Thus, during his tenure as pastor, Sunday School enrollment at White Rock increased from 150 people, with an average attendance of 70 or 80 people, to 520, with an average attendance of 480.[15] Equally important, members of the church were extremely cooperative, which made it easier for him to lead and accomplish goals. An increase in Sunday School membership naturally required an expansion of

White Rock Baptist Church
Renovations, 1910,
Courtesy of White Rock Baptist
Church Archives, Durham, N.C.

---

[14]Reverend Dr. Miles Mark Fisher, *Friends,* 32.

[15]Ibid., 52.

facilities. Therefore, Dr. Shepard, other members of the church's leadership, and members of the congregation approved improvements to the Sunday School annex and then modernized other parts of the church. According to one member who witnessed the improvements, "No church, white or colored, in Durham, [had] the same conveniences and modern appliances."[16] A new edifice was also built, which was opened to the public in 1911. The renovations were so major that the church leadership was forced to use a tent as a temporary place of worship.

Reverend Shepard was also committed to enlisting young men in the work of the church. Therefore, the church was remodeled, and a wing called the Baraca Room was added to the Mobile Avenue side of the sanctuary. This annex provided seating capacity for 250 men.

The Baraca Class started with six students and, within a month, the class grew to 105, with an average attendance of 64. The motto of the class was, "Young Men Helping Young Men, All Standing by the Bible."[17] The class assisted the sick members, helped in the general work of the church, and instilled in young men the need to save their money. The class did a lot of good for the church and had a great deal of influence in helping members.

Reverend Shepard also made other renovations to the church. In the basement, a kitchen and classrooms were added. The North wall of the main sanctuary was removed, expanding the seating capacity to 800, including the balcony. The renovation was completed, in 1911, with a new church façade, a library, public baths, an elevated floor in the main sanctuary and the installation of a pipe organ, at a total cost of $20,000 to $26,000.

The new pastor also tried to lay a religious foundation in all members by making special efforts to acquaint them with the Bible. He often emphasized that the Bible was not a toy to decorate the center tables of parlors, but instead a guidebook to be

---

[16]Ibid., 53.

[17]Ibid., 62.

read in daily family devotion and applied to their lives. In other words, the Bible had to be their daily companion.

During Pastor Shepard's tenure, membership and monetary collections increased. Everything seemed to be going well for a church founded by recently freed slaves just a little over four decades earlier. Much progress had been made in the church in such a short period of time. With Dr. Shepard as the lead pastor, many church members, especially those in leadership positions, tirelessly worked with him and other churches across the state. The White Rock Baptist Church of 1900, known for its chaos and confusion, had undergone considerable change by 1910. It was a church that was undoubtedly grounded in Biblical Scripture and many of its members conducted their lives according to the Great Commission. Gone was the chaos and confusion that were so pervasive in the church before Reverend Shepard arrived.

In September 1911, Reverend Shepard became seriously ill. He died seven weeks later on November 19, 1911. Thousands of African Americans and Whites, from across North Carolina, of all socioeconomic backgrounds, attended his visitation services held on the eve of his funeral.

White Rock was also filled to capacity during his funeral. According to some sources, there was not a dry eye in the sanctuary.[18] One dignitary after another spoke fondly of Dr. Shepard—a man that they considered as one of the best Gospel preachers in North Carolina's African-American community.

After Dr. Shepard's death, the church that had made so much progress was in limbo again. White Rock's leadership began a search for another pastor. In the meantime, one of its members and Durham's first African-American doctor, Dr. Aaron Moore, donated property to the church for a future Sunday School. He was determined to continue the work that Dr. Shepard had begun.

---

[18]J.A. Whitted, *History of Negro Baptists in North Carolina* (Raleigh, North Carolina: Presses of Edwards and Broughton Printing Company, 1908), 112.

Over the next two years after Dr. Shepard's death, several reputable clergymen preached at White Rock. One such person was Reverend Dr. James E. Shepard, the founder and first president of the National Religious Training School and Chautauqua. He was also ordained as a preacher at White Rock in 1912, the year after his father died.

Reverend Dr. Edward McKnight Brawley (1913-1919)

After having several pastors to preach over a two-year period, Reverend Dr. Edward McKnight Brawley was invited by the Deacons to be the next permanent full-time pastor of White Rock. He was known as a teaching preacher, largely due to his background. It seems that the church's leadership was in search of a religious leader that would focus on teaching more than

preaching. Reverend Brawley was the ideal person.

Born a free man, in March 1851, in Charleston, South Carolina, Reverend Brawley began his education at the age of four, when a private tutor taught him to read and prepared him for school. He only attended school until he was about eight or nine years old because his school for African Americans closed in response to John Brown's raid.[19] In 1861, Brawley's parents sent him to Philadelphia to attend school. He

Reverend Dr. Edward M. Brawley, Ninth Pastor, Courtesy of White Rock Baptist Church Archives, Durham, N.C.

---

[19]John Brown, a White abolitionist, led a raid on Harper's Ferry, Virginia, in 1859, as part of an armed slave revolt. The goal was to take over a United States arsenal at Harpers Ferry. Brown's party of 22 was defeated by a company of U.S. Marines, led by First Lieutenant Israel Greene. Colonel Robert E. Lee was in overall command of the operation to retake the arsenal. John Brown had originally asked Harriet Tubman and Frederick Douglass to join him in his raid. Tubman was prevented from joining because she was ill and Douglass declined, as he believed John Brown's plan would fail. And it did. For additional details about the raid, see the following: Horace Greeley, *The American Conflict: A History of the Great Rebellion in the United States of America, 1860-1864.* Volume 1 (Chicago, Illinois: O.D. Case and Company, 1866), 279; James McPherson, *Battle Cry of Freedom: The Civil War Era* (Oxford, United Kingdom: Oxford University Press, 1988), 201; Stephen Sears, *Landscape Turned Red: The Battle of Antietam* (New York, New York: Houghton Mifflin Company, 2003), 116; and Marian Taylor, *Harriet Tubman: Antislavery Activist* (Langhorne, Pennsylvania: Chelsea House Publishers, 2004), 68-69.

first attended a grammar school and, after three years, entered the Institute for Colored Youth. He remained there until 1866. In April 1865, he was baptized into the Baptist church, became involved in Sunday Schools, and made plans for the ministry. Brawley then returned to Charleston, in 1869, and was apprenticed to be a shoemaker; but, in 1870, he enrolled at Howard University as the school's first regularly enrolled theology student. After three months, he left Howard and enrolled in the preparatory department of Bucknell University in Lewisburg, Pennsylvania, becoming the school's first African-American student. He was given a partial scholarship by the president of Bucknell. He personally paid the remainder of his college expenses by teaching vocal music and preaching during the summers. In the fall of that same year, Brawley finished his preparation and enrolled in the University, graduating June 30, 1875. He earned an A.M. from Bucknell University in 1878, and an honorary Doctor of Divinity from Simmons College of Kentucky in May 1885.[20]

In 1873, Reverend Brawley was licensed to preach by the White Baptist church in Lewisburg and, on July 1, 1875, he was ordained in that particular church and commissioned by the American Baptist Publication Society (ABPS) as missionary for South Carolina. Finding a lack of Sunday schools in the area, he established Sunday school organizations and, in May 1877, formed these bodies into a state Sunday School Convention, of which he became corresponding secretary and financial agent.[21] Among his successes was securing funding for the Benedict Institute (today known as Benedict College) and working to open missions in Africa. During this period and later he was frequently an invited and well-received speaker at the annual national convention of the American Baptist Publication Societies. After eight years, Reverend Brawley resigned due to ill health and took

---

[20]William Simmons and Henry McNeal Turner, *Men of Mark: Eminent, Progressive and Rising* (Cleveland, Ohio: G.M. Rewell and Company, 1887), 908-912.

[21]William Montgomery, *Under Their Own Vine and Fig Tree: The African-American Church in the South, 1865-1900* (Baton Rouge, Louisiana: Louisiana State University Press, 1995), 113-114.

a six-month vacation.[22] During those eight years, he helped found 550 Baptist churches in South Carolina with 350 preachers and nearly 100,000 members.[23]

In January 1877, Brawley married Mary Warrick of Virginia. During that year the couple had a child, but by December both mother and child died. In December 1879, he married Margaret Dickerson of Columbia, South Carolina, and the couple had nine children, including nationally recognized prolific author and educator Benjamin Brawley.[24]

In October 1883, Reverend Brawley became president of Alabama Baptist Normal and Theological School, whose name was later changed to Selma University. He was well-loved as president and gave half of his salary to aid poor students.[25] He also founded the Alabama Baptist Women's Convention to provide monetary support to the school.[26] After three years, his second wife's health began to decline; therefore, Reverend Brawley resigned from Selma University and returned to South Carolina.

In January 1887, he began to publish the weekly paper, the *Baptist Tribune* and was district secretary for the south for the American Baptist Publication Society (which will be discussed in detail in a later chapter), a position he resigned from in 1890 to become pastor of the First Baptist Church in Petersburg, Virginia.[27] In 1890, he published a collection of works entitled, *The Negro Baptist Pulpit: A Collection of Sermons and Papers by Colored*

---

[22]William Simmons and Henry Turner, *Men of Mark*, 908-912.

[23]Allen Ballard, *One More Day's Journey: The Story of a Family and a People* (New York, New York: McGraw-Hill, 1984), 120-121.

[24]Arthur Caldwell, ed., *History of the American Negro* (Atlanta, Georgia: A.B. Caldwell Publishing Company, 1921), 470-471.

[25]William Simmons and Henry Turner, *Men of Mark*, 911.

[26]Wilson Fallin, *Uplifting the People: Three Centuries of Black Baptists in Alabama* (Tuscaloosa, Alabama: University of Alabama Press, 2007), iv.

[27]Daniel Culp, *Twentieth Century Negro Literature: Or a Cyclopedia of Thought on the Vital Topics Relating to the American Negro* (Atlanta, Georgia: J.L. Nichols and Company, 1902), 254-256.

Baptist Ministers. The work included 28 essays.[28] Shortly after, he resigned his pastorate to resume work for the Society. In 1899, he was pastor of a church in Darien, Georgia, when the city experienced a major race riot. Reverend Brawley was an outspoken leader in calls for peace and in the innocence of African-American people imprisoned in the event's aftermath.[29] By 1902, he had become Editorial Secretary of the National Baptist Publishing Board.[30]

In 1908, he helped found Morris College in Sumter, South Carolina, and in April 1911, the school was incorporated. He became the college's first president.[31] A year later, he resigned from Morris College to become pastor at White Rock Baptist Church.

During Reverend Brawley's career, he was pastor of many churches before his appointment at White Rock Baptist Church in 1913. For example, he served as pastor of Tabernacle Baptist Church in Selma, Alabama, Springfield Baptist Church in Greenville, South Carolina, and First Baptist Church in Fernandina, Florida.[32] Additionally, other than *The Negro Baptist Pulpit*, he wrote many other books, pamphlets and tracts.

One of the most significant achievements during Reverend Brawley's six-year tenure at White Rock was the establishment of a library in the basement of the church. In 1916, the library was moved to the corner of East Pettigrew and Fayetteville Street. Once the library relocated, it was named the Durham Colored Library—the forerunner of what is now Durham's Stanford L.

---

[28]Shirley Logan, *We are Coming: The Persuasive Discourse of Nineteenth-Century Black Women* (Carbondale, Illinois: Southern Illinois University Press, 1999), 167-168; and Martha Simmons, *Preaching with Sacred Fire: An Anthology of African American Sermons, 1750 to the Present* (New York, New York: W.W. Norton and Company, 2010), 247-256.

[29]"Author Unknown, "Race Riots his Theme." *Evening Star Newspaper* (Washington, D.C.), October 20, 1899, 16.

[30]Daniel Culp, *Twentieth Century Negro*, 256.

[31]Glenn Starks, *Historically Black Colleges and Universities: An Encyclopedia* (Santa Barbara, California: ABC-CLIO, 2011), 152.

[32]Arthur Caldwell, *History of the American Negro*, 471.

Warren Public Library. Also, while serving as pastor, he taught part-time as professor of Evangelism and Old Testament at Shaw University, in Raleigh, North Carolina.

Reverend Brawley resigned from White Rock Baptist Church in 1919, a year after World War I ended. He was fondly remembered by members as a "teacher of the Bible in the church."[33] After his resignation, he moved to Raleigh, North Carolina and began to teach full-time at Shaw University. He died on January 13, 1923, in Raleigh, and was buried in Durham, North Carolina.[34] Once again, White Rock's Trustees began their search for a new pastor.

Reverend Dr. James Kirkland (1920-1924)

Once again, in 1919, White Rock's leadership began its search for a new pastor. A year later, in 1920, Dr. James Kirkland, of Darlington, South Carolina, became the tenth pastor. He was the third pastor of Macedonia Missionary Baptist Church, in

Darlington, before he resigned to accept the pastorate of White Rock. While at Macedonia, Dr. Kirkland was regarded as a "man of great vision who planted the seed that inspired the congregation to build" the new church structure that still exists today.[35]

When he arrived at White Rock, Durham, like most cities and towns across America, began to experience prosperity. In post-World War I

Durham, businesses in both African-American and White communities began to flourish, and the more people earned, the more they paid in tithes and offerings.

Dr. Kirkland primarily focused on improving

Reverend Dr. James Kirkland, Tenth Pastor, Courtesy of White Rock Baptist Church Archives, Durham, N.C.

---

[33]Dr. Miles Mark Fisher, *Friends*, 9.

[34]North Carolina, Deaths, 1906-1930. Salt Lake City, Utah: Family Search, 2013.

[35]Macedonia Missionary Baptist Church Website, "Church History," June 17, 2018.

worship services during his four-year tenure. Among his achievements were the installation of two additional pipe organs, one which was made in England,[36] and the construction of a modern parsonage at 1219 Fayetteville Street. Dr. Kirkland resigned in 1924 and returned to Darlington, South Carolina.

Reverend Dr. S. L. McDowell (1924-1930)

That same year, White Rock's leadership welcomed Reverend Dr. S.L. McDowell as it eleventh pastor. Reverend Dr. McDowell had spent a considerable amount of time in Ontario, Canada, where he was licensed to preach and later ordained to the ministry. In 1910, he became pastor of University Avenue Baptist Church in Toronto, Ontario, Canada, where he remained for a number of years before beginning his tenure at White Rock.

Reverend Dr. McDowell arrived in Durham in 1924 to begin his tenure as the eleventh pastor. Dr. McDowell, who had earned both a Bachelor of Theology and a Doctor of Divinity, was regarded as a person interested in "reaching the masses." In the six years that he served as pastor of White Rock, Reverend McDowell did what he could to help people in Durham's community. According to Reverend Dr. Miles Mark Fisher, Reverend McDowell "wore out several Ford cars taking people to their engagements."

Reverend Dr. S.L. McDowell, Eleventh Pastor, Courtesy of White Rock Baptist Church, White Rock Baptist Church Archives, Durham, N.C.

He was also a "church administrator," converting the house donated by Dr. Aaron McDuffie Moore into "a church office." He also employed a "church secretary." Additionally, other changes made during Reverend McDowell's tenure included holding prayer meetings on "Wednesday and Saturday nights" at "his house" located next to the church, hosting the local Ministerial Alliance, and publishing a "directory of the church with a short history in

---

[36]Ibid.

1926."[37]

During Reverend McDowell's tenure, church member Charles Spaulding became actively involved in the National Negro Business League (NNBL), which included people like Booker T. Washington before his death. Spaulding to the inner circles of the NNBL, serving as secretary-treasurer as well as chair of the executive committee during the 1920s.[38] The NNBL had several institutional allies, one being churches. Given Spaulding's position in the organization, White Rock was one of the major religious institutions.

In the 1920s, one of the major goals of NNBL was to secure membership from Black-owned businesses. To assist in the effort, Reverend McDowell would give special evening sermons on business cooperation at White Rock. As a consequence, many of the African- American business owners at the church joined.[39] Reverend McDowell left White Rock in 1930. The Trustees began their search, once again, for a pastor.

Reverend Dr. William Ransome (1931-1932)

Reverend Dr. William Ransome, Twelfth Pastor, Courtesy of White Rock Baptist Church Archives, Durham, N.C.

Although White Rock's leadership and members expected the next pastor to remain for a longer period of time than his recent predecessors, Reverend Dr. William Ransome stayed for only one year. Heavily credentialed with Bachelor of Arts, Master of Arts, Bachelor of Law, and Doctor of Divinity degrees, Reverend Ransome was inarguably an intellectual. Although he remained at White Rock only from 1931-1932, he accomplished a great deal. During his tenure, he established the following initiatives: (1) alphabetical church groups; (2) women ushers; (3)

---

[37]Reverend Dr. Miles Mark Fisher, *Friends,* 10.

[38]Walter Weare, *Black Businesses in the New South: A Social History of the North Carolina Mutual Life Insurance Company* (Durham, North Carolina: Duke University Press, 1993), 15.

[39]Ibid., 146.

a forum or lyceum; (4) a church aid society; (5) a revival; and a (6) $1000 financial campaign. Reverend Ransome also encouraged more fellowship among members.[40]

He left White Rock to return as pastor of First Baptist Church in South Richmond, Virginia. Reverend Dr. Ransome spent most of his remaining years working for civil rights and racial equality for African Americans. A prolific author and writer, he also served as the lone African-American religious editor of the *Baptist Herald*, in Richmond, Virginia. In this role, he covered Black Baptist life in Virginia for the Baptist General Association of Virginia and Allied Bodies.[41]

Reverend Dr. Ransome was succeeded by internationally recognized pastor, scholar, educator, and author, Reverend Dr. Miles Mark Fisher. Based on a letter that Dr. Ransome sent Dr. Fisher prior to the latter's arrival at White Rock, he seemed somewhat instrumental in helping White Rock to secure Dr. Fisher. An excerpt from his February 1932 letter to Dr. Fisher reads: "I have said much concerning you. . . I have gratuitously inherited all that [my predecessors at White Rock] had accomplished. Here was an adequate church plant conservatively valued at about $85,000, and a congregation to worship in it. These people were accustomed to worship, patience, struggle, social vision, business, academic preparation, and spirituality and had outgrown rallies and revivals and church bartering. White Rock was the first church in age among Negroes in Durham."[42]

Conclusion

Clearly, White Rock Baptist Church had changed considerably since it was first organized in 1866 by Margaret Ruffin Faucette and a handful of other ex-slaves. Mrs. Faucette, whose husband, William had died by the late 1860s, lived until

---

[40]Ibid.

[41]Douglas Thompson, *Richmond's Priests and Prophets: Race, Religion and Social Change in the Civil Rights Era* Tuscaloosa, Alabama: The University of Alabama Press, 2017), 62.

[42]Reverend Dr. Miles Mark Fisher, *Friends,* 10.

she was 99 years old. She also remained a member of White Rock all of her life, witnessing the ministry of at least the first nine pastors. A church that was first comprised of a group of ex-slaves from all walks of life eventually transformed into a religious institution for Durham's African-American elite. One thing, however, remained constant at White Rock. From its organization in 1866 to the present, the church's leadership and congregation focused not only on improving its ministries within the church but also reaching out to members of the African American community to help improve their lives. They began immediately following emancipation by focusing on outreach with newly-formed African-American churches.

Chapter Four

A Divine Connection:
White Rock Joins Other Black Baptists in Work with Organizing Baptist Churches

"For just as we have many members in one body and all the members do not have the same function, so we, who are many, are one body in Christ, and individually members one of another." -Romans 12: 4-5 (KJV)

After eating supper with Margaret Faucette and Sally Husband, Reverend Zuck Horton, a recent widower and first pastor of White Rock Baptist Church,[1] returned home so that he could finish his speech for the annual Baptist Educational and Missionary Convention (BEMC).[2] The Convention was first organized in Goldsboro, North Carolina, in 1867, primarily by pioneers Reverend Horton, Reverend Harry

---

[1]When Reverend Zuck Horton became the pastor of White Rock Baptist Church, it was known as First Baptist Church. First Baptist became known as Colored Missionary Baptist Church in 1877 and White Rock Baptist Church by 1880.

[2]For a brief period of time, in 1867, the founding members of the Baptist Educational and Missionary Convention, were known as the General Association of the Colored Baptists of North Carolina. Over the years, the organization went through several additional name changes: Union Baptist Convention and the General Baptist State Convention of North Carolina.

Cowan, Reverend Thomas Parker, Reverend R.H. Parker, Reverend Edward Eagles, Reverend William Warwick, and eight other Black preachers across the State of North Carolina, to assist African-American churches with their organization efforts and to engage in missionary work among newly freed Blacks.[3] The handful of African-American preachers who planned and organized the first BEMC in North Carolina had little or no experience in Christian work, were recently freed from slavery, had no money, and at least two of them did not have a church in which to hold worship services. What these men did have, however, was strong faith in God and a fundamental belief that their purpose in life was what God had ordained and equipped them to accomplish in order that they might bring Him the greatest glory.

Reverend Harry Cowan, One of the Pioneers in Black Baptist Work, 1867, Courtesy of White Rock Archives, Durham, N.C.

On that cold, autumn day in September 1867, Reverend Horton was writing a speech for the Convention, which would host its first general session the following morning. He put the final touches on his opening remarks and then began to reflect on how far he had come since the days of slavery. He thought about what it was like as a slave on the Horton Estate of the Stagville Plantation, located in present-day northeast Durham County. The horrors of slavery were still visible in Reverend Horton's leather-brown face and on his partially scarred body. Yet, he had a smile on his face because he knew that the slaveholder may have once owned his body but never his soul. Reverend Horton proclaimed what believers knew then and still know, that his soul belonged to God.[4] Furthermore, he believed that it was God's mercy that helped him to survive the treacherous storms of life during

---

[3]J.A. Whitted, *A History of the Negro Baptists of North Carolina* (Raleigh, North Carolina: Presses of Edwards and Broughton Printing Company, 1908), 34. The Baptist Educational and Missionary Convention underwent several name changes. Today, it is the General Baptist State Convention of North Carolina.

[4]Ezekiel 18:4, *Holy Bible*, English Standard Version.

slavery and would continue to help him as a free man. While in this state of deep reflection, Reverend Horton fell asleep.

Night finally faded into day. Reverend Horton slowly forced his frail, arthritic body out of bed. He was extremely excited about spending time with his fellow preachers at the BEMC. He and the other African-American preachers believed that it was extremely important that ex-slaves and free Blacks understood that they were no longer defined by slavery or the racist ideology espoused by White America but rather by the new things that had come from God. The horrors of slavery and the oppression that ex-slaves, and even free Blacks, had endured for many years did not define their purpose in life or their destiny in post-Emancipation America. This, therefore, was the message that Reverend Horton and his colleagues repeatedly conveyed, in different formats, to the Convention's attendees.

In less than two years after slavery, ex-slaves in the Durham township of Orange County had not only organized the community's first Black Baptist church, which was White Rock, but also appointed a preacher who wanted to help his congregation fulfill God's purpose in their lives and assist in the development of Black Baptist churches and the education of Black preachers across North Carolina. Equally remarkable is that during this same period, Durham and other communities across North Carolina had begun to witness firsthand the power of God. The seemingly powerless, enslaved and so-called docile Negro was quickly being replaced with a more confident Christian believer who had been empowered by God to fulfill his or her true purpose in life.

***

Reverend Horton and other pioneers of the post-Civil War Black Baptist Movement in North Carolina also felt that the White slaveholder had tried to take what God had ordained for them. Similarly, they believed that Whites had attempted to strip them not only of their identity but also their humanity. As a consequence, between 1867 and 1900, the annual BEMC conventions included sessions for recently freed Black preachers who wanted guidance and advice on either organizing their first Baptist church or enhancing churches already established. Given the two aforementioned goals of the Convention's organizers, John 10:10 best defined the theme of the three-day event during the first decade after the Civil War. In this Scripture verse, Jesus states, "The thief comes only to steal and to kill and to destroy; I came that they may have life, and have it abundantly." Horton and other African-American preachers must have cited this Scripture when encouraging aspiring Black preachers and other Christians to continue allowing God to use them. Historical church records show that they frequently cautioned Convention participants that although slavery was over, Whites would not stop trying to take and destroy what Jesus had given them, which was freedom and renewed life. They reasoned that all Satan — better known as the former slaveholder — wanted to do was to ruin the lives of African Americans who were believers by confiscating their identity in Jesus Christ. They further encouraged participants not to continue to define themselves by their experiences as slaves and suggested that African Americans assembled at the BEMC read 2 Corinthians 5:16-17 if they were not certain of their identity as free men.[5]

To further make their point, Reverend Horton and other Convention organizers also frequently cited 2 Corinthians 5:16-17. In this Scripture, Paul describes in his letter to the church at Corinth exactly who people are as believers in Jesus Christ, when he avows, "From now on we recognize no one according to the flesh; even though we have known Christ according to the flesh, yet now we know Him in this way no longer. Therefore, if anyone is in Christ, he is a new creature; the old things passed away; behold, new things have come." Since most of the attendees often thought about their physical appearance when reading this

---

[5]Matthew Harper, "The End of Days: African American Religion and Politics in the Age of Emancipation," *North Carolina Historical Review* (April 2003), Volume 80, No. 2; J.A. Whitted, *History of Negro Baptists in North Carolina* (Raleigh, North Carolina: Presses of Edwards and Broughton Printing Company, 1908), 33; and White Rock Baptist Church Records, "Correspondence from the Baptist Educational and Missionary Convention," Folder 128, General Administrative Materials, Southern Historical Collection, University of North Carolina, Chapel Hill, N.C.

Scripture, Horton and his colleagues, therefore, felt compelled to elucidate its meaning. They made clear that when Paul says, "we recognize no one according to the flesh," he is saying one is not evaluated merely by his or her external, physical appearance. Rather, one is assessed based on his or her authentic core. In other words, Reverends Horton, Cowan as well as some of the other African-American preachers at the Convention reasoned, one must recognize or acknowledge people according to who they are inside, not based on their physical attributes.

In an effort to further clarify 2 Corinthians 5: 16-17, session leaders would further maintain that one's authentic core is the brand-new creation or self. Believers, they reasoned, are re-created in Jesus Christ. In other words, Jesus placed a brand-new essence, core or spirit inside of believers. More importantly, they argued, in order for the preachers at the BEMC to fulfill their God-given purpose in life, they must abide in Jesus Christ and fully embrace those things that have come from God. They must rediscover who they are because slavery and/or racial oppression had been their identity. They had been defined by their slave status or their function in antebellum life, which had influenced how little they thought of themselves as human beings. These beliefs continued to be prevalent among ex-slaves in the immediate post-Civil War era. Reverend Horton and other organizers of the BEMC knew that if they were going to be successful in addressing the multitude of African-American's needs, they had to change how ex-slaves thought and felt about themselves. They used the Bible to do so, making it the ex-slaves' daily companion, that is, a book to turn to when they needed reassurance, guidance or a friend. Additionally, Horton and others deduced that the ex-slave-turned-preachers must never look at each other or themselves again as slaves or an innately inferior people. Within each of them, instead, was a brand-new creation and God was the only one who could define them. The Convention's attendees, the majority of whom were ex-slaves, were inspired and motivated by this message.[6] In order to get

---

[6]Ibid.

much needed work done, Reverend Horton, Reverend Cowan and other leaders at the Convention needed every living body engaged in the activities. These men also realized that they were working with ex-slaves who had been told all of their lives that they were an inferior race—that they had no real self-worth.

Horton and the other preachers leading the BEMC sessions and meetings often reminded those in attendance that they must allow God to tell them who they are, especially as they lead their respective congregations. To do so, they must connect with God. The session leaders urged the participants to read and study the *Holy Bible*. Their entreaties did not begin or end at the Convention. Horton, Cowan and the other preachers, who were rapidly becoming leaders in the local Black community, made the same plea to their respective congregations.[7]

For the other organizers of the BEMC, it was critical that aspiring African-American preachers had a relationship with God themselves before preaching to the masses. It was also equally important that they were in constant prayer and studied God's Word, especially since they were also responsible for helping non-believers in Christ to become believers. The leaders always reminded Convention attendees, especially in sessions for aspiring preachers, they needed to fully commit themselves to God so that their thoughts would align with His thoughts.

There were also a few White Baptist preachers in attendance at the Convention. The organizers of the meeting believed that they needed White preachers to help them in planning the program for the Convention and offer advice for its future operation. Blacks felt that White preachers provided valuable assistance.[8] It was evident that the organization of Black churches was imperatively necessary, and the BEMC was determined to do so.

---

[7]White Rock Baptist Church Records, "Correspondence from the Baptist Educational and Missionary Convention," Folder 62—Sermons, General Administrative Materials, Southern Historical Collection, University of North Carolina, Chapel Hill, N.C.

[8]J.A. Whitted, *A History of Negro Baptists of North Carolina*, 16.

Creating Unexpected Alliances to Fulfill God's Purpose

Although preachers at the BEMC cautioned Convention participants to be aware of ill-intentioned Whites, they were quick to add that there were some Whites who had always supported religious instruction for African Americans. Because they regarded the BEMC as part of God's purpose for them, these men believed that anything one could do on his or her own was too small to be God's plan for that individual. Therefore, they reminded their colleagues that even the organizers of the BEMC needed help.

They would often compare themselves to Moses in the wilderness who eventually learned that he could not fulfill his God-given purpose on his own. It took Moses forty years in the wilderness to learn the lesson of dependence. He required a setback in order to be set up for his purpose. But when his purpose was revealed, God showed up in an extraordinary way. Reverend Horton and the others learned from Moses' story that they needed to allow God to work with and through them. This would often require that they collaborate with individuals with whom they did not want or expect to cooperate. This attitude was predicated on their belief that, regardless of their race, these individuals were a part of God's plan. To make their point, the organizers of the BEMC would give accounts of the many illustrations in the Bible of how God brought people, events, circumstances and other things together at the right time.

The pastors who organized the BEMC, therefore, worked collaboratively with Whites, many from the North who had served as missionaries to slaves and educated African-Americans preachers long before slavery ended. Some African Americans at the Convention wanted to continue these valuable relationships after gaining their freedom, and the White missionaries were willing to oblige. Also, many of the leaders of the Convention knew that members of their race could benefit immensely from the experiences and expertise provided by White missionaries. They began by collaborating with the American Baptist Home Mission Society (ABHMS)—a White organization that would not only be able to authorize the organizers of the Convention to serve as missionaries to members of their own race but also send White missionaries to North Carolina to assist the organizers in their proselytizing efforts until they had enough of their own people ready to assume such a major undertaking. This was indeed a divine connection.

The Baptist Educational and Missionary Convention, American Baptist Home Mission Society and Establishment of Shaw University

Reverend Dr. Henry Tupper, Founder of Shaw University (aka as Shaw Collegiate Institute), 1865, Courtesy of Public Domain.

Officials of the American Baptist Home Mission Society sent Reverend Henry Martin Tupper, who had recently been honorably discharged from the Union Army, to assist Horton and the other 13 African-American preachers. Having been interested in mission work since childhood, Dr. Tupper, accompanied by his wife, arrived in Raleigh on October 10, 1865, only six months after the end of the Civil War. His primary responsibility was to teach religion to ex-slaves in the city who had been left bitter and in poverty because of slavery and the recently fought Civil War. Dr. Tupper's goal changed, however, once he arrived in Raleigh and saw the religious needs of the African-American community. After giving the matter considerable thought, he decided that a school was needed to train ministers and educate the Black masses in the State. Reverend Horton and the other African-American preachers were elated that Dr. Tupper wanted to provide a formal education for those Black ministers who were quick to assert that they had been called by God to preach. One of their major challenges was having enough educated ministers. So, they welcomed Reverend Tupper with open arms. However, everyone did not feel the same as Horton and the other leading African-American preachers. Not everybody approved of such a school. In fact, some opponents of education for African Americans were quite hostile.

Despite increasing hostilities and opposition, by December 1, 1865, Dr. Tupper had succeeded in organizing a class of ministers. The theology class was taught in the old Guion Hotel (where the North Carolina Museum of History now stands in Raleigh, North Carolina). Since most of the initial attendees were illiterate, the class consisted primarily of lessons in reading and writing.

In February of the following year, with the aid of a few of his former followers who had been slaves, Dr. Tupper built a two-story wooden school and church, on the corner of Blount and Cabarrus Streets, in Raleigh, on a lot for which he paid with his own savings. The school became known as Raleigh Theological Institute and the church was called Second Baptist Church.[9] Meanwhile, Mrs. Tupper aided by establishing a school for Black women. The entire project was at first financed with money secured from a night school taught by Dr. and Mrs. Tupper, for which students had to pay five cents per night.[10] This method did not prove to be satisfactory, however, and appeals for help were sent to Northern friends. Among the first to respond were Andrew Porter, of Monson, Massachusetts, and Elijah Shaw, a woolen manufacturer, of Wales, Massachusetts. Additionally, a few churches and Sunday Schools became interested and sent aid. Despite financial assistance from Porter, Shaw and Sunday Schools throughout North Carolina, Dr. Tupper still needed extra funds. But, he did not discontinue his plans because of inadequate funding. Instead, he continued with his plans and eventually completed construction of the school. He finished building the school just in time to begin training aspiring Black preachers that had been sent to the school by Reverends Horton, Cowan and Parker. As part of their mission, these men desperately needed a place that would offer a formal education for Black preachers, and God made it happen. Horton, Cowan and others knew that just as God had prepared them to fulfill their purpose, He also prepared others like Reverend Tupper and his wife to assist them. This was a divine connection planned by God.

---

[9]From these humble beginnings, two institutions were eventually born—Shaw University and the historic Tupper Memorial Baptist Church.

[10]*Shaw University Bulletin*, Diamond Jubilee Souvenir, Raleigh, NC, 1940, 12.

On January 1, 1869, Reverend Tupper admitted Raleigh Theological Institute's first class of fifteen seminary students. Reverends Horton,[11] Cowan and the others were extremely thrilled and looked forward to having 15 newly trained preachers. They knew that there were many more African-American preachers who could benefit from training at the Raleigh Theological Institute. For that reason, Horton and the other organizers of the Baptist Educational and Missionary Convention that year agreed to join other groups and individuals who decided to make annual monetary donations to Dr. Tupper and the Institute. Needless to say, Tupper and the Institute benefited from the donations.

Shaw Collegiate Institute, 1871, Courtesy of White Rock Baptist Church Archives, Durham, N.C.

A year later, the school had outgrown its facilities and Tupper began making plans to expand. Accordingly, Tupper's fundraising efforts and additional monetary support from Elijah Shaw as well as the American Baptist Home Mission Society and the Baptist Educational and Missionary Convention attendees provided him with enough money to purchase an estate in the center of Raleigh. The building was erected, in 1870 and 1871, by Dr. Tupper and his students from bricks baked on the campus. Upon relocating, the school changed its name to Shaw Collegiate Institute. In 1875, the school officially became incorporated as Shaw University, which offered a baccalaureate degree to students graduating from what eventually became known as a Divinity School (replacing the Theology Department). The school was precisely what African-American preachers who advocated for some type of formal

---

[11]Reverend Zuck Horton was extremely ill and, although he could barely function, he was excited when he heard the news. Furthermore, although ill, he continued to be involved as he could in the annual Conventions. Samuel "Daddy" Hunt, White Rock Baptist Church's second pastor, began to become involved in the Baptist Educational and Missionary Conventions, assuming a strong presence like his predecessor.

theological training had wanted since gaining their freedom. From its founding until the present, Shaw's Divinity School has educated more African Americans for the ministry than any other program or institution. Moreover, the School provided an opportunity for pastors at area churches in North Carolina to teach. Many of White Rock's clergy either received their terminal degree in theology from Shaw or taught as an instructor in the Divinity School.

Shaw University had a very important relationship with the various Black Baptist conventions over the years. Convention members provided, among other things, financial support to the university. As a matter of fact, the Convention attendees and organizers included funds for the Institute as part of their regular annual budget.

While Tupper was the most prominent missionary sent to North Carolina by the ABHMS, he was not the only one. The Society dispatched many other White missionaries to churches in towns and rural areas across the state to assist African-American preachers. Some of the Whites that the Society sent also served as missionaries in African-American churches.[12]

The actions of the ABHMS helped the executive officers of the BEMC to fulfill another one of their many goals. A second goal that the executive officers had was to provide religious education and resources to Baptist congregations across North Carolina. These men were convinced that this goal had been revealed by God as part of His purpose for them. They believed that God wanted them to be deliverers of their people and that the Black masses were ready to be delivered.

Reverends Cowan, Horton and the other African-American preachers therefore decided, during the planning sessions, to be obedient and allow God to use them to bring salvation to ex-slaves and former free Blacks. African Americans had longed for the right to be able to read the Bible and to study God's Word.

---

[12]J.A. Whitted, *A History of the Negro Baptists of North Carolina,* 22.

Therefore, they felt that it was the right time to help members of their race learn more about God and His purpose for their lives. Furthermore, they wanted other African Americans to know that God's purpose for them was much larger than what they had envisioned.

As these men embarked upon this part of God's plan, they often thought about the Israelites who had been crying and complaining for years about their endless suffering. Although Moses was there with them, it was forty years before they were ready to follow him out of the wilderness.[13] Like Moses, these men felt that God wanted them to lead other Blacks out of the wilderness of not knowing God to a place where they would learn about almighty God, their Lord and Savior. To successfully do so, the preachers and leaders of the BEMC had to depend on several divine connections. For one, members of the BEMC believed that God wanted them to collaborate with the American Baptist Publication Society (ABPS).

God's Other Divine Connection for Black Baptists: Baptist Educational and Missionary Convention Organizers Collaborate with the American Baptist Publication Society and Take a Lead in the Black Sunday School Movement

The ABHMS was not the only organization to collaborate with North Carolina's African-American preachers in their quest to fulfill God's purpose for their lives. After hearing of their plans and the work that African American preachers were trying to do, the ABPS, with headquarters in Philadelphia, Pennsylvania, decided to ask leading African-American preachers again if they could assist them. Their previous request had gone unanswered and the preachers did not provide a reason. The ABPS was interested in *beginning* its colportage[14] and missionary work

---

[13]See Exodus 3, *Holy Bible*, New International Version.

[14]Colportage is defined as the distribution of publications, books, and religious tracts by carriers called "colporteurs" or "colporters." The term does not necessarily refer to religious book peddling.

among the ex-slaves.[15] This Society, first organized in 1824, was primarily responsible for North Carolina's Sunday School organizations. It had worked exclusively with White Baptists in the past because slaves were not allowed to read or write. Now that slaves were free men and women, the ABPS was willing and ready to work with them.

Finally, the organizers of the first BEMC welcomed the support of the ABPS, accepting their offer to assist them with their efforts. The American Baptist Publication Society stepped in and immediately began to provide the BEMC's executive leaders with training on how to organize Sunday Schools as well as with the distribution of Sunday School literature. Both groups began working together just before the first Convention and continued to do so over the next few years; at least until the organizers and other Black preachers who later joined them could provide the necessary assistance to other aspiring and practicing Black pastors on their own.

In the meantime, a second more important way that the ABPS offered to assist Reverends Cowan, Horton and the other preachers was to train them or other African Americans to serve in a lead role within the ABPS by coordinating efforts to organize Sunday Schools in African-American churches and distributing Sunday School literature. The ABPS officials also told Cowan, Horton and the others that there could possibly be other positions within the organization for African Americans. The preachers immediately welcomed such an opportunity, which they regarded as a blessing from God. Unfortunately, Reverend Zuck Horton, White Rock Baptist Church's first pastor and one of the 14 pioneers in the Black Baptist Movement in North Carolina, died before the ABPS made this opportunity available to African Americans.

White Rock's subsequent pastors in the Convention's earliest years, Reverends Samuel Hunt, Frederick Wilkins, T. W.

---

[15]Ibid., 26. Colportage is defined as the distribution of publications, books, and religious tracts by carriers called colporteurs.

Woodward and Allen P. Eaton, continued to play a major role in planning and organizing the annual Baptist Educational and Missionary Conventions. The church's fourth pastor, for example, Reverend T.W.H. Woodward, one of a few Black pastors in the State actively involved in the work of the BEMC of North Carolina, served as the District Missionary for Eastern North Carolina for two years. Reverend Woodard resigned from his position, in 1884, due to failing health.[16] Nonetheless, his work had a lasting impact on the Eastern section of the State.

By the time White Rock Baptist Church's sixth pastor, Reverend Allen P. Eaton, became its preacher in 1886, the ABPS had put a plan into place to appoint African-American preachers to join their organization and play a leading role in conducting its work among Black Baptists. According to the Society's guidelines, Black preachers had to be appointed by their members before they could serve. The Society's members only selected African-American men who "proved themselves to be men of rare ability, Christian piety and devotion."[17] They also wanted men who were intellectually and culturally prepared because such men, the ABPS members thought, set the pattern for other African-American preachers. For that reason, many African-American clergy believed it was an honor and privilege to be appointed by members of the Society.

The executive officers of the annual BEMC recommended White Rock preacher, Reverend Allen Eaton, for the position. Whites accepted him, without reservations, because they felt that he met the criteria. Therefore, Reverend Eaton became the first African-American preacher in North Carolina to be appointed by American Baptist Publication Society officials to work within the Society. He was primarily responsible for organizing Sunday Schools for Black churches, distributing Bibles, tracts and other literature to Black Baptists across the State, and approving Sunday School Conventions for all Black North Carolina Baptists. This

---

[16]J.A. Whitted, *A History of the Negro Baptists of North Carolina*, 48.

[17]Ibid., 26.

was a significant role and appointment, especially at a time when race relations in America were becoming worse.

Additionally, to fill another need, Reverend Eaton was appointed by members of the ABPS to serve as the inaugural President of the Black Baptist State Convention of North Carolina,[18] founded in the late 1880s. His primary role in this position was to host Sunday School Institutes for the State's African-American Baptists. It was during this time that White Rock became known across North Carolina as having one of the best and largest Sunday Schools in the State.

Another White Rock pastor who played a major role in the Black Sunday School Movement in North Carolina was Reverend Dr. Augustus Shepard. The church's eighth pastor was a graduate of Shaw University in 1880 and a protégé of Shaw's longtime president, Reverend Dr. Henry Tupper. They eventually became best friends.

As soon as Augustus Shepard graduated from Shaw University, Dr. Tupper responded to a request from the ABPS by recommending him to be appointed as General Sunday School Missionary and Colporteur of North Carolina. Although Augustus Shepard, at the time, had planned to graduate from Shaw University and then serve as a full-time pastor, he realized that church work among African-American Baptists in North Carolina was in a "crude state." Despite the efforts of the Baptist Educational and Missionary Convention and the American Baptist Home Mission Society in the last decade, there were still "comparatively few men with any degree of intellectual ability, and the field was ripe for a great harvest."[19] Reverend Shepard

---

[18]The Black Baptist State Convention of North Carolina was a name change for what began briefly as the General Association of the Colored Baptists of North Carolina. It soon became known as the Baptist Educational and Missionary Convention. Additional name changes included the Baptist State Convention of North Carolina, Union Baptist Convention and, as of 1929, the General Baptist State Convention of North Carolina.

[19]J.A. Whitted, *Biographical Sketch of the Life and Work of the Late Reverend Augustus Shepard, D.D.* (Raleigh, North Carolina: Edwards and Broughton Printing Company, 1912), 32.

was, consequently, ready to do what he could to continue the efforts made by various groups to educate African-American pastors and to teach them how to be leaders. Therefore, he accepted the position and began the work among the Black masses that he knew needed to be done.

While serving as General Sunday School Missionary and Colporteur for North Carolina, Augustus Shepard traveled across the State informing African-American preachers of his plans, which were well-received. He was not only involved in Sunday School work but church work as well. Ex-slaves, eager to learn more about God's Word, requested more advanced Sunday School work, and Dr. Shepard responded accordingly. He hosted Sunday School Institutes that both male and female missionaries were required to attend, to learn as much as they could, and then return to their respective churches better prepared and more inspired to do the work of Sunday School teaching. It was not long before Sunday Schools across the State were filled with more lettered men and learned women who received much of their instruction and inspiration from the institutes. Because of these influences, many men and women were sent forth as missionaries and pastors to not only meet the needs of African Americans in North Carolina but also in other states and in Africa.

Reverend Dr. Shepard's efforts eventually led to the establishment of the Black Baptists State Sunday School Convention of North Carolina. Likewise, he formed auxiliary conventions throughout the State, many of which are still in existence and continue to perform great service for the State Sunday School Convention. Reverend Shepard also distributed thousands of Bibles and Gospel tracts throughout North Carolina, providing Black churches with much-needed and valuable resources.

Hundreds of African-American preachers and ministers were supplied with literature, which proved to be of inestimable value in preparing them for their work. By the time Reverend Shepard arrived as pastor of White Rock Baptist Church, he was well prepared to reorganize and revive its Sunday School which, at the time, was experiencing some difficulty. Reverend Shepard's efforts in this area is an excellent example of how God's purpose for an individual is often much larger than what the person envisioned. Furthermore, Shepard's work as a disciple, also illustrates that God's Word is personal and designed to expand His Kingdom. God prepared Reverend Shepard for his next experience by leading him to a place where his gifts, skills, passion, and true purpose emerged.

| Dr. James Hubbard, Courtesy of White Rock Baptist Church Archives, Durham, North Carolina | Dr. Aaron Moore, Courtesy of White Rock Baptist Church Archives, Durham, North Carolina | Dr. James Shepard, Courtesy of White Rock Baptist Church Archives, Durham, North Carolina |

By the late 1920s and early 1930s, White Rock's Sunday School was one of the most organized in the city. It became known as the "great Sunday School" and had advanced to department status within the church. The Sunday School Department excelled under three prominent White Rock and Durham community leaders during this era: Dr. Aaron Moore, active church member and the city's first African-American doctor; Dr. James Hubbard, active church member and Trustee of the North College for Negroes; and Dr. James E. Shepard, active church member and president of nearby North Carolina College for Negroes.[20] These men served in other major roles at White Rock while serving the Durham community. For example, Dr. Moore served also as a Deacon at the church, Dr. Hubbard was a

---

[20]Miles Mark Fisher, *Friends: Pictorial Report of Ten Years Pastorate, 1933-1943* (Durham, North Carolina: Service Printing Company, 1943), 10-12.

long time Trustee, and Dr. Shepard would serve as guest preacher from time to time. These men are excellent examples of how believers use their God-given talents to serve people in the church through various ministries as well as in the community.

Baptist Educational and Missionary Convention's Missionary Groups Establish Divine Connections and Expand God's Kingdom Abroad

In the decade and a half following the inaugural meeting of the BEMC, some of its members decided that it was time to convert Africans to Christianity. As core members of the Convention over the years, some of White Rock's members played a major role in this Kingdom building effort. The men who organized the BEMC began to realize that God wanted them to engage in proselytizing not only in the United States but also in Africa. Therefore, they allowed God to work with them and through them to expand His kingdom to areas of the African continent they believed were unfamiliar with God and His gift of salvation.

Efforts to convert Africans to Christianity began in the late 1890s in North Carolina as members of the BEMC connected with the National Baptist Convention (NBC). The latter convention was organized on September 24, 1895, in Atlanta, Georgia by a group of men who had found three competing conventions. Reverend William Colley, of Virginia, ex-slave Reverend Dr. William Simmons, who was President of the State of Kentucky University, and ex-slave W. Bishop Johnson, of Washington, D.C., brought African-American Baptists from around the country together to form the National Baptist Convention and to encourage people to become members. The heart of the new convention was that the three former conventions would serve as the three boards of the National Baptist Convention: Foreign Missions, Home Missions, and Education.[21] This reorganization provided more structure for

---

[21]Walter H. Brooks, "The Evolution of the Negro Baptist Church," *Journal of Negro History*, Volume 7, Number 1(1922): 11-22; Wilson Fallin, Jr., *Uplifting the People: Three Centuries of Black Baptists in Alabama* (Tuscaloosa, Alabama: The University of Alabama

the Black Baptist churches. White Rock's sixth and seventh pastors, Reverend Allen P. Eaton and Reverend H. Henderson, respectively, were very much involved in the negotiations and final decisions regarding the organization and purpose of the National Baptist Convention. They were the representatives of the Baptist Educational and Missionary Convention of North Carolina at the Atlanta, Georgia convention.

Two years after the NBC was organized, African-American Baptists who had attended its initial meeting met in Washington, D.C. and formed the Lott Carey Foreign Mission Convention as one of the goals of its Foreign Missions board. Their goal was to see more missions to Africa. The Convention included delegates from North Carolina, Virginia, Maryland, District of Columbia, Pennsylvania, and other Eastern states. Women were organized into a separate organization known as the Women's Auxiliary Convention. In the end, the Lott Carey Foreign Mission Convention and Women's Auxiliary were successful — baptizing at least 300 native Africans in the first five years. Needless to say, North Carolina's Black Baptists were excited about engaging in foreign missionary work along with other Baptists across the United States.

North Carolina was one of the first states involved in the Lott Carey Foreign Mission (LCFM). White Rock Baptist Church had several members involved in LCFM work, including one of White Rock's First Lady, Mrs. Sally A. Eaton, and Durham's first African-American physician, Dr. Aaron McDuffie Moore. Dr. Moore's work for the Lott Carey Foreign Missionary Convention took him to Haiti where he founded the Haitian White Rock Baptist Church with funds he had raised in the United States. He also raised funds for missionary work in Africa. White Rock members Reverend Allen P. Eaton, Mrs. Sally A. Eaton, Reverend Augustus Shepard, Mrs. Hattie Shepard, Dr. Aaron Moore, Mrs. Minerva Womack, Mrs. Cottie Dancy Moore, and Tempie Jordan Whitted also engaged in foreign mission work as well as mission

Press, 2007), 52-53.

work within the church and in Durham's African-American community in the late 19th and early 20th centuries. They were well-known in both the city of Durham and in the State of North Carolina for their mission work.

Baptist Educational and Missionary Convention Engages in Additional Kingdom Building and Organizational Work

In the first twenty years, the BEMC not only engaged in missionary work at home and abroad but also tirelessly worked to organize Black Baptist churches and Black Baptists. This was done in two main ways.

Baptist Educational and Missionary Convention organizers and active participants, which included many White Rock pastors and members, first became involved in developing a strategy to bring the different religious sects together. Baptists, both Black and White, represented the largest Protestant denomination in the State after the Civil War. Baptists were, and still are, unique among Christian sects in their rejection of infant baptism (waiting instead until individuals are old enough to choose for themselves) and their requiring of full immersion as the method of baptism. They also refute any religious or moral authority other than that of the Bible as interpreted by individual believers. Baptists also believed then and now that a true church can be formed only by a congregation of believing, baptized members who together are the sole source of authority for the congregation.

Because of this unique approach to their faith, Baptists historically have developed into a variety of sects, each espousing a theology that is distinct in some way. There were several different Black and White Baptist groups in North Carolina after the Civil War. The different groups included Missionary Baptists, Free Will Baptists, General Baptists, Particular Baptists, Calvinistic Baptists, and Primitive Baptists. Therefore, African-American Baptists attending the annual Baptist Educational and Missionary Conventions in North Carolina wanted to find a way to connect the different Baptist sects with one another so that Baptists, as a whole, could achieve certain designated goals.

To address this issue, the BEMC decided to establish associations, which would allow delegates from various churches to meet at certain times to achieve specific goals. Member churches of each of the associations agreed to cooperate with one another. This structure also ensured that all Baptists, regardless of basic theological beliefs, would work together on mutually agreed upon goals. Between 1886 and 1915, African-American Baptists created at least forty associations.[22] White Rock became a member of the New Hope Missionary Baptist Association with forty other churches located in several North Carolina towns, including Durham, Apex, Holly Springs, Chapel Hill, Morrisville, Hillsborough, Carrboro, Mebane, Pittsboro, New Hill, and Fuquay Varina.

The New Hope Missionary Baptist Association was organized to: (1) support State Missions through the Baptist Educational and Missionary Convention (later named the General Baptist State Convention); (2) support Foreign Mission through the Lott-Carey Convention; (3) support the Women's Auxiliary of the General Baptist State Convention; (4) support the Colored Orphan Asylum of North Carolina (later named the Central Children's Home of North Carolina); (5) support the National Baptist Convention; and (6) support Shaw University. It is still in existence today as one of the more active Baptist associations.

Conclusion

In summary, the first pastor of White Rock Baptist Church, Reverend Zuck Horton, and other African-American preachers from across North Carolina began planning a convention as early as 1867 to help newly-freed African Americans organize Baptist churches, train African-American Baptist preachers, and provide religious instruction for members of Black churches. Barely educated themselves, these men believed that that they were fulfilling their God-given purpose. Consequently, they allowed God to use them to build His Kingdom. But, in the process, they

---

[22]J. A. Whitted, *A History of the Negro Baptists of North Carolina,* 45-47.

realized that they could not do it alone. Therefore, they worked with others that God had placed in their lives. In the end, thousands of ex-slaves and former free Blacks across North Carolina became Christian disciples and glorified God through Kingdom building.

A significant development from this Convention was the perceived "empowerment" of women. Often regarded as second-class citizens, women were given an opportunity to form a Woman's Convention that would focus not only on gender-specific issues in the African-American religious community but also issues important to the Black community in general. They did not disappoint their African-American male counterparts. Their work was also considered by believers as part of God's plan. The Woman's Convention work allowed them to use their God-given talents to engage in missionary work and further advance God's Kingdom. Their work is examined more fully in Chapter 5.

Chapter Five

Standing in the Shadows:
The Role of White Rock Baptist Church Women in Early African American Baptist Convention Work

"So in Christ Jesus you are all children of God through faith, for all of you who were baptized into Christ have clothed yourselves with Christ. There is neither Jew nor Gentile, neither slave nor free, nor is there male and female, for you are all one in Christ Jesus."
– Galatians 3: 26-29 (NIV)

A s she walked briskly up the stairway to her small makeshift office at North Carolina Mutual and Provident Association, Susie Veta Gille Norfleet was excited about her life. So much had happened since she first stepped off of the train in January 1906 to begin her new position at the insurance company. She never thought that nine short years after arriving in a small, Southern town she would be married and still working at an insurance agency that provided opportunities for women to advance. She also thought about how Black and White people in Durham regarded her as being different from other African-American women when she first

Susie Veta Gille Norfleet, Courtesy of White Rock Baptist Church Archives, Durham, N.C.

arrived. To many people, she represented a different "image of [African-American] womanhood."[1] At the time, she was a "graduate of Wilberforce University, classically educated, professionally skilled, and single;" moreover, unlike members of the old African-American aristocracy, Norfleet did not care about one's lineage or complexion but rather how to generate and accumulate wealth.[2] Always well-dressed, polished and genteel, Norfleet represented the best of the late 19th century "new woman."

Susie Norfleet's contemporaries said that she brought culture and class to Durham, which was basically an unrefined town. Perhaps Leslie Brown, a scholar and historian, best describes Durham's reaction to Susie V. G. Norfleet. She said,

Susie V. Gille . . . created a sensation in Durham. She wore a white, high-collar, puff-sleeved blouse and layers of African American skirts. She had arrived on the Jim Crow car and probably was covered in soot. She pulled her railroad trunk with straight-backed dignity, asked directions in schoolmarm English, and made her way through the muck . . . Susie Gille was the personification of respectability and of the best attributes of African Americans . . . As a woman, she was to model a public expression of a private life above reproach and in repudiation of any hint of impropriety . . . she was quite an attraction. Stories tell of adults and children descending on her office just to watch 'the flying fingers of the colored girl from the North who typed without even looking at the keys.[3]

Susie did not intend, on this particular day, to remain at work for long. It was her first wedding anniversary and she wanted to

---

[1]Dr. Leslie Brown, *Upbuilding Black Durham: Gender, Class and African American Community Development in the Jim Crow South* (Chapel Hill, North Carolina: The University of North Carolina Press, 2008): 110.; William J. Kennedy, Jr., *The North Carolina Mutual Story: A Symbol of Progress, 1898-1970* (Durham, North Carolina: North Carolina Mutual Life Insurance Company, 1973), 27, 72, 77, 87; and Ira Reid, *The Urban Negro Worker in the United States, 1925-1936* (New York, New York: Alexander Press, 1930), 7.

[2]Ibid.

[3]Ibid., 110-111; Walter Weare, *African American Business in the New South: A Social History of the North Carolina Mutual Life Insurance Company* (Urbana, Illinois: University of Illinois Press, 1972), 76-77; and Viola Richard Turner, Interview by Walter Weare, 15 April 1979 and 17 April 1979.

celebrate her marriage to her dear husband, Moses Norfleet. However, she had several errands to run, including dropping off food for the missionary group at her church, White Rock Baptist. She regretted having to miss her missionary circle's dinner meeting because she had been actively involved for a long time in her church and state missionary group as well as any auxiliaries with which they may have been affiliated. But, she thought that perhaps the other missionaries would not frown on her missing one meeting. Susie Norfleet, as she had become affectionately known, would assure her missionary group that she had already prepared her presentation for the annual Woman's Baptist Home (later "and Foreign") Mission Convention scheduled for the following week. This was an important meeting because the Woman's Baptist Convention (WBC) had become determined to become independent of the male-led and male-dominated larger Baptist Educational and Missionary Convention (BEMC). Women felt that their voices needed to be heard at these important annual meetings. The young, energetic Susie G. Norfleet had no reservations about making sure that her voice was an important part of the discourse. After all, she had learned from some of the best—Hattie Shepard, Essie Trice, Minerva Womack and Sylvia Williams. Furthermore, she understood the significance of the Woman's Baptist Home Mission Convention (WBHMC) because many of her foremothers had fought for this historical moment.

***

Approximately fifteen years after its inaugural meeting in 1867, BEMC members decided to invite women to join. Their decision to allow women to organize their own conventions and missionary societies within their larger Convention may have been motivated by the late 19th century women's movement. The men who organized and led the Convention did not expect women to focus on issues outside of the domestic realm, which is reflected in the Woman's Convention's first name. However, men failed to see the growing evidence of the women's movement as they engaged in political activism and opposition to injustices against North Carolina's African Americans. Women believed that since the Black Baptist church provided an institution for African

Americans to identify with, it served as the ideal platform for them to spread their message and promote their cause. Women who planned the WBHMC shared these and similar views with attendees at the annual Convention as they reported on goals and activities of their respective church missionaries.

Prior to the Woman's Baptist Home Convention, many African-American middle-class women, like White middle-class women, had begun to not only publicly advocate for the right to vote but also to form women's clubs that allowed them to learn from each other, share female values, and work toward common goals. However, African-American and White women's clubs were separate, with similar as well as uniquely different missions.

Middle-class African American women, for example, who comprised the majority of women actively involved in the BEMC's auxiliaries and missionary societies, were also known as "club women." In their respective women's clubs, formed in the late 1870s, these women immediately adopted a distinctive mission—a mission that they later translated into their work with the Convention. They described their mission as "the moral education of the race with which [they] identified."[4] They saw their role as being moral beacons for African Americans. Consequently, these women focused on purity, good mental health, and improving the home training of children. They also worked on changing the image that White America had of African-American women, that is, they were allegedly "moral[ly] loose."[5] These missionaries always tried to project positive images of themselves by aligning with African-American club women.[6] In

---

[4]Nancy Woloch, *Women and the American Experience* (New York, New York: The McGraw-Hill Companies, Inc., 2002), 201.

[5]Ibid., 202.

[6]The African American woman's club movement emerged in the 1880s, or late 19th century, and comprised a number of local reform organizations dedicated to racial improvement. These grassroots organizations were made up primarily of middle-class women who were part of the larger progressive reform effort. These clubs formed social organizations to provide services, financial assistance, and moral guidance for the poor. Many of these clubs grew out of religious societies and were a response to intensified racism in the late 19th century. These club women, many who were also missionaries in

doing so, the missionaries adopted the more politicized agenda of club women by "preaching and enlightening their flocks on the connection between the political position of" African Americans in "society and perceptions about African American morality."[7] Therefore, regardless of the types of issues that missionaries at the WBHMC addressed, the central issue for them was the race's "standard of morality." Hence, while attending the Woman's Convention and the Women's Club meetings, African-American women often spoke about teenage pregnancy or children being born out of wedlock, regarding such issues as "shameful and disgraceful" and ultimately designed to "destroy the African American race."[8]   They embraced middle-class values such as temperance, thrift, hard work and piety, and continued to focus on these principles during their missionary work with the BEMC.

So, when, in 1884, the BEMC executive officers decided to invite some of the more active pastors' wives to join them and organize a convention exclusively for women to focus on issues important to them as God's disciples, many women were ready and several African-American preachers' wives favorably responded. These ministers' wives became "helpmeets to their husbands."[9] Women from White Rock Baptist Church were among the charter members of the BEMC's first women's convention. Reverend Allen P. Eaton's wife, Sallie A. Eaton, was one of the early organizers of the Woman's Baptist Home Mission Convention (WBHMC) of North Carolina. Mrs. Eaton and the other female organizers, many who were preachers' wives, believed that women could, just as African-American men, contribute to the work of building, organizing and improving African-American churches. Likewise, another White Rock First

---

African American Baptist churches, such as White Rock, taught the poor how to keep a household, manage a budget, and raise their children. These are the same principles that were adopted by many of the missionaries.

[7]Dr. Leslie Brown, *Upbuilding Black Durham*, 101; and Miles Mark Fisher, *Friends*, 19.

[8]Dr. Leslie Brown, *Upbuilding Black Durham*, 101; and Glenda Gilmore, *Gender and Jim Crow: Women and the Politics of White Supremacy in North Carolina, 1896-1920* (Chapel Hill, North Carolina: University of North Carolina Press, 1996), 314.

[9]Dr. Leslie Brown, *Upbuilding Black Durham*, 103.

Lady, Mrs. Hattie Shepard, who was the wife of Reverend Dr. Augustus Shepard, became one of the original organizers of the women's missionary convention.

It was not easy, however, for women to realize their goals and/or agenda. The women, for example, encountered much resistance from African-American male preachers when they visited their churches and homes on behalf of the work of the Woman's Convention.[10] Yet, they continued their work. The first officers of the WBHMC were: President Lizzie Neely of Salisbury, North Carolina; Corresponding Secretary Lizzie Saunders of Henderson, North Carolina; and Treasurer Mary Tinsley of Oxford, North Carolina.

The initial goals of the Woman's Baptist Home Mission Convention of North Carolina were to: (1) establish and improve Baptist Home Mission Societies in all the Baptist churches and destitute sections of the State; (2) assist in the support of the Colored Orphan Asylum of North Carolina; (3) engage in foreign mission in Africa; (4) generate interest in the Bible; and (4) increase youth involvement in Sunday School.[11] Furthermore, fundraising was one of their major goals. The first Convention, in which White Rock's First Lady, Mrs. Eaton, played a prominent role, proved to be successful in fundraising and achieving its goals.

Additional goals were set over the next few years as these women began to see themselves as a women's movement within the African-American Baptist church. As time passed, the WBHMC set its own agenda and made "social, moral, and economic needs of women and their families" central to their overall agenda. The Woman's Convention also established missionary circles in all Baptist churches in socio-economically disadvantaged areas of the state; promoted Sunday Schools, Bible reading, and the significance of attending church in the African-

---

[10]Ibid., 102.
[11]Ibid., 114.

American community; and cooperated with the Northern Baptist Home Mission Society. The Convention also created and maintained a Women's Training School for Missionaries at Shaw University.[12]

In order to achieve many of their goals, organized missionary groups, both locally and on the state level, needed funds, which most of them did not possess. Therefore, largely through the fundraising efforts of women, members of African-American churches, like White Rock, were able to build schools, provide clothes and food to poor people, establish old folks' homes and orphanages, and make available a host of needed social welfare services.[13] These women were also quite influential in opposing racial prejudice and other social injustices during this time. They formed a type of sisterhood which attempted to bring justice to many of the inequalities faced by African Americans.

Additionally, the Woman's Baptist Home Mission Convention of North Carolina was an auxiliary of the larger Woman's Baptist Organization of North Carolina, which had also received the endorsement of the state's leading pastors in the BEMC. Mrs. Pattie Shepard, the wife of Reverend Robert Shepard, of Oxford, North Carolina, and Hattie Shepard's sister-in-law, headed the Woman's Baptist Organization (WBO) for 16 years. She is given credit for the success of the WBHMC because of her ability to lead women as well as for the subsequent progress that was made. Under her leadership, "the Convention grew rapidly in departmental work and influence."[14] Mrs. Pattie Shepard also personally selected Mrs. Sallie A. Eaton, one of White Rock's first ladies, to work side by side with her in the

---

[12]James Whitted, *A History of the Negro Baptists of North Carolina* (Raleigh, North Carolina: Edwards and Broughton, 1908), 113-114, 62; Johnnie McLester, *A Brief History of the Women's Auxiliary to the Lott-Carey Baptist Foreign Mission Convention*, N.p., N.d.

[13]Evelyn Brooks Higginbotham, *Righteous Discontent: The Women's Movement in the African American Baptist Church, 1880-1920* (Cambridge, Massachusetts: Harvard University Press, 1993), 2.

[14]M.W. Williams and George Watkins, *Who's Who Among North Carolina Negro Baptists: With a Brief History of Negro Baptist Associations* (Place of Publication Unknown: Publishing Company Unknown, 1940), 369.

WBO as the Secretary. Mrs. Shepard, Mrs. Eaton and the officers of the Convention comprised the Executive Board.

Unlike the men's convention, most of the women's work was done through the Executive Board.[15] Instead of their sessions being devoted to discussions of business, they presented papers and delivered speeches on what they considered as useful topics, sang songs, and gave devotions. Moreover, men were surprised when women began to exercise autonomy. These women regarded themselves as activists who had their own ideas about how to address the myriad of issues confronting recently freed African Americans. Their leader, Pattie Shepard, "known for her flow of language and her great executive ability, swayed great audiences wherever she appeared not only of the gentler sex, but of the opposite as well." Of course, the men did not always listen. When this happened, many of these women, including Pattie Shepard, Hattie Shepard, and Sallie Eaton, "appeared on the floor of associations and the Baptist Educational and Missionary Convention as well as at the churches," determined to have their views heard.[16] These women insisted on being independent of men. Despite men's efforts to make the Women's Convention an "auxiliary of the men's convention, women resisted." They believed that they could accomplish more if they remained separate from men.[17]

Some of White Rock's earliest first ladies, like Hattie Shepard and Sallie Eaton, as well as other women in the church, such as Minerva Womack, Essie Trice, and Sylvia Williams, were active in the Woman's Baptist Home Mission Convention before organizing missionaries and implementing other Convention-supported initiatives in their local communities. As active participants in the Woman's Baptist Home Mission Convention of

---

[15]Ibid., 112.

[16]Dr. Leslie Brown, *Upbuilding Black Durham*, 103; James Whitted, *A History of the Negro Baptists of North Carolina* (Raleigh, North Carolina: Edwards and Broughton, 1908), 112-113.

[17]Dr. Leslie Brown, *Upbuilding Black Durham*, 104; Evelyn Brooks Higginbotham, *Righteous Discontent*, 94; James Whitted, *A History of the Negro Baptists*, 117-118.

North Carolina, their work was divided into home visitations, Bible instruction, charity distribution, organizing, and strengthening and building up societies that were already organized. These women believed that the greatest need of African American people after they gained their freedom and secured homes was home training. In other words, they taught women how to maintain clean homes, properly arrange furniture, properly set tables, and appropriately discipline children. A key component of their training was Bible Study in which they taught women about being virtuous and pious. African American women who received such training were encouraged to have the Bible as the centerpiece of their coffee tables. The Bible would usually be opened to Proverbs 31, which served as a constant reminder of the attributes of a righteous and honorable woman. The missionaries of the WBHMC of North Carolina undertook this major task. They measured their success, in part, by how well homes of African-American Baptists looked as well as by the Christian piety and zeal demonstrated by women within those homes.

Another member who served as leader of both the local missionary circles was the wife of Durham's first African-American doctor, Sarah "Cottie" Dancy. Since her husband was a licensed physician, she had the resources that some other African American missionaries lacked but were so desperately needed for successful missionary work. For instance, Cottie Moore fed the hungry using her personal finances. Her husband's patients also benefited from her care, and "the community members who called on her in emergencies relied on her wisdom and alliances."[18]

Cottie Dancy Moore, Missionary and Wife of Dr. Aaron Moore, Courtesy of White Rock Baptist Church Archives, Durham, N.C.

The women of White Rock Baptist Church, first ladies as well

---

[18]Dr. Leslie Brown, *Upbuilding Black Durham*, 35; and John Dancy, *Sands Against the Wind: The Memoirs of John Dancy* (Detroit, Michigan: Wayne State University Press, 1966), 70.

as members, maintained a strong presence in the North Carolina Woman's Baptist Home Mission Convention even as the Baptist Educational and Missionary Convention underwent name changes. They also continued to engage in missionary work at the church and in Durham's African-American community through the various missionary circles that had been mandated by the Woman's Convention. They also made and collected food, clothes and fuel while simultaneously "distributing assistance as lessons of morality and faith."[19]

Minerva Womack, Missionary, Courtesy of White Rock Baptist Church Archives, Durham, N.C

Several women of White Rock were also actively involved in missionary work on the local level. Four women—Essie Trice, Minerva Womack, Hattie Shepard, and Sylvia Williams—gained attention for their missionary work within the church and the local Durham community. As a consequence of their tireless efforts and those of the many women who also volunteered their time to work with them, the church's missionary department became one of the most active and effective among African-American churches. Prior to 1933, White Rock Baptist Church's missionary circle was one of its primary ministries. Its membership supported church initiatives and advanced racial self-help by focusing its energy on the needs of people in Durham. Hence, the church's missionary circle, under the leadership of some of the more prominent missionaries in North Carolina, developed a successful model used by other churches in Durham.

At White Rock, Hattie Shepard, Essie Trice, Minerva Womack, and Sylvia Williams organized a missionary circle that would extend into the Durham community in a unique way. Shepard presided over the church's Senior Missionary Society. In addition to missionary work, she and other missionaries in her Circle were involved in race work, which required a great deal of

---

[19]Dr. Leslie Brown, *Upbuilding Black Durham*, 33.

energy, a significant number of volunteers, and a fundamental desire for change.

Shepard, Trice, Womack, and Williams established three missions in Durham (auxiliaries of the Senior Missionary Society) in an effort to reach and minister to a larger number of African  Americans. The first auxiliary was the Grant Street Mission, which was placed under the leadership of its president, Minerva Womack, who had learned from one of the best missionaries in Durham, Essie Trice. The second auxiliary, East End Mission, was placed under the leadership of Mollie Crews. Both of these missions were strategically placed in poorer neighborhoods. The third auxiliary was a citywide endeavor known as the City Missionary Society, which was comprised of members of local African-American Baptist churches. It was placed under the leadership of White Rock missionary, Sylvia Williams. Both Tempie Whitted and Susie Gille Norfleet were two of the more active members of this particular mission group.[20] These three local missions supported White Rock's Senior Missionary Society, which focused on providing support for the church's Sunday School orchestras. Furthermore, these missionaries "preached not only the gospel of salvation but the gospel of cooperation, community, and coordinated efforts."[21] The four women who presided over the missions worked extremely well together. Their influence could be seen all over Durham. Three of them—Hattie Shepard, Minerva Womack and Sylvia Williams—continued their mission efforts in Durham and statewide, thereby becoming known in some circles as the "troika." White Rock's missionary circle eventually changed its name to the Shepard, Womack and Williams Missionary Circle to recognize their noble efforts and the

First Lady Hattie Shepard, White Rock Baptist Church Archives, Durham,

---

[20]Saundra Hartsfield Interview with Minerva Fields, November 17, 2017.

[21]Miles Mark Fisher, *Friends*, 12, 19; and Dr. Leslie Brown, *Upbuilding Black Durham*, 101.

legacy that they built in Durham.

For Shepard, Williams, Womack and others, civic work was central to their missionary work. They frequently worked with other gradually emerging missionary circles in Durham. Their meetings provided spaces where they could, as African American female leaders, speak "with a respectable public voice and gain the support of a broader public." Hattie Shepard, Minerva Womack, Sylvia Williams, Cottie Moore, and Mollie Crews could not have done missionary work alone. They had to rely on volunteers in White Rock and at other churches across Durham affiliated with the three auxiliaries if they were going to increase their efforts. Susie Gille Norfleet, Tempie Whitted, Maggie Kennedy, Annie Day Shepard and several other women from White Rock volunteered their time, actively working with the church's Senior Missionary Society as well as the three auxiliaries in the community and the Baptist Woman's Home and Foreign Missionary Convention of North Carolina.

Conclusion

North Carolina's leading African-American women, many who were members of White Rock Baptist Church, did not engage in Kingdom building exclusively within the Woman's Baptist Home Mission Convention or their respective missionary circles. Instead, they continued their work in other outreach ministries within their respective churches, especially as they engaged in building a strong African-American community after slavery. To them, this work was equally important because it, too, was a part of God's plan and allowed them to use their God-given talents to engage in missionary work and further advance God's Kingdom. Their work in these ministries and in community building will be discussed in a later chapter.

PART 3

White Rock Men and Women Were
Leaders in the Development of
Durham's Black Community

Chapter Six

Angels of Mercy: The Colored Orphan Asylum of North Carolina

"Take heed that ye despise not one of these little ones; for I say unto you,
That in heaven their angels do always behold the face of my Father which
is in heaven." – Matthew 18:10 (KJV)

Twelve-year-old L'il John lived at the Colored Orphan Asylum, located a few miles on the outskirts of Oxford, North Carolina. He had lived there since the death of his parents when he was seven years old. He loved the beautiful red brick building with its nice wooden doors. He loved the creak of the floors above him as he studied his books, and he loved the swoosh sound of the great oak branches on the roof above him as he lay in bed every night. L'il John slept in a room with five other male orphans, on a narrow wooden bed with crisp, white sheets that were changed every other day by Miss Bessie, the housekeeper. He looked forward to the chicken broth in the mornings and sandwiches at noon and pot roast in the evening for supper, with boiled potatoes and vegetables. L'il John loved knowing that on Sundays, after church, there would be apple pie for dessert, and for birthdays and adoption days there would be cake. He loved chocolate cake.

L'il John also missed his parents very much; however, he loved the orphanage. He took pride in keeping the crisp, white sheets straight on his narrow bed and, with humility, swept the dining hall conscientiously every Monday evening and Friday morning, which were his scheduled times. He loved Miss Bessie, and Miss Mazie the cook, and Mrs. Jacobs the matron who sat in her office and presided over the overall operations of the orphanage. L'il John remembered when Mrs. Jacobs was new, and Mrs. Johnson before that. He had been at the orphanage for a long time, which may be one of the reasons why he loved it. The Colored Orphan Asylum was home for L'il John.

L'il John dreamed though, and in the mornings while he straightened his crisp, white sheets, and during the days while he studied and completed his school assignments, and during the evenings while he bathed and dressed and after dinner on Monday evenings while he swept the floor of the dining hall, L'il John dreamed that one day he would be adopted. Although he longed to find another family, he often thought about how his life would be different if he had not been assigned to the Orphanage. It had literally saved his life.

Before arriving at the orphanage, L'il John, alone and afraid, lived on the streets of Durham—hanging out in smoke-filled billiard halls with older boys because he had nowhere else to go. He was headed down the wrong path, having already experienced two encounters with the criminal justice system before he was eight. Now, at twelve years old, he was truly on a different path—earning good grades, learning the importance of having good work ethics, and exercising appropriate judgment as well as embracing respectable moral standards. The Colored Orphan Asylum had changed the lives of countless young girls and boys like L'il John since it was first officially organized by two Oxford, North Carolina natives—Reverend Dr. Augustus Shepard and Black United States Congressman Henry Plummer Cheatham.

Reverend Shepard eventually became White Rock Baptist Church's eighth pastor. During his tenure, the church became the biggest supporter of the orphanage—recommending two to three times more young children and raising more funds than any other Black church in Durham, Wake and Granville counties.

***

"The Negro Problem": Reasons an Orphanage was Needed for African American Youth

In the two decades after the Civil War and emancipation of slaves, thousands of African American and White children in North Carolina were living in abject poverty. In 1873, to resolve this issue for White youth, a Masonic-supported orphanage for them was constructed in Oxford. No similar organization existed for African-American children. Although a bill was introduced in the North Carolina Legislature for State support of an orphanage for African-American youth, it failed to pass.

Local governments in the various counties were the first to attempt to address the problem of not having a safe place for African-American orphans. Their attempts, however, failed because most of the politicians, who were White, felt that they were no longer liable for African Americans. Slavery was over and African Americans were no longer their responsibility. Consequently, local governments stopped providing housing, food and clothing for orphaned African-American children. Black churches in the State then stepped up to meet the challenge of caring for vulnerable, and often homeless, African-American progenies. Black American church leaders felt compelled, especially after other efforts were unsuccessful, to determine how to best care for young orphans in their respective communities.

During the Orphan Movement in North Carolina, middle-class leaders who adopted the philosophy of "racial uplift" emerged within the African-American church and Black community. Emancipation and the demise of slavery had fueled their optimistic pursuit of education, full citizenship and economic independence—all crucial markers of freedom. But these aspirations for social advancement came under assault by powerful Whites, many of them politicians, seeking to regain control over African Americans. One way in which Whites attempted to maintain control was refusing to provide assistance to Black orphans. As far as they were concerned, this was a "Negro problem" that needed to be solved by Blacks. Subsequently, African-American leaders, who did not want to be considered as the White man's problem, adopted racial ideology to forge and maintain a positive identity in America that they felt reduced their identity to the alienating phrase, "the Negro problem."[1]

In towns like Oxford, Durham and Raleigh, African-American leaders felt a sense of responsibility to care for the children, thereby becoming their "angels of mercy." Two leading proponents of racial uplift ideology were Oxford natives Reverend Dr. Augustus Shepard and United States Congressman Henry P. Cheatham. When Whites refused to help African-American orphans, these men recommended that an orphanage was built to house the children. Since African-American churches were generally engaged in discourse about this important issue, Reverend Shepard decided to first present his idea to the North Carolina Black Baptist Association in the late 1870s; however, the majority of the Association's membership was initially opposed because they did not believe that it would be a successful initiative; subsequently the problem remained unresolved. Reverend Shepard, nonetheless, continued to seek support for an orphanage.

Reverend Dr. Augustus Shepard Gains Approval of an Orphanage for African-American Youth

In August 1882, at a regional meeting in Henderson, North Carolina, Reverend Shepard presented the idea of an orphanage for Black youth again to members of the Shiloh and Wake Baptist Associations. In his passionate plea to the meeting attendees,

---

[1]Kevin Gaines, *Uplifting the Race: Black Leadership, Politics and Culture During the Twentieth Century* (Chapel Hill, North Carolina: The University of North Carolina Press, 1996), 73.

Reverend Augustus Shepard described how he and his wife, Hattie, witnessed first-hand evidence of the dire need for an orphanage to provide African-American children with the basic necessities of life—food, clothing, shelter and an education. He eloquently spoke of how in communities across North Carolina, children who had no parents were typically apprenticed out, or "bound out, by the county court. This process involved sending a child to live in the home of a family where that child would be housed, fed and taught to read and write. In exchange, that child was taught a trade and used those services to work for the family until he or she was 21 years of age. Boys were often taught the trade of being a planter, blacksmith or carpenter and girls were often taught the trade of being a domestic. Reverend Shepard hastened to add that this apprenticeship system had replaced the institution of slavery.[2] He further provided statistical data on how growing African-American opposition to the apprenticeship system had led to its decline, thereby becoming a major contributing factor to the drastic increase in African-American orphaned children in Wake, Granville and Durham counties.

Before a vote was taken at the meeting, Reverend Shepard had a second opportunity to make a plea for approval of an orphanage by the group. This time he shared with them what he had observed in African-American communities as he traveled across the State as a long-time Sunday School missionary for North Carolina. He witnessed first-hand the poverty and criminal activity among African-American youth. Reverend Shepard told them that he saw the pressing need for some kind of institution that would lift hundreds of destitute African-American orphan children of the State from the gutters of vice and misery and a life of helpless poverty. He believed that with proper care, these young boys and girls might be trained to be good and useful citizens; and instead of being a dark blot upon civilization and Christianity, they might become blessings in the communities in which they lived. He also discussed how his heart became so

---

[2]Southern Historical Collection, Wilson Library, University of North Carolina, Chapel Hill, N.C.

burdened with the thought of some place for the care and attention of the orphans that he would often spend sleepless nights and anxious hours trying to devise some definite plan for an institution to support them. A lively discussion and debate ensued. A vocal proponent of an orphanage movingly spoke of how Reverend Dr. Shepard, who was once a pastor of a church in Henderson, "had a regular 'praying ground,' where he would resort night after night, and plead with God for the orphan children."[3] Discussion and debate continued. Finally, a vote on the recommendation was taken and, much to Reverend Shepard's surprise, association members decided it was time to form an orphanage. They subsequently approved an orphanage to be built in a small town not too far from Henderson, known as Oxford, North Carolina.

Steps Taken to Make the Orphanage a Reality

In 1883, Reverend Shepard consulted some of the best Christian men of the State about the feasibility of a plan to care for these helpless children. These men included, among others, United States Congressman Henry Plummer Cheatham, then a teacher in the public schools of Henderson, North Carolina; Reverend Shepard's son, Dr. James E. Shepard, who later became founder and President of North Carolina College for Negroes in Durham North Carolina; Dr. Charles C. Spaulding, President of North Carolina Mutual Life Insurance Company and active member of White Rock Baptist Church, both in Durham, North Carolina; Judge B. K. Lassiter, Recorder's Court, Oxford, North Carolina; Dr. David Jones, President, Bennett College for Women, in Greensboro, North Carolina; and Reverend N.A. Cheek, Pastor, Belton Creek Baptist Church, in Oxford, North Carolina.[4]

Since the Wake Baptist Association and the Shiloh Baptist Association[5] were the first organized Christian bodies to

---

[3]Ibid., 37.

[4]"Colored Orphan Asylum of North Carolina," Oxford, N.C., Pamphlet, 1900, 3-4.

[5]Baptists are unique from Christian sects in their rejection of infant baptism (waiting

demonstrate interest in building an orphanage for African-American youth, they were asked to appoint delegates to meet with Reverend Shepard and the group of Christian men mentioned above. Their goal was to turn the plan into reality — to officially organize an Orphanage Association, which was first organized as "The Colored Baptist Orphan Association of North Carolina."

A few months later, in order to take in and care for all the needy African-American orphan children of the State, the delegates, led by Reverend Shepard, agreed to accept children regardless of their religious beliefs. Consequently, they unanimously agreed to remove

Colored Orphan Asylum, Oxford, N.C.,
Courtesy of Public Domain.

from the Colored Baptist Orphan Association of North Carolina's title the word "Baptist."[6] So, when the doors of the Asylum were eventually opened for the reception of children, the neediest orphan children could attend, regardless of denomination.

Once Reverend Shepard and the delegates approved of building an orphanage, they created a Board of Directors that made decisions on behalf of the Colored Orphan Association

instead until individuals are old enough to choose for themselves) and their requiring of full immersion as the method of baptism. They also refute any religious or moral authority other than that of the Bible as interpreted by individual believers. Baptists also believe a true church can be formed only by a congregation of believing, baptized members who together are the sole source of authority for that congregation. As a result of this individualistic approach to their faith, Baptists historically have developed into a variety of sects e.g., General Baptist, Southern Baptists, Missionary Baptist, Free Will Baptist, Calvinistic Baptist, Primitive Baptists), each espousing a theology that is unique in some way. They are often connected to each other through Baptist associations, which are meetings of delegates from various churches that have agreed to cooperate to achieve certain designated goals. The different associations in North Carolina include, among others, Gray's Creek Association, High Point Missionary Baptist Association, the Beulah Association, and the New Hope Association.

[6]*Colored Orphan Asylum of North Carolina*, Oxford, N.C., Pamphlet, 1900, 3-4.

[hereafter referred to as the Association]. The members of the board were Reverend Augustus Shepard, Reverend Joshua Perry, Reverend M.A. Patillo, Reverend Isaac Alston, Reverend J.W. Levy, Mr. M. T. Thornton, Mr. H. E. Long, Mr. Henry Lester, and the Honorable Henry Cheatham. The board, comprised of primarily ministers, determined the Colored Orphan Asylum of North Carolina's curriculum and policies. Reverend Augustus Shepard served as the first President of the Association.

Securing Donors and/or Funding for the Orphanage

After officially being formed, the Association began to seek funds that would be used to purchase land, construct a building and pay operational expenses. During the first couple of years, 1883 to 1885, its members agreed to rely on volunteers to serve as staff members. When the Association approached some of the more prominent African Americans in North Carolina for financial support, they were surprised that they had strong reservations about giving money or their time to helping the orphanage. A significant number of African-American men believed that the Colored Orphan Asylum would not be successful. More specifically, "many of [the] good men [of Oxford and Durham] said at first that it was impossible for the colored people to set up and successfully run such an institution."[7] Some African Americans even went as far as not having anything at all to do with the orphanage; they did not want their names associated with a project that, they felt, was destined to be a failure.

Although African Americans like Charles Spaulding and churches like White Rock supported the orphanage without any reservations, during its earliest days, individual support came primarily from the supposedly more Christian Whites who believed in its purpose. Tobacco industrialist and philanthropist

---

[7]Andrew Leiter and Natalia Smith, *Colored Orphan Asylum of North Carolina* (Oxford, N.C.: Public Ledger Print, 1900), 4, in the North Carolina Collection, University of North Carolina, Chapel Hill, N.C.

Washington Duke, textile and energy philanthropist Benjamin Newton (B.N.) Duke, manufacturer and financier philanthropist George Watts, and industrialist philanthropist Julian Carr, all of Durham, were the largest regular individual contributors to the Asylum. The first time that Benjamin Duke, for instance, visited the Asylum and toured some of the buildings, he expressed his satisfaction by leaving a check for $100. He later said, "If some more of our great-hearted philanthropists would visit [the Colored Asylum] and see the work that is being carried forward and the pressing needs, we know that they too would be constrained to give of their means to help further the great cause."[8]

Reverend Dr. Augustus Shepard,
Founder of Colored Orphan
Asylum
at Oxford, N.C.,
Courtesy of Public Domain.

Another source of funding for the orphanage was in the form of private donations from churches. Reverend Augustus Shepard used his influence with members of the various conventions to secure funding. The Baptist Sunday School Convention, which was led for years by Reverend Shepard, as well as many of the Baptist Sunday School Conventions, North Carolina Baptist Educational and Missionary Convention and some of the Baptist Associations across North Carolina made it one of their goals, in their organic laws, to give a certain amount of money annually to the Asylum for its support. The Baptist Home Mission State Convention, for example, made an annual contribution of $75 to the orphanage as stated in its charter.[9] Methodists and Presbyterians provided financial support when needed; however, Baptists, by far, provided more support for the orphanage than any other Protestant denomination.

Reverend Augustus Shepard and Congressman Henry

---

[8]Ibid., 5.

[9]Ibid., 4.

Cheatham employed other ways to solicit funds for the institution. *First*, Reverend Shepard made an appeal to the people of North Carolina in an 1890 pamphlet titled, "An Appeal for Help to the People of the State in Behalf of the Colored Orphan Children of North Carolina." The document took a meek tone in its address to the readers. It was filled with Christian references and revealed both optimism and the dire need for support. Reverend Shepard

U.S. Congressman Henry P. Cheatham, 2nd Congressional District, N.C., Courtesy of the Public Domain

wrote, "We . . . earnestly ask that every church, Sunday School and individual will pray the blessing of God upon the work," further adding that orphans "are coming in as rapidly as we can provide for them."[10] Reverend Shepard also expressed the Association's desire to "open an industrial department as soon as possible."[11] This suggested that African Americans in North Carolina were experiencing similar challenges to those of Black Southerners elsewhere: during this period, the "Great Migration" from South to North left many homeless, economically insecure, and detached from extended families who once acted as support networks. The Great Migration occurred between 1900 and 1916 when six million African Americans left the rural Southern part of the United States to relocate to the urban Northeast, Midwest, and West.

The "Appeal" also suggested that the founders of the Colored Orphan Asylum acted in the spirit of Booker T. Washington, who promoted industrial and vocational education for young Black Southerners. In his autobiography, *Up from Slavery*, Washington, a good friend of Reverend Augustus Shepard and Congressman Henry Cheatham, promoted practical skills over abstract knowledge when he stated, "[w]e want to teach them to study

---

[10]Reverend Dr. Augustus Shepard, *An Appeal for Help to the People of the State in Behalf of the Colored Orphan Children of North Carolina* (Oxford, N.C.: Colored Orphan Asylum, 1890), 1.

[11]Ibid.

actual things instead of mere books alone."[12]   Washington believed that students should work for their education, demonstrating initiative and dedication to a hard day's work in addition to academic inspiration. Shepard, Cheatham and other proponents of the Colored Orphan Asylum at Oxford embraced this belief or philosophy.

The "Appeal" pamphlets were sent to virtually every religious institution in all North Carolina counties.   In the document, Reverend Shepard also informed the churches that the fifth Sunday in August 1890 had been set aside by the Association as a day of "prayer and offerings for the Colored Orphan Asylum at Oxford, N.C.," and requested that "every church, Sunday-school and individual . . . pray the blessings of God upon the work, and take a collection, or make an offering, the same day, and forward the Same to Mr. Henry Hester [Treasurer], Oxford, N.C., who [would] acknowledge the same on receipt." The letter continued, "The outlook for the future prosperity of this institution was never more encouraging than the present time. . . We have the poor with us, and while we can let us do them good. Will you, as an individual, pray and give, and urge others to give. . . The scripture says, 'He that hath pity upon the poor lendeth unto the Lord, and that which he hath given will He pay him again.' — Prov. 19:17."[13] Reverend Shepard closed his appeal by asking them to pray and help on any Sunday if the fifth Sunday in August was not convenient for them.

Second, they not only made appeals through newspapers and circulars but also depended on assistance from children and staff at the orphanage. During the summer months, Reverend Shepard hired women staffers as traveling agents, each traveling with three or four orphans, giving concerts, holding meetings and soliciting what aid they could from churches and individuals.

---

[12]Booker T. Washington, *Up From Slavery: An Autobiography* (Garden City, N.Y.: Doubleday and Company, Inc., 1901), 126.

[13]Reverend Dr. Augustus Shepard, *An Appeal for Help to the People of the State in Behalf of the Colored Orphan Children of North Carolina* (Oxford, N.C.: Colored Orphan Asylum, 1890), 1.

Their efforts yielded positive results. For example, the orphanage soon began receiving annual donations between $100 to $121 from the Grand Lodge of Colored Free Masons of both Oxford and Durham.

In 1883, the first iteration of the Grant Colored Asylum[14] was prepared and built. Four years later, the institution was renamed and incorporated as The Colored Orphan Asylum of North Carolina. The orphanage was chartered as a nondenominational institution to care for children deprived of their parents with the goals of providing them with training along religious, moral and industrial lines, and to prepare them for life as productive citizens.[15]

Further, when Henry Cheatham was elected as a Republican member of the United States House of Representatives from 1889 to 1893, he used his diplomatic skills to persuade enough members of the North Carolina Legislature to approve funding for the Asylum. In 1891, the Legislature granted an annual appropriation of $1,000 to the institution; in 1893, it was increased to $1,500. Congressman Cheatham left the United States House of Representatives in 1893 and returned to Oxford to work with the orphanage as its Superintendent. He continued to petition his friends in the North Carolina Legislature for financial assistance. Consequently, in 1895, the state legislators approved $3,000 annually for the Asylum, increasing it to $5,000 a year in 1897.[16]

Eventually, Reverend Shepard, Congressman Cheatham and other proponents of the Colored Orphan Asylum collected enough funds to purchase twenty-three acres of land, located one and one-half miles from Oxford, next to Fishing Creek Township,[17] at a cost of $1,565.00.[18] The lot included a small

---

[14]The asylum was first named the Grant Colored Asylum.

[15]*Report to the Board of Directors of the Colored Orphan of North Carolina* (1963); Andrew Leiter and Natalia Smith, *Colored Orphan Asylum*, 6.

[16]Ibid., 6.

[17]This township was inhabited primarily by Native Americans. Some of them

building with three rooms and a small barn. However, the building did not have any furniture and the Association had no money to buy such. Nor did it have money to pay employees or to buy additional items needed for the children. But, Shepard and his supporters refused to give up; instead they did what they knew would work—they prayed and prayed. Finally, according to White Rock Church member, Dr. Bernetta McGhee White, writing on the subject, "a Negro woman came forward and offered the use of her furniture and her services as matron of the institution without pay . . . support came from churches, from the Negro masons, from what the children could earn tending the six acres under cultivation, and from washing and ironing done by the matron herself."[19] After raising additional funds and receiving promised annual donations, Shepard, Cheatham and the Association constructed a two-story building for boys, a large dining hall, a cook room, a two-story building with a sewing room for girls, and a laundry. A few years later, in 1898, the Board of Directors approved the purchase of a one-acre lot for $100 across the road from the original land purchased and, on that lot, they erected a two-story building with nine rooms. The building was used for the Superintendent's home.

As more funds were donated, the Association purchased a 144-acre farm, within a hundred yards of the Asylum, for $1,440. Four horses, two mules and six cows were also purchased by the Association's leadership. On this farm, children were assigned gender-specific duties. Boys were trained to raise corn, wheat, oats, peas, beans, sorghum, potatoes and cotton.[20] Girls, on the other hand, were taught to cook, sew, wash, iron and perform

---

worked with Reverend Shepard and others on the Colored Asylum project. Reverend James W. Levy, of the Native American community, was among the founding Board members of the Asylum.

[18] *Report to the Board of Directors of the Colored Orphan of North Carolina* (1963); Andrew Leiter and Natalia Smith, *Colored Orphan Asylum*, 6.

[19] Dr. Bernetta McGhee White, Roll Call: Central Children's Home Membership, 1900-1920, cited from Washington Duke Papers, in Rare Book, Manuscript and Special Collections Library, Duke University, Durham, North Carolina; Used with permission granted the author 5 May 1998 by William Erwin, Jr., Senior Reference Librarian.

[20] Andrew Leiter and Natalia Smith, *Colored Orphan Asylum*, 6.

general housekeeping duties. Everyone—the superintendent, president, board of directors, staff and students—was required to invest either their time, energy or funding to the Association. This essentially meant that they would all take ownership for its success or failure.

The Grand Opening: Fulfilling God's Purpose

After the first building was constructed, the Association prepared for its official opening. Applications for admission were made available to those interested in having orphans accepted. From the outset, the Colored Orphan Asylum was bombarded with many applications, which only increased over the years. This demonstrated how much of a need there was to place parentless and homeless African-American children in safe and structured environments. Adults who submitted applications on behalf of orphaned children did not mince words when expressing how the child that they were recommending could benefit from being a resident of the orphanage. The applicants often provided "heart-touching tales of

Girls at the Colored Orphan Asylum, Oxford, N.C., 1880s, Courtesy of the Public Domain.

wretchedness" on behalf of boys and girls who suffered "hunger" and were left in the cold.[21] They would often conclude by reassuring the Association that many unsuccessful attempts had been made to place the child or children in a safe environment. Most of the adult applicants were missionaries from the African-American Baptist churches. The Woman's Baptist Home Mission Convention of North Carolina had decided to assist the Oxford Orphan Asylum as one of their many goals. African-American churches, like White Rock, had missionary groups that referred orphans to the Asylum. The Colored Orphan Asylum maintained a waiting list that was used to accept new children when a

---

[21]Ibid., 8-9.

resident was adopted or reached the age of 21 and was subsequently released. The orphanage, when operating at full capacity, enrolled at least 200 children per year.

The children, housed at the Colored Orphan Asylum, attended classes five days a week, Monday through Friday. They studied the 3R's in the early days — Reading, 'Riting and "Rithmetic. Technical training was also crucial to the mission of the orphanage. Early 20th century Superintendent B. W. Parham, in making a plea for financial support, avowed, "[u]nless we can develop these boys and girls into good citizens, both willing and able to earn a living and to make their contribution to the welfare and progress of the State [of North Carolina], we have done very little." Parham concluded with the observation that "[w]e do not solve social problems by the court or the jail or the chain gang," and he urged North Carolinians to support the "great work" of the Colored Orphan Asylum.[22]

Placing God First: Orphanage with a Christian Focus

Baptist influence could also be seen in the instruction that children received. The Association's Board of Directors was comprised primarily of Baptist preachers who wanted the instruction to be religious and moral.   Pastors of different churches were invited to preach during Sunday services. Moreover, at least twenty minutes were spent every morning in prayer and reading the Scripture. The children also had Sunday School every week and prayer meeting every Thursday evening.[23]

The orphans were also taught to be kind to each other, respectful of each other and truthful and honest.   They were required to be neat and clean at all times — all middle class moral standards and a key component of the "racial uplift" movement.

---

[22]T.K. Borders, Dr. E.E. Toney, B.W. Parham and J.W. Medford, *1939 Pamphlet* (Oxford, N.C.: Colored Orphan Asylum of North Carolina, 1939), 4, 7.

[23]Ibid., 8.

On Sundays, they attended church or devotional services. A preacher from one of the Black Baptist churches was often invited to deliver a sermon. When male orphans were not in class during the week and on Saturdays, they worked in one of the shops on the premises or in the fields harvesting crops. Female orphans spent their time learning how to cook and clean house and how to wash and iron clothes.

Given its mission and focus, the Association made sure that its superintendents were Christian men who had connections in the community that could financially benefit the orphanage. A good example of this would be the appointment of Reverend Robert Shepard as superintendent of the Asylum. After a succession of superintendents, Reverend Augustus Shepard decided it was time to appoint someone who would commit to a longer tenure and was a great fundraiser. He believed that his brother, Robert, was the ideal person. Furthermore, his brother's wife, Pattie, was actively involved in the Woman's State Convention, which had adopted support of the Asylum as one of its major goals. Dr. Augustus Shepard, a full-time pastor at Second Baptist Church in Raleigh at the time, was being invited to speak at more African-American churches. His son, James, had also informed him that he would nominate him as pastor of White Rock Baptist Church at the end of the three-year moratorium that the courts had placed on the hiring of preachers at the embattled church. Despite White Rock's internal chaos, becoming the pastor of the prestigious church was an honor for many contemporary African-American preachers. Dr. Augustus Shepard, in particular, believed that White Rock would be a great opportunity for him as he devoted more time to his ministry. Thus, he needed reliable help with the orphanage.

Reverend Augustus Shepard, therefore, decided to invite his brother, Reverend Robert Shepard, to serve as superintendent of the orphanage. This was a key appointment at a critical time in the history of the Colored Orphan Asylum. Instability in the superintendent's role sent the wrong message to potential donors that Reverend Augustus Shepard was trying to secure.[24] When approached about the position, Reverend Robert Shepard initially had reservations. He had recently married his second wife, Pattie, and questioned whether he would have the time with his responsibilities as a new husband and father. After all, both he and his wife were very much involved with the Baptist Educational and Missionary Convention and Woman's Baptist State Missionary Convention of North Carolina. He wanted to do well if he accepted the position.   After giving the matter considerable thought, however, Reverend Robert Shepard agreed to become the superintendent and was subsequently approved by the Association. This was one of the best decisions that Reverend Augustus Shepard could have made for the orphanage.

During Robert Shepard's leadership, private donations to the institution increased. He not only solicited the help of various prominent people, both African American and White, to assist him in this endeavor but also targeted individuals who would be able to provide support consistently over a period of years. Prominent people across the State wrote letters of support that he used to secure funding and material resources needed for the institution. For example,

> Office of the Clerk of the Superior Court
> Granville County, N.C.
> Oxford, N.C.
> December 11, 1899

To Whom It May Concern:

I have known for several years Rev. R. Shepard, Superintendent of the Colored Orphan Asylum of this place, and during all these years he has borne a good character, being respected by both races for his upright Christian walk.

---

[24]Ruth Edmonds Hill, ed., *The Black Woman Oral History Project* (Berlin, Germany: Walter de Gruyter, 2013), 303.

J. G. Hunt
Clerk Superior Court

Oxford, N.C., Dec. 11, 1899

To Whom It May Concern:

I will state that I have known Rev. R. Shepard for eight or nine years as manager of the Colored Orphan Asylum of North Carolina, and it gives me pleasure to state that I believe him to be a good man. Honest and upright, a man who has made a most excellent Superintendent of the Asylum for colored orphan children at this place. He has been economical on his management and has about 125 to 150 children now at the Asylum. Any one [sic] who sees fit to aid him in any way I am confident the money will be most judiciously expended.

Very sincerely,
J. G. Hall, Druggist

The Colored Orphan Asylum of North Carolina is located at Oxford, and has been in existence since 1887. It seems to do for the colored children of the State what is done for the white children in the various orphan homes of North Carolina. At present there are one hundred and thirty children in its care. There ought to be at least one thousand, judging by the number of white children cared for in the different Asylums.

Reverend Robert Shepard has had charge of this work for years. He has the confidence of the people and is well suited to his work. We commend him and this deserving charity to the people generally.

JNO. S. Hardaway
Pastor White Baptist Church
Oxford, N.C.

While others wrote letters of support for Reverend Robert

Shepard, he wrote letters of his own asking for financial support of the Colored Orphan Asylum. He appealed, for instance, to the Duke family for support. In December 1898, he sent the following request to Washington Duke:

Will you please remember the poor colored orphans during the Christmas? We have 88 little needy children to feed and care for and many others who are desirous of entering the home whom we are compelled to refuse for want of means. I am sure you could not give to a more needy cause. Capt. & Mrs. Brady Williams referred me to you some time ago but, supposing you had many such applications, I felt embarrassed to do so until now. I can refer you to all the white as well as the respectable colored people as to the economical manner in which the Asylum is conducted. Whatever is given will be prayerfully received.[25]

According to Dr. Bernetta McGhee White, Reverend Robert Shepard made a second plea to Washington Duke on April 14, 1899:

I take the priveledge [sic] of addressing you this personal letter appealing to you for some assistance at this very needy time in the existence of the institution. The Asylum was never so needy as now. . . We need money, shoes, clothes, medicine. There are now one hundred and thirty of this unfortunate class in this Asylum. They must be fed, clothed, lodged, and taken care of. You know, if anybody does, what it takes to run a large institution. . . We are purchasing a large farm of 145 acres. We are behind in the payments which must be made now. Mr. Duke will you help us some in this? Every dollar you give you have helped to save somebody's child. You have a great reputation for your charity. You are one of charity's friends. I beg of you in the name of charity to assist us at this needy time. I would not write you were it not for the great need. Any am't will be gladly received. Please let us hear from you.[26]

---

[25]Dr. Bernetta McGhee White, Roll Call: Central Children's Home Membership, 1900-1920, cited from Washington Duke Papers, in Rare Book, Manuscript and Special Collections Library, Duke University, Durham, North Carolina; Used with permission granted the author 5 May 1998 by William Erwin, Jr., Senior Reference Librarian.
[26]Ibid.

Reverend Shepard's passionate 1899 entreaty did not fall on deaf ears. Washington Duke and other members of the Duke family became some of the largest benefactors for the orphanage. The Duke Endowment, for instance, was listed among the Colored Orphan Asylum's major philanthropists.

Reverend Augustus Shepard was also strategic in his Board of Directors appointments. He appointed people to the Board who could generate financial support from their respective churches and communities. Because of White Rock's position in the African-American community, from its beginning to the early 20th century, some of its members held positions on the Board of Directors. Both Dr. Aaron Moore and Charles C. Spaulding, for instance, served on the Board for years. Both were well-established members of the African-American elite who held important positions of authority at White Rock and in Durham's community. They used their positions in the church and community to raise funds and other resources for the Asylum. Consequently, White Rock became one of the major benefactors of the orphanage.

White Rock Baptist Church's Affiliation with the Colored Orphan Asylum at Oxford

So, when Reverend Augustus Shepard arrived as pastor of White Rock Baptist Church in 1901, the Colored Orphan Asylum of Oxford had been in operation for at least 18 years. The last few years under the leadership of Superintendent Reverend Robert Shepard and, later, Congressman Henry Cheatham were the best financially for the institution. Reverend Augustus Shepard had served on the Board of Directors since its founding and continued to do so. This particular position provided him with an opportunity to help set institutional policy and observe the orphanage's daily operations.

Reverend Dr. Shepard was already acquainted with prominent White Rock members as a consequence of his attendance at annual Baptist State conventions and his work with the orphanage. The church's longtime Sunday School superintendent, Dr. Charles C. Spaulding, Trustee Dr. Aaron Moore and missionaries Essie Trice and Minerva Womack had some interaction with Reverend Shepard and his wife, Hattie, as well as Reverend Robert Shepard and his wife, Pattie, prior to 1901. Both Spaulding and Moore served on the Colored Orphan Asylum's Board of Directors. Moreover, they all supported the orphanage in their respective capacities. Hence, when Reverend Dr. Augustus Shepard arrived at White Rock, it was not difficult to continue the church's involvement with the orphanage. In a 1923 radio address, Spaulding outlined the history of the orphanage and the Association's plans for the future before concluding with an appeal for racial pride and cooperation. He noted, "The moral and spiritual growth of a race is largely dependent upon the investment made in Youth [sic]."[27]

As previously stated, during Reverend Augustus Shepard's tenure at White Rock, the church became one of the largest benefactors—including an annual donation in its budget and providing material assistance when necessary. Furthermore, the church's missionary circle, which had become recognized as a model for others across the state, referred more children to the orphanage than any other Black Baptist church in North Carolina.[28] Over the next few years, several other members of the church served on the Board of Directors where they helped to shape the future direction of the orphanage. Reverend Dr. Shepard and his wife, Hattie, had to have been pleased with the way in which White Rock's members stepped up to offer their support of an institution that was so important to him.

Conclusion

God had given Reverend Augustus Shepard the vision for the Colored Orphan Asylum and Shepard had carefully recruited some of North Carolina's best foot soldiers to help him realize the

[27]Charles C. Spaulding, Civil Rights Digital Library, 30 December 2009.

[28]Annual Report of the Colored Orphan Asylum of North Carolina, (Oxford, N.C.), 1905. North Carolina Collection, University of North Carolina, Chapel Hill, N.C.

vision. He had allowed God to use him to help a group of people who could not help themselves. It was his relentless commitment to this endeavor as well as the divine connections that he made both in the community and at White Rock, in Durham, and First Baptist, in Raleigh, that eventually changed the lives of so many of their people. White Rock's members, in particular, would also demonstrate this same kind of tenacity to change the lives of their people, especially young people, in the area of education.

Chapter Seven

"Thy Word is a Lamp Unto My Feet, a Light Unto My Path:" White Rock's Disciples Seek an Education with Christian Principles for Blacks

"The heart of the prudent getteth knowledge; and the ear of the wise seeketh knowledge." –Proverbs 18:15 (KJV)

Speaking to a virtually all-White crowd of over two thousand people at the 1908 International Sunday School Association, in Louisville, Kentucky, Reverend Dr. James E. Shepard, the man who would later preach from time to time at White Rock Baptist Church, thanked them for all that they had done for his people and to let them know that "colored people only wanted a chance in the race of life." He further added, "They are not whining, but are trying to work out their salvation with fear and trembling." He continued by pointing out that his race needed further help until they could stand alone and they would return to them and their children the kindness that the Association had shown to them.[1]

---

[1]International Sunday School Association. *Organized Sunday School Work in America,*

In addition to asking Whites at the Conference to assist Blacks, Reverend Dr. James Shepard also advocated support from them for religious education. He was advocating this for African Americans at a time when nationally recognized Booker T. Washington, also a keynote speaker on the same program in Kentucky, promoted industrial education as being best for Blacks. In his address to conference attendees, Shepard told them that "religious education was essential to the Negro not only for salvation but to help him live as a man, to develop the best in him and to teach him to hold the worst in subjection." He emphasized that religious education did not detract from industrial education, or from higher education, for, he said, "to sweep a room well, to be able to bake bread, to plow all day behind a mule, each of these in its place is religious education."[2] He ended his speech with a plea to all assembled to "do [their] utmost to uplift the black race in the Southland, and when [they] do that the black race will sing [their] praises not only in this world but in the world to come."[3] Reverend Shepard received a standing ovation for his address. Less than two years later, he founded the National Religious Training School and Chautauqua for the Colored Race, which was the first public liberal arts institution for Blacks in the nation. It is no coincidence that Dr. Shepard founded a school to train ministers. After all, he was a minister and so was his father, Dr. Augustus Shepard, whom he greatly admired. His father was the eighth pastor of White Rock Baptist Church, and a Baptist minister who instilled Christian values in his children. Because of his father's influence, James E. Shepard had high ideas and moral standards. He was once asked who the most influential person in his life was; he replied, his father. He also had great respect for his father[4] and, in several ways, he followed in his father's

1905-1908, Twelfth International Sunday School Convention, Louisville, Kentucky, June 18-23, 1908. Chicago, Illinois: The Executive Committee of the International Sunday School Association, 1908, 554.

[2]Ibid., 550, 552.

[3]Ibid, 553.

[4]Lenwood G. Davis, ed., *Selected Writings and Speeches of James E. Shepard, 1896-1946: Founder of North Carolina Central University* (Madison, Wisconsin: Fairleigh Dickinson University Press, 2013), 93, 97.

footsteps.

Hence, Dr. James Shepard believed that members of his race would be enlightened by an education. However, he felt that the enlightenment should first come from the Bible. In other words, he was a major advocate for a Christian education before a secular education. Shepard once said that if recently freed Blacks wanted to walk safely in the woods at night, they would need light so that they would not fall over roots or into holes. This is analogous to a life in which people can walk through a dark forest of evil. But, the Bible can be that person's light to show them the way ahead so that they will not stumble as they walk. This parallel also reveals the entangling roots of false values and philosophies, which was the focus of many courses that Dr. Shepard initially offered at the Institute once it opened its doors. He encouraged students, laypersons and scholars to study the Bible so that they would be able to see their way clear enough to stay on the right path.

Shepard and other White Rock members that valued and supported the education of recently freed Blacks adopted this particular ideology. Like countless other Black North Carolinians, Shepard, Dr. Aaron McDuffie Moore, Cottie Dancy Moore, Dr. Charles Shepard, James R. Evans, Allen and Flonnie Goodloe, George and Maude Logan as well as several teachers in the church fought, through various means, for Blacks to have an education comparable to that of Whites. But, as usual, Whites vehemently opposed them and other proponents of Black education, thereby denying them that right.

***

During slavery, proponents of education for Blacks were determined to be successful. Many were devout Christians who believed that, despite the efforts by ill-intentioned Whites, if they lived their lives according to God's will, He would make it possible for them to receive an education. In other words, God would turn the satanic and bad in their lives into something that was divine and good. And so, early supporters of education for Blacks put their faith in Jesus Christ as they fought for this precious God-given right.

Blacks' Struggle for Education Began During Slavery: Looking Back

Although free public schools existed in North Carolina during slavery, they did not admit slaves or free black children. Slave masters understood that their social control of the slaves could not be based solely on physical coercion. Knowledge was power, and Whites in North Carolina and other Southern states feared that Black literacy would prove a threat to the slave system. Consequently, virtually all slave codes established in the United States set restrictions making it illegal to teach slaves to read or write. The North Carolina General Assembly, for instance, passed a statute, in 1830, to make it illegal to teach slaves.[5] Yet, when they had the opportunity, some people did teach Blacks.

Some brave teachers like John Chavis, for example, a free Black educator and Presbyterian minister, in Raleigh, North Carolina, ran a secret night school for slaves and free Blacks. Chavis opened a school in his home, in 1808, where he taught both White and Black children. He placed ads in the *Raleigh Register* to encourage enrollment. He initially taught both races together. After some White students objected, Mr. Chavis taught White children during the day and Black children in the evenings. He charged White students $2.50 per quarter, and Black students $1.75 per quarter. As an educator, Chavis taught full-time and instructed his college-bound White students in Latin and Greek, which were required classical subjects in the colleges and universities of that time.

Chavis' school was described as one of the best in the State of North Carolina. Students from some of the most prominent White families in the South studied at his school. His students were sons and brothers of State senators, chief justices, governors, and ministers of foreign countries. Because of who his students were, Chavis taught and preached until the Nat Turner Rebellion in

---

[5]Joyce Blackwell, *The Control of Blacks in North Carolina, 1829-1840* (Thesis, North Carolina Central University, Durham, NC, 1977),40; North Carolina General Assembly Statutes, 1830, University of North Carolina, North Carolina Collection, Louis Round Wilson Library Special Collections, Chapel Hill, North Carolina.

1831.[6] After Turner's uprising, however, Chavis was forced, by law,[7] to give up preaching and teaching school.

Furthermore, teachers found educating Black children faced not only imprisonment but also physical retaliation from Whites. For instance, Margaret Douglass, who was caught teaching Black children in Norfolk, Virginia, was convicted and imprisoned for her actions.[8] Likewise, in his autobiography, *Narrative in the Life and Adventures of Henry Bibb, An American Slave*, Henry Bibb, a slave in Shelby County, Kentucky, provided an account of what happened when a White girl on his plantation attempted to teach men in bondage: "Slaves were not allowed books, pens, ink, nor paper, to improve their minds. There was a Miss Davies, a poor white girl, who offered to open and teach a Sabbath School for slaves. Books were supplied, and she started the school; but the news got to [her] owners that she was teaching [slaves] to read. This caused quite an excitement in the neighborhood. Patrols were appointed to go and break it up [at] the next Sabbath."[9]

Frederick Douglass, Orator and Abolitionist, Courtesy of the Public Domain.

Despite the danger of teaching Blacks, there were still people who fervently believed that they should be taught how to read and

---

[6]Nat Turner, an American slave and preacher, led a two-day rebellion of slaves and free Blacks in Southampton County, Virginia, on August 21, 1831, for which Turner was tried, hanged and beheaded. He killed approximately 70 Whites, creating fear and terror in White communities along the eastern coast. Whites responded with legislation that prevented Blacks from preaching. Also, during the antebellum period, and even before, a free-Black population existed in North Carolina and other parts of the South. Before laws were passed to remove them from the South, they amassed wealth by owning land and other property. The first Black millionaire was Thomy Lafon who lived in Louisiana during the Revolutionary era.

[7]The North Carolina General assembly passed a law in 1830-31 that prevented Blacks from learning how to read or write and authorized heavy penalties for anyone who attempted or taught slaves. This law is discussed in chapter one.

[8]Albert P. Blaustein and Robert L. Zangrando, eds., "The Case of Mrs. Margaret Douglass," in *Civil Rights and the Black American: A Documentary History* (New York, New York: Washington Square Press, 1968), 31-33.

[9]Henry Bibb, *Narrative of the Life and Adventures of Henry Bibb, An American Slave* (North Charleston, South Carolina: CreateSpace Independent Publishing Platform), 79.

write. Some of these supporters and advocates included Frederick Douglass, Harriet Tubman and Sojourner Truth (nee Isabella Baumfree). Frederick Douglass, an extremely strong supporter of Black education, wrote to Harriet Beecher Stowe, author of the infamous *Uncle Tom's Cabin*, in 1853: "I assert then that poverty, ignorance, and degradation are the combined evils; or in other words, these constitute the social disease of the free colored people of the United States. To deliver them from this triple malady, is to improve and elevate them, by which I mean simply put them on an equal footing with their white fellow countrymen in the sacred right to *life, liberty, and the pursuit of happiness* . . . How shall this be obtained? I answer . . . by the establishment of an Industrial College in which shall be taught several important branches of the mechanic arts."[10]   This is the environment in which Margaret and William Faucette, Melissa and Gos Lee, Reverend Zuck Horton and his wife, Elizabeth, and Reverend Samuel "Daddy" Hunt lived and worked as slaves. Their dreams of one day being allowed an education were never realized during slavery.

Advocates for African-American Education Continue their Fight as Free Men and Women

Maude Logan, Courtesy of White Rock Baptist Church Archives, Durham, N.C.

Some of White Rock Baptist Church's members were the first people to fight for the education of African Americans in Durham in the decades following the Civil War and emancipation. In their non-secular and secular lives they often wore several titles at once, such as Christian missionary, wife, husband, mother, father, doctor, lawyer, politician, educator, business owner, and chief executive officer. Regardless of their worldly role, they put God first and allowed Him to combine these various positions together so that they could fight for the greater good which, in this particular case, included glorifying God as they fought for educational opportunities for

---

[10]Frederick Douglass to Harriet Beecher Stowe, March 8, 1853.

African Americans.

Some of the men and women that played a significant role in the Black education movement in Durham and across North Carolina in its early years were, among others, Dr. Aaron McDuffie Moore, James Rufus Evans, George Logan, Maude Logan, Allen Goodloe and Dr. James Shepard. They were determined to ensure the education of all Blacks, regardless of their socio-economic status.

George Logan, Courtesy of White Rock Baptist Church Archives, Durham. N.C

The education advocates faced a great deal of opposition from Whites who believed that God intended for Blacks to remain illiterate. Despite the amount of hostility that they encountered, and the amount of work involved to be successful, Moore, Evans, Goodloe, and the others believed just the opposite — that God wanted Blacks to be educated and, therefore, would give them the strength to endure. While Whites regarded education as merely a tool to empower Blacks, the newly freed slaves believed education would provide them with the opportunity to read God's Word, which would teach them how to be better disciples for Him.

Need for Grade Schools in Durham's Black Community after the Civil War and Emancipation

In 1886, Durham's city leaders, who were White, finally decided that they had a responsibility to provide schools for Blacks as well as Whites. A few years later, two grade school buildings (first through sixth grades) were erected for White children and one in Hayti[11] for Black children. The grade school for Black children, built in 1893, was the Whitted School, named after the school's first principal and White Rock member, J.A.

---

[11]The historic Black community in Durham, North Carolina. It was founded as an independent Black community shortly after the American Civil War on the southern edge of Durham by freedmen coming to work in tobacco warehouses and related jobs in the city. By the early decades of the 20th century, Blacks owned and operated more than 200 businesses.

Whitted. It operated out of temporary venues for the first few years. By 1901, both Black and White communities had grown, and the city had seven schools, three of them for African-American children. All four of the schools for White children were of brick, while the schools for Blacks were two-story wooden frame buildings. None of the seven had fire escapes; none had any playground equipment, such as swings, slides, or seesaws.

In 1906, a high school for White students was built on Morris Street, in Durham, but work for Blacks above the sixth-grade level continued to be done, for a while, at Whitted School.[12] When the Whitted School burned down in 1921, it was replaced, in 1922, by Hillside Park High School on Umstead Street.  Mary Hester Smith (known as Mary Hester at the time), a long-time member of White Rock Baptist Church, relocated with her parents to Durham in 1929 and enrolled as a seventh grade student at Hillside. She eventually graduated from the eleventh grade.[13] After college, she taught at both Hillside Park High School and Whitted School. Another White Rock member, J.A. Schooler served as principal of Hillside Park High School. In 1935, a new Whitted School was built on Concord Street. Many years later, Deacon Emeritus Dr. John Lucas, at White Rock, served as a principal at Hillside High School.

Mary Hester Smith, Member of White Rock Baptist Church and Former Teacher and Student at Hillside Park High School, Courtesy of White Rock Baptist Church Archives, Durham, N.C.

Former students of Whitted and Hillside Park claimed that the teachers were "highly qualified; some teachers had Ph.D.s because they could not get a job anywhere else."[14] Another student, Dr. Debra Parker, later a professor of Education at North

[12]James G. Leyburn, *The Way We Lived: Durham, 1900-1920* Elliston, Virginia: Northcross House, Publishers, 1989), 75.

[13]Mary Hester Smith, Interview by A. Leanne Simon, 8 August 2013, *Upbuilding Whitted School* Video, Durham, N.C.

[14]Eileen Watts Welch, Interview by A. Leanne Simon, 8 August 2013, *Upbuilding Whitted School* Video, Durham, N.C.

Carolina Central University, contends that they were two schools where "teachers made" the learning experience "successful". She further added, "They were awesome. We had class while teachers painted, cleaned the classroom and performed other tasks."[15]

Additionally, former students spoke glowingly of Hillside Park's principal, James Schooler. He was well-respected and, along with the teachers, was responsible for the school's success in its early days. One former student, Dr. Cecilia Steppe-Jones, vividly recalls how Mr. Schooler would "throw his keys down the hall and the person he hit or pointed to had to pick up the keys and bring them to him." She added, with a chuckle, "That was a sign that the student was in trouble."[16] Although Mr. Schooler was a strong disciplinarian, they believed that he was an extraordinary principal and school leader.

James Schooler, Principal of Hillside Park High School and Clerk, White Rock Baptist Church, Courtesy of White Rock Baptist Church Archives, Durham, N.C.

J. A. Whitted, Mary Hester Smith and James Schooler worked just as hard in the community as they did at Hillside Park and Whitted schools. They were active members of White Rock Baptist Church where they served in a variety of ministries. Mr. Schooler, for instance, was the church clerk and worked with the youth. Like many other church members, regardless of what they were doing in the community or how busy they were on their jobs, Whitted, Smith and Schooler always had time for their church.

Although civic leaders gradually began to invest in schools for African-American students living within the city limits of Durham at the turn of the twentieth century, they spent very little money and time in providing a place for Black students to receive an education in the county or rural areas. This was, however, a

---

[15]Interview Debra Parker, Interview by A. Leanne Simon, 8 August 2013, *Upbuilding Whitted School* Video, Durham, N.C.

[16]Interview Dr. Cecilia Steppe-Jones, Interview by A. Leanne Simon, 8 August 2013, *Upbuilding Whitted School* Video, Durham, N.C.

common practice throughout North Carolina.

White Philanthropists Join the Struggle for Black Education

Since Southern Whites were slow to provide schools and teachers for Blacks, White Northern philanthropists felt compelled to step in to address what Blacks believed was a significant problem. In 1892, John F. Slater, a textile manufacturer from Norwich, Connecticut, established a foundation with an initial donation of $1 million. Its sole purpose was "uplifting of the [recently] emancipated population of the southern states . . ., by conferring on them the blessing of a Christian education."[17] Several influential political and educational leaders joined the Slater Fund's board, which helped support the establishment of hundreds of schools in several Southern states.

John Slater, Philanthropist, Courtesy of Public Domain

Anna T. Jeanes, Philanthropist, Courtesy of Public Domain

In 1907, a Quaker named Anna Jeanes donated $1 million to create "The Fund for Rudimentary Schools for Southern Negroes." She appointed to her board of trustees several notable figures, including nationally renowned Booker T. Washington, founder of Tuskegee University. The funds were used to develop a network of Black educators who traveled throughout the South to oversee instruction for Black children. They became known as "Jeanes Teachers" or "Jeanes Supervisors."[18] They also led fundraising efforts, arranged healthcare, offered adult education and even started land co-ops to enable sharecroppers to purchase their own land. These White philanthropists and their surrogates traveled all over the South to assist in the education of Blacks. However, in some

---

[17]"African American Rural Schools in North Carolina," *Merrick Washington Magazine* (Summer 2015): 1-2.

[18]Ibid., 2.

Southern states, like North Carolina, they did not provide support because no one attempted to meet the requirements necessary for funding; that is, not until Dr. Aaron McDuffie Moore, one of White Rock Baptist Church's members, backed by several influential members of the congregation, decided to apply for financial assistance to help children in rural North Carolina. White philanthropists who wanted to help fund African-American education would be very instrumental in helping Dr. Moore achieve his goal of establishing schools for Blacks in rural North Carolina. Dr. Moore would need their generous donations to be able to implement his goals.

White Rock Baptist Church Members and the Rural Education Movement for African Americans

Dr. Aaron McDuffie Moore, White Rock Baptist Church's well-known Sunday School Superintendent and teacher, had strong faith in God and often talked about feeding his sheep. His sheep were those individuals that he felt could not take care of themselves. One of his colleagues and friends described Dr. Moore as a Christian who "personally sought the rejected and the needy so that God's mercy could be extended to them."[19] Dr. Moore was also a businessman and the city's first Black physician.

Dr. Aaron Moore, Durham's First Black Physician, Courtesy of White Rock Baptist Church Archives, Durham, N.C

The most important role that Dr. Moore believed that he had was that of being a devout Christian. Although he genuinely believed that being a medical doctor was his chosen career, Dr. Moore felt that God had a divinely ordained purpose just for him. This purpose included his passion, personality, skills, dreams, and hurts. He believed that God wanted him to provide educational opportunities for African Americans living in rural America. Therefore, Dr. Moore stepped forward to address the educational

---

[19]Louis D. Mitchell, "Aaron McDuffie Moore: He Led His Sheep," *Crisis Magazine*, Vol. 81, No. 7 (August/September 1980): 251-252.

needs of Blacks in Durham, and the State of North Carolina, at a time when it was desperately needed. He knew that if no one did anything, Black students in North Carolina, mainly in rural areas of the State, would not have an opportunity to attend school or get an education. Moore's work in rural education was ultimately responsible for dramatically improving literacy among African Americans and creating an educational system that uplifted generations of Blacks residing in rural North Carolina communities.

Moore also had a special interest in rural education because of his personal experiences and his desire to help the needy. He experienced first-hand the inadequacies of education for African Americans when he attended a rural school in Rosindale, North Carolina. As a child, Moore worked on his parents' farm and attended the county school whenever it was open. He later attended normal schools[20] in Lumberton and Fayetteville (cities in North Carolina), where he was trained to teach in Black public schools.

While attending normal schools, Moore was forced to leave school each year to assist with the planting and harvesting season, but he still maintained his passion for learning. After completing the normal schools, Moore spent three years teaching at one of the schools that he had attended.

Leonard Medical School, Shaw University, First Medical School for Blacks in the South, Courtesy of the Public Domain.

In 1885, Aaron Moore gained admission to Shaw University in Raleigh, North Carolina, intending to become a professor. While there he learned of the desperate need for Black physicians; so, school officials encouraged him to attend its new

[20] A normal school is a school created to train high school graduates to be teachers. Most such schools later became known as "teachers' colleges".

Leonard Medical College. He completed the four-year program in three years and was ranked second among the mixed racial group being tested when he passed the North Carolina Medical Board. Despite changing the direction of his career, Dr. Moore, Durham's first Black physician, continued to dedicate his life to educating his community because he believed that it was what God had ordained him to do. He had been given so many opportunities and, therefore, had a moral, civic and Christian responsibility to help the less fortunate of his race.

Like his friends who served in leadership roles at the meetings of what had been once known as the Baptist and Educational and Missionary Convention, and which had focused on formal education for Black preachers, Moore wanted to offer such educational opportunities to *all* Blacks. While serving as president of the Baptist State Sunday School Convention (BSSSC), Dr. Moore witnessed his share of dilapidated, make-shift schools with limited educational resources that recently freed slaves were expected to attend in urban areas. He also could not help but think about the children in his Sunday School class at White Rock Baptist Church—many whose parents were once slaves who had been denied the right to learn how to read. He wanted to help them. Therefore, while serving as White Rock's Sunday School superintendent, Dr. Moore urged all of the Sunday School teachers to encourage and invite *all* Black children—regardless of their denomination—to attend Sunday School because he felt that this was the only way to ensure that they would receive additional training and education.

Dr. Moore also believed that Sunday School lessons would teach students good Christian moral and ethical values. The values that the Bible taught, Moore and others believed, were the opposite of worldly values. For instance, Moore encouraged Sunday School teachers to focus their lessons on the following: kindness and respect for all people instead of power; humility instead of status; honesty and generosity instead of wealth; self-control instead of self-indulgence; and forgiveness instead of revenge. Besides, the Christian values promoted peace and good will among people in accordance with God's purpose. Ultimately, due to Moore's efforts as well as those of his teachers, White Rock Baptist Church was known to have the largest Sunday School in the city.[21]

Some of the children in Dr. Moore's Sunday School classes also initially attended the Freedman Bureau schools, which provided minimum educational training in often crude settings. But Dr. Moore felt that God wanted Black children to have the same type of education as White Americans and under similar or identical conditions. He knew, however, that Whites were not interested in educational equality for Blacks and Whites. Dr. Moore, therefore, realized that he would have to find a way to provide African-American children with the same educational opportunities as Whites. Moore assumed that with funds from the Jeanes and Slater foundations, which North Carolina had yet to receive, he could build new and better schools for African-American children in Durham—both in urban and rural areas. He began to review funding requirements for the two foundations with the personal goal of successfully gaining monetary support. He also explored ways to obtain Rosenwald funds. Little did he

know that the people with whom he would meet to discuss potential funding were divine connections that God had intentionally arranged.

Moore had known about the Rosenwald funds for a while. His close friend, nationally-recognized Booker T. Washington, had first told

Booker T. Washington, Race Leader, Courtesy of the Public Domain.

him about the Rosenwald Foundation. Once he learned more about it, Moore was convinced that he needed the funding to construct school buildings for Blacks, first in Durham and, later, throughout North Carolina. Dr. Moore knew that Booker T. Washington and Julius Rosenwald were good friends. Therefore, if Washington was willing to help him, Dr. Moore knew that this was his best chance of securing funding from the Rosenwald Foundation.

---

[21]Gazella Lipscomb ad R. K. Bryant, Jr., "A Directory of White Rock Baptist Church and Its Members," Loose Leaf Handout, September 7, 1999.

After his meeting with Dr. Moore in 1914, Booker T. Washington approached Julius Rosenwald, son of German-Jewish immigrants, who was President of Sears, Roebuck and Company at the time, about not only providing Dr. Moore with funds but also to provide enough monetary resources to improve education for all Blacks in the South. At the time, Rosenwald was serving on the Board of Trustees of Tuskegee Institute where he often told his colleagues on the Board that he was committed to uplifting Blacks. As far as Booker T. Washington was concerned, he was merely asking Julius Rosenwald to honor his commitment.[22]

Finally, in 1917, two years after Booker T. Washington's death, Julius Rosenwald agreed to provide funding to support Black education. He declared, "The horrors that are due to race prejudice come home to the Jew and Negro more forcefully than to others of the White race, because of the centuries of persecutions that they have suffered and still suffer." However, he made it clear that Blacks had to meet the requirements for possible funding. Rosenwald first agreed to fund six, small schools in Alabama. Eventually his program was expanded as he financed over 5,300 schools, shops and teachers' homes in 15 states.[23]

Julius Rosenwald, Philanthropist, Courtesy of the Public Domain.

To receive a Rosenwald fund or grant, communities were required to raise matching funds and the local school boards had to purchase the land, as well as provide teachers with salaries and supervision. According to historian Joanne Abel, "The Black community was doubly taxed; once for their regular taxes and then they provided additional funds, as well as contributed labor and materials."[24] To build the schools, communities were given blueprints and strict requirements for construction. Inspectors ensured that they met the standards. The schools were designed

---

[22]For a detailed account, please read Booker T. Washington, *Up From Slavery: An Autobiography* (New York, New York: Doubleday, Page and Company, 1907.

[23]Ibid.

[24]Ibid.

by William Hazel, head of Tuskegee Institute's architectural and mechanical drawing division; George Washington Carver, Tuskegee's noted agricultural scientist; and Robert Taylor, professor of architecture at Tuskegee. The goal was to make the Rosenwald buildings state of the art.

Dr. Moore read the guidelines for receiving Foundation funds. Since Booker T. Washington was no longer alive and available to assist him, Dr. Moore knew that if he wanted to meet the requirements of the grant, he had to essentially work a miracle. As a believer, he knew that his faith in God and fervent prayer would help him to be successful, not his degrees or money. Since God was positioned first in his life, Dr. Moore knew that everything else would fall in place. This was not his agenda; it was God's agenda as promised in the book of Colossians 1: 16-17, which says, ". . . all things have been created through Him and *for Him*, He [God] is before all things, and in Him all things hold together." Dr. Moore knew that living out his God-given purpose in life was all about proper alignment. So, if he was going to provide education to rural Black children in Durham, a forgotten group, then he needed to trust in God and allow Him to work through him and to use him. As Moore began to take the next steps in a plan created by God uniquely for him, he prayed to God for guidance and a willing spirit to work with those individuals whom God had placed in his life.

To begin this initiative, Dr. Moore had to first document the current problems that were prevalent in rural areas. He began by personally paying the salary for George Davis, North Carolina's first inspector for Black rural schools; furthermore, he worked with the State's Education Department to provide direction and support.[25] The inspector noted the terrible conditions of the school buildings, the poorly educated teachers earning extremely low salaries, dilapidated furnishings, short school terms, poor student attendance, and insufficient resources.

Dr. Moore also assumed the task of raising thousands of

---

[25]"African American Rural Schools in North Carolina," 3.

dollars from a Black community that was already struggling. At this point, not only could Dr. Moore envision securing the funds he needed but so did those White Rock members who helped him, which included among others, James Evans, Charles Spaulding, and Nancy Faucette Cooper. He needed enough financial support to not only match the Rosenwald funds and to show that Blacks were trying to financially support a portion of the cost of their own education, but also to supplement the salaries of the Jeanes supervisors.

Although he focused on the Durham community, Dr. Moore also worked to ensure that African-American communities across North Carolina would receive funding for schools. For that reason, he encouraged other communities across the State to strive to meet the requirements of providing the labor and materials to build the schools, as well as contributing much needed funds and increasing the amount of time their children attended school. This was a major sacrifice to many Blacks because children were needed to help on their family farms. Nonetheless, to receive funding from the Rosenwald Foundation, African-American children were required to spend an additional two months in school. Black families were confronted with making a difficult decision — one that could have an adverse financial impact. While Dr. Moore understood the importance of his fight for African Americans to receive an education comparable to that of Whites would upset the critics, he was more concerned about the long-range effects on the African-American community if they did not receive similar educational opportunities. Blacks were already losing ground in this fight. Therefore, he continued to wage a very contentious battle for African-American education.

Nancy Faucette Cooper, Educator, Courtesy of White Rock Baptist Church Archives, Durham, N.C.

Dr. Moore held a series of community meetings for African Americans in Durham and throughout the state. He informed the families of their rights as citizens and provided them with documentation that showed the disparity between White and Black children's education. He also forewarned them of the sacrifices that they would have to make if they wanted to improve their children's quality of education. Dr. Moore wrote a powerful tract in support of rural education for Blacks entitled, "Negro School Rural Problem: Condition-Remedy." The following is an excerpt from the tract:

The biggest thing that we can do, and this seems to me to be our mission, is to empty our lives and character into our children, thereby making them better and wiser citizens than we are, or had the opportunity to be . . . There is much that we can do and must do for ourselves, and we call upon, every teacher, preacher, farmer and business man to arouse themselves, and let us reason together.[26]

Owing to his efforts, Aaron Moore gained robust backing from the North Carolina Teachers' Association (formed by Black educators in 1881). The relationship that he developed with the Association was so strong that they made him treasurer, a position he maintained for years. Dr. Moore drew upon every political and personal contact he knew to obtain sponsorship for the cause. He also felt that he would be more successful in securing foundation funds if he could demonstrate support from North Carolina's legislators.

Dr. Moore, therefore, with nothing but unremitting faith in almighty God, took on the insurmountable task of convincing the North Carolina State Legislature to expand funding for the education of African Americans. By the time he made his case to state legislators, Dr. Moore had documentation of the issues and support from the Rosenwald, Slater and Jeanes foundations. He also had funding and backing from Black communities all over the state. Alliances with some White community leaders and support from many North Carolina educators, including the state superintendent, bolstered his plan.

Equally important, Dr. Moore had the support and advice of several members of White Rock Baptist Church who knew best what he was trying to do. Since Dr. Moore always made a

---

[26]Ibid., 3; Dr. Aaron McDuffie Moore, "Negro Rural School Problem: Condition-Remedy," quoted in "African American Rural Schools in North Carolina," 3.

conscious effort to put God first, he needed the advice of the church's believers. Many of them were trained and practicing educators. The church members that Moore relied on included, among others, Maggie Pool Bryant, Dr. James E. Shepard, Dr. Charles Shepard, Trustee and Deacon James Rufus Evans, Charles Spaulding, and Annie Day Shepard. Impressed with Dr. Moore's relentless commitment to gaining funds for Black education, the North Carolina General Assembly finally gave their support by approving a small amount of funding to help with resources for new schools for Blacks being built across the State. No community was more proud of Dr. Moore than Durham, a community that disproportionately benefited from his efforts.

While the Slater and Jeanes foundations supported mainly teachers and resources for Black education, Rosenwald funds were used to also support the construction of school buildings. By the mid-1920s, Rosenwald schools appeared throughout the South, including Durham, North Carolina, and provided the much-needed education that ex-slaves desperately wanted and needed. Likewise, many of these schools were welcomed by the United States Federal Government, which had tried to resolve the issue of African-American education with the short-lived Freedman's Bureau.

The Rosenwald schools were initially hastily organized affairs, often dependent upon a variety of cast-off books as texts, but they proved immediately and immensely popular. Moore and other leading contributors, like Black businessman and community leader John Merrick and White Rock Baptist Church members Dr. James E. Shepard and Charles Clinton Spaulding, were excited about the funds and the schools that were constructed. Eventually, the one room school houses for Blacks became two rooms with a kitchen, and were stocked with more than enough learning resources. The improved schools were considered state-of-the-art during that period.

Schools for freed Blacks in just about every town in North Carolina were crowded to overflowing. One teacher walked into his little schoolhouse to find three hundred Blacks assembled for a lesson. "I never knew anything like the craving the[y] . . . have to learn," he said. Old people came to night schools after a day of work, fired by "eagerness and youthful enthusiasm." In one Rosenwald school there were "representatives of four generations in a direct line . . . a child of six years, her mother, grandmother, and great grandmother, the latter being more than seventy-five years of age."[27] The desire for education was powerful and universal.

Ultimately, Dr. Moore's work on behalf of education for Blacks worked. He not only received funding for African-American education from the Rosenwald, Slater and Jeanes foundations but also from the Black communities across the State as well as local and state politicians. His strong advocacy for a Christian education resulted in a curriculum in Rosenwald Schools that focused on the four R's: Religion, 'Riting, 'Rithmetic, and Reading. These courses were offered through eighth grade. After completing eighth grade, students could graduate and either attend college or seek employment.

Rural students who attended Sunday School at White Rock Baptist Church could build upon lessons learned in the Rosenwald schools or vice versa. This was a major accomplishment for many rural Black students in Durham and across North Carolina who would have remained in ignorance and darkness if these educational opportunities had not been provided. Moore, Evans, Spaulding, Shepard, Poole and many other White Rock members wanted to ensure that not only adults who were once ex-slaves but, also their children, would know the Lord and the work that He had done. Moreover, Rufus Evans and others tirelessly worked to provide educational opportunities for ex-slaves, and frequently warned Blacks of what would happen, according to Scripture, if they did not receive an education. As noted in Ephesians 4:18-19, without a Christian-based education, freed Blacks would remain ". . . darkened in their understanding," and, therefore, would be "excluded from the life of God because of the ignorance that [was] in them. . . ."

---

[27]Jeffrey Crow, Paul Escott and Flora Hatley, *A History of Blacks in North Carolina* (Raleigh, North Carolina: Office of Archives and History, 2002), 81.

Because of the efforts of a handful of White Rock members like Dr. Moore, James Rufus Evans, Hattie Shepard, Dr. James Shepard and many other unsung heroes and heroines, as well as funds that they received from foundations, North Carolina eventually constructed over 800 Rosenwald school buildings, more than any other state in the country. This was a major accomplishment, considering the State was one of the last to secure funds from the three foundations. Also, this would not have been possible without Dr. Aaron Moore's leadership and his ability to secure support from several of his friends at White Rock. However, in order for Dr. Moore to be able to secure the support of church members, he needed the endorsement of the church's pastor. During the height of his movement for Black education in Durham, Dr. Moore had the support of three of the church's pro-education pastors: Reverend Dr. Augustus Shepard, Reverend Dr. Edward McKnight Brawley and Dr. James Kirkland. These men were living examples of how education could change the lives of Blacks. If Blacks were to continue to make progress, they all reasoned at one time or another, education was key. Therefore, they gave Dr. Moore the support he needed, whether it was monetary or exercising their persuasive oratorical skills to secure the support from members of the congregation.

One of the most well-known Rosenwald schools, located near Durham County, in Hillsborough, North Carolina, for which Dr. Moore and his supporters were responsible for building was the historic Russell School. It still exists today as one of several North Carolina institutions on the Historic Register. The two-room school was named for one of the major

Russell School (Renovated), 2001 St. Mary's Road, Hillsborough, N.C., National Historic Register, Courtesy of the Public Domain.

neighborhood supporters, Thomas Russell. While the school was open, hundreds of children were educated, bringing to fruition the vision and dedication of Dr. Moore and others who believed that high-quality education should be available to everyone.[28] The school movement in African-American neighborhoods was truly a community effort. Julius Rosenwald contributed more than $4.3 million, and Black communities—comprised of many ex-slaves—raised more than $4.7 million.[29]

Because of the seeds planted by Dr. Aaron McDuffie Moore, numerous White Rock Baptist Church members, Jeanes supervisors and the Rosenwald Foundation, many generations of rural and urban African-American students in Durham and across North Carolina received an education. Due to the notable gains made by Dr. Moore in rural education for ex-slaves, he was aptly named the "Father of the Rural School Movement for Negroes in North Carolina." Of all the titles that Dr. Moore could claim or that were bestowed upon him, he cherished this moniker best because it was the result of his God-given passion and purpose.

Moore often compared himself to Jeremiah when people questioned why he, a gifted and well-to-do physician, would want to spend most of his time fighting an uphill battle for African-American education instead of seeing patients in the comforts of his home. He frequently responded that he had passion like Jeremiah and then would ask his critic if he or she ever had anything to burn within them until they acted on it. That, he would respond, was fire or passion. "It wakes me up at night," says Moore, "or keeps me from going to sleep in the first place. It causes me to think about the subject when the subject is not even on the table. It is the very fuel of my purpose. It keeps me going even when I want to be uncalled. You, too, will know it's your passion when it's something you would do even if you were not paid to do it."[30] This sentiment expressed by Dr. Moore truly captures the type of passion that he and countless others

---

[28]Mary Hoffschwelle, *Preserving Rosenwald Schools* (Washington, D.C.: National Trust for Historic Preservation), 2.

[29]Ibid.

[30]Dr. Aaron McDuffie Moore, "Negro Rural School Problem: Condition-Remedy," quoted in "African American Rural Schools in North Carolina," 28.

exhibited as leaders of the "Rural Education Movement for Blacks in North Carolina."

Dr. Moore's dual positions as president of the Sunday School Convention of North Carolina and superintendent of White Rock Baptist Church's Sunday School Ministry provided him with an opportunity to see firsthand the need for formal education for urban and rural Blacks. He made considerable progress in achieving educational opportunities for Blacks in grades one through six, and later high school. However, Dr. Moore felt that Black students could not start learning too soon. Therefore, he began to promote the idea of having a kindergarten at White Rock since he could not convince the legislators to approve such an important program for youth. Shortly after sharing his idea with some members of his church family, Dr. Moore began such a class on his own in the basement of White Rock Baptist Church. He organized the first Kindergarten in the city and his daughter, Mattie Moore, was the teacher.[31] Many of the children who attended kindergarten at White Rock were academically prepared for first grade.

White Rock Members Want More Than a Grade School and a High School for Durham's Blacks

Dr. Moore was inarguably one of the leading members of White Rock Baptist Church and the Durham community to tackle issues related to education in the Black community. However, he was not the only one. Another member who tirelessly fought to gain educational opportunities for members of the Black community and who was mentioned in the scenario at the beginning of this chapter was Reverend Dr. James E. Shepard. Another believer in Jesus Christ, he specifically thought that education for Blacks and his ministry work as a Christian were inextricably linked. He was a man with many occupations—minister, educator, businessman, politician, pharmacist, civil servant and race leader. But like Dr. Moore and other members of

---

[31]Gayzella Lipscomb and R. K. Bryant, Jr., "A Directory of White Rock Baptist Church and Its Members."

White Rock, those were mere titles. Shepard was a disciple of God first and genuinely believed that he had been placed on earth to fulfill God's purpose and build His Kingdom. He was very clear about his God-given purpose in life.

Dr. Shepard knew that it was God who had first planted in his mind the concept of post-secondary education for African Americans. Shepard also knew that once God gave him this idea, He would wait to see what Shepard would do with it. And Shepard was more than ready to show God how he would handle the vision that He had given him. Shepard also knew that he had been entrusted by God with something that had the potential to be so much larger than what Dr. Shepard could ever envision. After all, as Shepard reflected on his life, he believed that God had been preparing him for this from the time he was born.

James E. Shepard was born in Raleigh, North Carolina, on November 3, 1875, to Reverend Dr. Augustus and Mrs. Hattie Whitted Shepard. He was the eldest of twelve children. Four of his siblings died in early childhood and eight survived, three boys and five girls.[32] James Shepard was reared in an educationally rich environment. His father, Dr. Augustus Shepard, graduated from Shaw University and was a minister. All the Shepard children attended Shaw University as well. Charles Haddon Shepard, James Shepard's younger brother, graduated from Shaw University's Leonard School of Medicine and became a physician and surgeon.

Dr. Shepard's father always emphasized the need and importance of education in his household. After all, his dad, Reverend Dr. Augustus Shepard, was an example of what Blacks could achieve if they were educationally prepared to meet the challenges of society. This was very important for a race of people less than ten years out of slavery. From as far back as anyone could remember, James Shepard was always interested in

---

[32]Lenwood G. Davis, ed., *Selected Writings and Speeches of James E. Shepard, 1896-1946: Founder* of North Carolina Central University (Madison, Wisconsin: Fairleigh Dickinson University Press, 2013), 2; *Historical Data Sheet*, North Carolina Central University Archives (1978), 1.

education. Like Dr. Moore, this, too, was his spiritual passion.

Dr. James E. Shepard, Founder of Present-Day North Carolina Central University, Courtesy of White Rock Baptist Church Archives, Durham, N.C.

He graduated from Shaw University in 1894 with a degree in pharmacy at the age of nineteen. Dr. James Shepard became one of the first Black pharmacists in North Carolina.[33] Dr. Shepard first worked as a pharmacist in Danville, Virginia. A year later, in 1895, he relocated to Durham, North Carolina, and worked as a pharmacist with the Durham Drug Company. While at Durham Drug Company, Dr. Shepard met Dr. Moore and they subsequently formed a professional and religious relationship. The following year, he married Annie Day Robinson.[34]

In 1897, Shepard moved to Washington, D.C., to take the position, Comparer of Deeds, in the Recorder of Deeds Office.[35] Earlier in the year, President William McKinley's administration had appointed former United States House of Representatives Henry Plummer Cheatham Recorder of Deeds for Washington, D.C. This was considered at the time as a high position in the Federal Government. Cheatham later appointed Shepard to the Comparer of Deeds' position. Shepard's position brought him in close contact with many Federal Government officials, including future President Theodore Roosevelt, all who would later become God's divine connections in Shepard's life. Shepard served in the position for one year before returning to North Carolina to accept a higher federal position.

In 1898, President William McKinley appointed Shepard Deputy Collector for the United States Internal Revenue Service in

---

[33] *Historical Data Sheet,* North Carolina Central University Archives (1978), 1.

[34] See James E. Shepard Papers, 1905-1990, University Archives, Records and History Center, , James E. Shepard Memorial Library, North Carolina Central University, Durham, N.C.

[35] Jessie Smith, *Black First: 2000 Years of Extraordinary Achievements* (Detroit, Michigan: Visible Link, 1994), 170.

Raleigh.[36]   Shepard was the first African American to be appointed to that position. He remained in the position until 1905, when his appointment expired.

In 1900, Shepard, a real estate dealer, joined the National Negro Business League, founded by Booker T. Washington. He owned a real estate company, which made him eligible to join the League. Shepard loaned money, invested in property, and had collections as one of his specialties.

In every position that James Shepard held, it was obvious to people around him that he was first, and foremost, a Christian. Also, in each position, God was preparing him for what would become his most impactful position of all, that is, founder and Chief Executive Officer of a college to train ministers and to teach morality and ethics to a people who were either recently freed slaves or descendants of ex-slaves. The divine connections that Dr. Shepard made in each of the positions that he held over the years would prove to be beneficial as Shepard encountered the many challenges of not only starting a college but keeping the college open. What sustained Dr. Shepard was his passion and vision, two gifts that God had given him in an effort to strengthen and motivate him through the difficult times. These precious gifts gave him the strength to proceed and to get up each day and wage yet another battle to make his God-given vision and passion a reality.

Shepard, an avid Bible reader, probably called on God many times given the numerous challenges that he encountered while trying to establish an institution that focused on religious training for African Americans.   Having been reared in a Christian environment with a father who was a Baptist minister, it would not have been unusual for Dr. Shepard to appeal to God for assistance. So, when it was time to fulfill his ultimate purpose of establishing a college to train ministers, filled with and guided by

---

[36]H. Leon Prather, Sr., *Resurgent Politics and Educational Progressivism in the South: North Carolina, 1890-1913* (Rutherford, New Jersey: Fairleigh Dickinson University Press, 1997), 104. See also Elizabeth Irene Seay, "A History of North Carolina for Negroes," Unpublished M.A. Thesis, Duke University, 1941, p. 92.

the Holy Spirit, Shepard took the steps necessary along his life journey to make it a reality.

In 1905, when Dr. Shepard was appointed Field Superintendent of Work Among the Negroes by the International Sunday School Association, God was preparing him to take the next step towards the purpose He had for his life, which was establishing a religious training school that would give God glory and expand His Kingdom. Many of the individuals who attended the Sunday School conventions would eventually attend Dr. Shepard's school. In this position, his assignment was "to improve Sunday Schools in management, methods and equipment and to endeavor to bring the denominations into a close understanding for cooperation to uplift the race."[37] Such improvements to Sunday Schools were done to improve the religious instruction of Blacks. Shepard held that position until 1909.

During the first year of his appointment, Dr. Shepard spoke at the 1905 convention that was held in Toronto, Canada, from June 23 to June 27. His topic, "Work Among the Negroes," explained that the work of the International Sunday School Association, as far as African Americans were concerned, must be largely among children between the ages of five and fourteen, and to make Christian citizens of them. He offered suggestions as to what that work might be and then closed by thanking them for supporting his race. Dr. James Shepard made similar speeches both at home in the United States and abroad.

Dr. Shepard believed that the Sunday School presented a most inviting field for work, and felt that if the nations were to be strong and lifted permanently, it must be done through and by the Sunday Schools. He conveyed this belief everywhere that he presented. He would often argue that the races of the world needed a Christian education, for "with a Christian education would come Christian tolerance and love," which he believed,

---

[37]Ibid., 94.

would "lessen friction, bridge the chasm of hate, and make a way for peace."[38]

Over the next few years, Reverend Dr. James Shepard made a compelling case as to why religious education was important for African Americans. Again, this was a part of God's plan for the larger (and ultimate) purpose that He had for Dr. Shepard. For instance, in the speech he made before the 1908 International Sunday School Convention, Dr. Shepard mentioned that religious education was industrial education, liberal arts education, and higher education. "Religious education," he argued, "checked the human waste, which was found on the chain-gang, and in jails, in the penitentiaries, and on the streets, and stores up energy for the salvation and uplift of the people."[39] He reasoned that if one wanted to save the Black race, they had to be given a religious education.

Like his father, when Dr. James E. Shepard traveled across the country in his position as Field Superintendent in Work Among Negroes, he came in direct contact with Black ministers as well as other religious leaders. During his travels, he observed that many of the Black ministers were poorly trained and ill-prepared as leaders. For that reason, he realized that if the African-American community was to make progress under its ministers' leadership, the ministers must be trained in religious affairs. It was, in part, because of the ministers' lack of training that Dr. Shepard conceived of the idea of establishing a school for the training of minsters and other religious leaders and teachers.

Two years after the International Sunday School Convention, in Toronto, Canada, and while still serving as superintendent, James E. Shepard published a pamphlet entitled, *The True Solution*. In this work, he presented a plan for the establishment of a Bible school for African Americans. He wanted to have a school like the Northfield Bible Training School[40] that 19th century evangelist

---

[38]Ibid., 94.

[39]Ibid., 95-96.

[40]Northfield Bible Training School, established after the Civil War by Evangelist

Dwight L. Moody had founded in western Massachusetts. In his work with the International Sunday School Association, Dr. Shepard met Evangelist Moody on several occasions. He was an admirer of Mr. Moody's work and school, which was established to "train men and women in the Bible and thus change the inner life and with this life changed, send them out to change others, and rear a new people, loving, right fearing God, and respecting their fellow man."[41] According to the plan, the school would have a literary department that would be designed for illiterate ministers. A course in advanced methods, the art of reaching and teaching men would be given. The establishment of a course for Sunday School teachers and home missionaries would be offered. A special course would be taught for foreign missionaries, teaching the language, habits, and customs of the people studied, and a brief knowledge of medicine and industrial work, to prepare them for service. His idea found support in Durham, including that of the *Recorder:* "Dr. James E. Shepard has been at work on a plan for some time, and that his efforts are in a measure successful is cause for all members of the colored race in Durham and their white friends to rejoice."[42]

That same year, 1907, Shepard laid the foundation for the school which became the National Religious Training School and Chautauqua for the Colored Race. His initial investment of $25,000 was from his good old friend from White Rock, Dr. Aaron McDuffie Moore, John Merrick, and the Merchants Association in Durham, North Carolina. The school was incorporated on June 30, 1909.

One of the first things that Shepard did was to form an

Dwight Lyman Moody and his wife, trained men and women in evangelistic outreach and ministry work. The Institute initially served women and, later, opened its doors to men. Moody also focused on educating the poor and minorities and admitted students from diverse religious backgrounds. He had an amazing ability to bridge the gap between denominations.

[41] I Lenwood G. Davis, ed., *Selected Writings and Speeches of James E. Shepard, 1896-1946: Founder* of North Carolina Central University (Madison, Wisconsin: Fairleigh Dickinson University Press, 2013), 96.

[42] Jim Wise, *Durham,* 105.

advisory board known as the Board of Trustees. The 35-member board included Dr. James E. Shepard, President-Elect, Durham, North Carolina; Dr. James B. Dudley, President of A&M College, Greensboro, North Carolina, Chairman; Mr. John Merrick, President, North Carolina Mutual and Provident Association, Durham, North Carolina, Vice Chairman; Dr. Aaron McDuffie Moore, Physician, Durham, Secretary; General Julian Carr, President of the First National Bank and mill owner in Durham, Treasurer; and Dr. W. M. Gilbert, Physician, New York, New York, Chairman of the Special Finance Committee.[43] An analysis of the Board of Trustees reveals a number of interesting things. First, there were no females on the board, which is not surprising since very few females were involved in matters of this kind during that time. Second, the board consisted of members from ten states and Washington, D.C. Third, half of the members were religious leaders. Fourth, the second largest number on the Board consisted of capitalists and businessmen. Fifth, educators comprised the next largest number on the board. Sixth, there were two physicians (both Blacks), a United States Senator and one United States Circuit Court Judge.[44] The Board of Trustees served in an advisory capacity and Dr. Shepard sought their advice on all matters regarding policies and fiscal issues.

The objectives of the National Religious Training School and Chautauqua for the Colored Race were as follows: "To provide religious, industrial and literary training to colored youth of North Carolina and other states of the United States, and especially to train men and women in the Bible, and to teach practical industries, such as agriculture, horticulture and domestic science and similar branches. The fundamental idea being that young men and women will be taught to work, and that religion and work go hand in hand. Also [sic] to teach any and all subjects

---

[43]Benjamin Newton Duke Papers, Box 37. Material Housed in the Rare Book, Manuscript and Special Collections Library, Duke University.

[44]Ibid. See also: Lenwood G. Davis, ed., *Selected Writings and Speeches of James E. Shepard, 1896-1946: Founder* of North Carolina Central University (Madison, Wisconsin: Fairleigh Dickinson University Press, 2013), 8.

and branches commonly taught in normal training schools and colleges."[45]

Once the Board of Trustees and plan for the school were in place, Reverend Dr. James Shepard began to solicit funds. When Dr. Shepard traveled around the country to secure funds for the school, he often had to answer two questions: "Why such an institution?" and "Do colored people need such an institution?" He would always reply, "There is no similar one for the Colored race in America and all industrial and college education that will cause the betterment of the real conditions of the race must be founded upon a moral and religious training."[46] He also said that the rallying cry of the race must be "change the man and the environment will be changed by the man."[47] This belief resonated with those in the community. Because it was so difficult to obtain funds from the North Carolina State legislature and private donors for a school with a religious focus, Dr. Shepard called on members of his church, White Rock Baptist, and the North Carolina Black Baptist Convention for support. They did not disappoint him, each making generous donations. However, despite their large, consistent financial contributions, it was not enough. Dr. Shepard simply could never seem to find enough money.

The school continued to struggle over the years because of the lack of adequate finances. The institution often operated on credit notes signed by Dr. Shepard. At one time, the institution was auctioned off, forcing the school to close for a short time. Eventually, Mrs. Margaret Olivia Slocum Sage, the wife of robber baron[48] Russell

Margaret Slocum Sage, Philanthropist, Courtesy of the Public Domain.

---

[45]Ibid., 108.

[46]Benjamin Newton Papers, Box 35, Material Housed in the Rare Book, Manuscript and Special Collections Library, Duke University.

[47]Lenwood G. Davis, ed., *Selected Writings and Speeches of James E. Shepard, 1896-1946: Founder* of North Carolina Central University (Madison, Wisconsin: Fairleigh Dickinson University Press, 2013), 9.

[48]Robber baron is a derogatory term applied to certain later 19th century American businessmen who used unscrupulous methods to get rich.

Sage, made a personal contribution of $15,000.[49]

Her contribution along with those made by Board of Trustee members enabled Dr. Shepard to buy the school back and re-open its doors to students.

However, the school was reorganized and became the National Training School, as previously mentioned, and, in 1923, it became known as the Durham State Normal School when the State of North Carolina assumed control. In 1925, the school survived a major fire and subsequently became the North Carolina College for Negroes — the first state-supported liberal arts college for Blacks in the nation. The North Carolina General assembly changed the name to the North Carolina College at Durham in 1947, the same year that Dr. Shepard died, and to North Carolina Central University in 1969.

Dr. Shepard's school was often compared to Tuskegee Institute, Booker T. Washington's school. Shepard was quick to deny any similarities. He said that Washington's school was essentially industrial in nature while his school was spiritual. Moreover, Shepard wanted an educated ministry, "one with an illuminated conscience and an informed heart that would lead the race and work out its soul salvation."[50] For the most part, especially in the school's earliest years, Shepard achieved his goal. His efforts brought enlightenment to a people who were not aware of God's message of salvation and helped many African Americans to understand that God had a purpose for them in life which, when followed, would glorify Him and expand His Kingdom. The National Religious Training School and Chautauqua for the Colored Race, founded by one of White Rock's members and frequent preachers, and supported, in large part, by the church's membership since its inception, was God's purpose and plan for Dr. Shepard. Consequently, four and one-half decades after slavery, thousands of Black North Carolinians

---

[49]Elizabeth Irene Seay, "A History of North Carolina for Negroes," Unpublished M.A. Thesis, Duke University, 1941, p. 58.

[50]*Durham Morning Herald,* August 13, 1909, 1.

had the opportunity to pursue a post-secondary education that had primarily a religious focus.

Well Done, My Good and Faithful Servant – Matthew 15: 21

Over the years, Dr. James E. Shepard received many honors and awards for his efforts. In 1912 alone, for example, he received several major honors. He was ordained a minister of the gospel at White Rock Baptist Church, in Durham, North Carolina, on January 14, 1912, and frequently preached at the church after his father died. This is also the same church where he was a member and first shared his ideas about the school with members Dr. Aaron McDuffie Moore, Dr. Charles Spaulding, James Evans and a number of other deacons, trustees and educators at the church.[51] Furthermore, many of White Rock's members were employed at the college as administrators, faculty and staff once it became fully operational and, as such, felt compelled to support the National Religious Training School and Chautauqua.

Reverend Shepard had previously taken some theological courses at Shaw University. He had been licentiate for some time. Therefore, many people were excited when he was ordained at White Rock in 1912. One account given during his ordination services stated that "Shepard had preached a few Sundays ago and preached a very acceptable and inspiring sermon that was quite in keeping with dignity and ability with which he peculiarly endowed."[52] The editor of the *Scranton (Pennsylvania) Tribune* heard an earlier address by Shepard at the First Presbyterian Church of Scranton and declared: "In a matchless address of forty minutes, Dr. Shepard held the large audience spell bound as he made a plea for his Race."[53] Years later, the editor of *Winchester* (Massachusetts) *Star*, commenting on Shepard's oration said, "Dr.

---

[51]"Dr. Shepard an Ordained Minister," *Washington (DC) Washington Bee,* June 29, 1912, p. 1. See also: "Dr. James E. Shepard, Negro Educator, 72." *New York Times,* October 7, 1947, p. 27; and Lenwood G. Davis, ed., *Selected Writings and Speeches of James E. Shepard, 1896-1946: Founder* of North Carolina Central University (Madison, Wisconsin: Fairleigh Dickinson University Press, 2013), 10.

[52]Ibid.

[53]"Equal Chance for the Negro," *Scranton (PA) Republican,* October 30, 1911, p. 8.

Shepard was a speaker of persuasive eloquence, clear insight and judicial mind."[54]

Additionally, in 1912, Shepard, a loyal Republican, attended the National Republican Convention held in Chicago, Illinois, upon the request of former President Theodore Roosevelt who was a friend and admirer of Dr. Shepard and supporter of the school. So, Roosevelt sent out a lot of literature concerning the school, "thereby aiding it with his influence."[55]

Dr. Shepard received another honor in 1912, when Muskingum College, which is affiliated with the Presbyterian Church (USA), in New Concord, Ohio, conferred the degree, "Doctor of Divinity," upon him. He was the first and, at that time, the only person of color to be honored with a degree by Muskingum College; the vote among the faculty was unanimous.[56]

This is just a small sample of the earthly awards and recognition that Dr. Shepard received. While he cherished each of them, his most cherished award and reward was to one day hear from Jesus Christ that he had been a good and faithful servant. Nothing else really mattered to Dr. Shepard.

Another Good and Faithful Servant Also Faithfully Performed God's Work: Dr. Moore, a Disciple of God First, Physician and Businessman Second

While traveling the State raising funds, meeting with legislators and researching the educational needs of rural communities, Dr. Moore remained committed to White Rock Baptist Church. Actually, his missionary work at the church was first in his life. He was devoted to the religious activities of the church, both financially and educationally. He believed in the

---

[54]"Dr. Shepard Speaks," *Winchester* (MA) *Star,* April 27, 1923, p. 6.

[55]"Dr. Shepard in Chicago," *Durham Morning Herald,* June 13, 1912, p. 8.

[56]J. A. Whitted, *Biographical Sketch of the Life and Work of the Late Rev. Augustus Shepard, D.D. Durham, North Carolina* (Raleigh, North Carolina: Edwards and Broughton, 1912), 22.

power of prayer, and felt that it replenished his own spiritual fountain.

Moore was so popular in Baptist circles in North Carolina that he was elected president of the Sunday School Baptist Convention. Additionally, as previously stated, an active worker at White Rock Baptist Church while leading the rural education movement in North Carolina, Dr. Moore was also elected chairman of the Deacon Board of Directors, superintendent for life of the Sunday School, and president of the church library which became part of the public library many years after his death. He also helped raise $26,000 for the remodeling of White Rock, which was completed in 1910. The church had a new front Baraca Room, inclined floors, pipe organ, library, public baths for a nominal fee, and night classes in bookkeeping and stenography, all which Dr. Moore avidly

Trustee William Kennedy, Jr., Courtesy of White Rock Baptist Church Archives, Durham, N.C.

supported. He knew that these were areas in which members of the African-American race had to improve if they wanted to be successful participants in the democracy. "Youth must recognize individual responsibility," Dr. Moore maintained, "to the race, the nation, and to humanity and prepare themselves to become a working unit in their development."[57] Not only did Dr. Moore preach this belief; he lived and died by it. As a manifestation of this belief, his Sunday School class was passed on to the tutelage of William Kennedy, Jr., a member of the church and longtime advocate for African-American education. Dr. Moore was so committed to God and his church that he made a place in his will for an enlargement program. He gave to the church a double house and two lots adjoining the church. Hence, Moore was committed to helping people—both in the church and the community, which was demonstrated by his incessant activity.

Furthermore, Moore saw travel as an education and

---

[57]Louis D. Mitchell, "Aaron McDuffie Moore: He Led His Sheep," *Crisis Magazine*, Vol. 81, No. 7 (August/September 1980): 254-256.

encouraged Blacks to do so. He exemplified his beliefs in the importance of travel by his many trips with his family to Chicago for the Great Fair in 1892,[58] numerous visits to New York City, trips across country with his daughters, trips to Florida with John Merrick, and excursions to Puerto Rico and Cuba. Additionally, his fond interest in foreign mission work extended to the work of the Lott Carey Foreign Mission Convention in the Republic of Haiti, where White Rock Baptist Church had a special interest. He went to Haiti at his own expense and subsequently persuaded his Sunday School to raise sufficient funds to buy land on which the convention erected a church building in Saint-Marc, a large port town in western Haiti.[59]

White Rock Baptist Church's Link to Durham's First Library for Blacks

Dr. Moore's work in the rural education movement exposed another problem in the African-American community that he felt compelled to address. An avid reader and lover of books, he often expressed concerns about the lack of good reading material. The Durham Public Library, which opened its doors on February 10, 1898, did not allow Black patrons. This concerned Dr. Moore and other White Rock members such as William Kennedy, Jr., James Shepard, James Evans, and Maude Logan. They felt that African Americans also needed a place to go to read and check-out books. Consequently, they decided to provide such an opportunity to Blacks, in 1913, by establishing a library in the basement of White Rock Baptist Church. The library opened with 799 books that had been donated by Drs. Aaron Moore and James E. Shepard.[60] As previously mentioned, at the time that Dr. Moore and the others

---

[58]The Great Fair, also known as the World's Fair, was held in Chicago to celebrate the 400th anniversary of Christopher Columbus's arrival in the New World in 1492. The exposition covered more than 600 acres, featuring nearly 200 new buildings of predominantly neoclassical architecture, canals and lagoons, and people and cultures from 46 countries.

[59]Louis D. Mitchell, "Aaron McDuffie Moore: He Led His Sheep," *Crisis Magazine*, Vol. 81, No. 7 (August/September 1980): 256.

[60] "History of the Durham County Library and the Stanford L. Warren Library," North Carolina Digital Collections, State Archives of North Carolina, August 14, 2007, 1.

opened the State's second public library in North Carolina for African Americans,[61] Moore was superintendent of the church's Sunday School.

John Merrick, Durham Businessman, Member of Saint Joseph's AME Church, Courtesy of White Rock Baptist Archives, Durham, N.C.

The church library experienced partial success. Although all Blacks were encouraged to use the library, many of them refused to do so if they were not a member of the church or a Baptist. The library remained in the church for three years. On August 14, 1916, Dr. Moore and his good friend, ex-slave-turned-businessman John Merrick, moved the library from White Rock Baptist Church to a building Merrick owned at the corner of Fayetteville and Pettigrew streets.[62] It became the Durham Colored Library, which was supported by community donations during its first year. Its first librarian and only employee was Hattie Wooten. Because of the name change and new location, Moore, Merrick and their supporters quickly witnessed an increase in the number of Blacks visiting the Durham Colored Library. An increase in the number of library visitors required more funding if they were to expand, which the library's founders lacked. Therefore, Dr. Moore, John Merrick, and Reverend Dr. James Shepard made several pleas to Durham city and county governments as well as major benefactors in the city for monetary support.

In 1917, the City of Durham began granting the library a meager monthly appropriation; however, the institution still relied heavily on community financial support. In 1918, the library began receiving $30 per month from the city of Durham and, that same year, the North Carolina General Assembly incorporated an association to be called Durham Colored Library, Inc.[63]

---

[61]The first public library for Blacks in North Carolina was the Brevard Street Library in Charlotte. It was in operation from 1905 until 1961.

[62]Ibid.; Dawn Baumgartner Vaughan, "He Co-founded N.C. Mutual and a Library in the Jim Crow South. Now a Biography is in the Works," *The Herald Sun.* June 12, 2017.

The library soon became popular and, as its usage increased, it became apparent that the library was outgrowing its cramped quarters. Although the Library's Board of Trustees had discussed possible relocation of the library for some time, it was not until 1939 that they were able to build a new library at the corner of Umstead and Fayetteville streets, in Durham. The new building was financed mainly by a $24,000 loan from North Carolina Mutual Insurance Company, the first Black insurance institution in the country. Several individuals contributed significant amounts of money, including long-time board president, Dr. Stanford Leigh Warren, who donated $4,000 to purchase the lot at the corner of Fayetteville and Umstead streets, in Durham, for the new library building. The opening of the library, renamed after

Stanford L. Warren, on January 17, 1940, brought about a dramatic expansion of services. The new library contained a collection of books on and by African Americans as a non-circulating special collection. The library introduced bookmobile services in 1942.[64]

Durham Colored Library, Started in Basement of White Rock Baptist Church, Courtesy of White Rock Baptist Church Archives, Durham, N.C.

Dr. Moore, the architect of the North Carolina rural education movement for African Americans and founder of the State's second public library for Blacks, died before Stanford L. Warren Library opened its doors to the public in 1940. He was known not only in Durham but statewide and nationally for his work as a community servant when he lost his struggle with life on April 29, 1923. After nearly sixty years on earth, as Louis Mitchell states, he went "over

---

[63]Dawn Bumgartner Vaughan, "He Co-Founded N.C. Mutual;" for a detailed history of Stanford L. Warren Library, see Beverly Washington Jones' *Stanford L. Warren , 77 Years of Public Service: A Phoenix in the Durham Community* (Durham, N.C.: Durham County Library, 1990).

[64]Beverly Washington Jones, *Stanford L. Warren.*

Jordan."[65] His life's work left Durham, the state and the nation in a much better place. Hence, when he died, Black and White people all over North Carolina were at a loss for how to proceed. Which of White Rock Baptist Church's members, or members of the African-American community-at-large, if any, would continue the movement for Black education? While a great deal had been accomplished, much more needed to be done. Which White Rock members would represent Blacks and their causes before local and state legislators? What Black North Carolinians and White Rock members would establish relationships with national figures to accomplish the goals of the Black community? These and other questions loomed large as members of Durham's community as well as Black communities across the State tried to cope with Dr. Moore's death.

Following the departure of Dr. Aaron McDuffie Moore, who was born to free, Black, land-owning parents during the Civil War, there was, as Louis Mitchell vividly describes, a hushed pause not only in Durham but across North Carolina. Mitchell best summed up the impact that Dr. Moore's death had on people when he eloquently stated:

There descended on the state a choking sense of loss. There was grief everywhere. What Dr. Moore's immediate family lost was a brother, an uncle, a cousin, a father, and a husband. White Rock Baptist Church lost a faithful and committed member, and a gentle soul with a deep compassion for those who suffered regardless of whether they were members of the church. Durham lost a religious leader, pioneer, philanthropist, believer in men, businessman, and an educator. In short, North Carolina lost a brave man who learned as a young man the ancient and enduring tensions of racism. He dared to confront that evil element—in his own calm way—with a conviction that there was better on this earth for his people and for those who dealt out persecution upon his people. Endowed with a fervent belief in the fundamental goodness of man, this active, far-seeing, gentle soul, whose very choice of profession—medical doctor—symbolized his deep compassion for the

---

[65]Louis D. Mitchell, "Aaron McDuffie Moore: He Led His Sheep," *Crisis Magazine*, Vol. 81, No. 7 (August/September 1980): 248-249.

suffering, in the end gave of himself, all he had, as he worked diligently both in his community and church caring for his sheep.[66]

Indeed, Dr. Moore left a legacy unmatched by many. He was an excellent example of a member of Durham's Black elite committed to racial uplift whether it was in his church, White Rock, or the community.

Conclusion

Today, the grade schools (many known as Rosenwald schools), North Carolina Central University and Stanford L. Warren Library stand as a testament to the faith and commitment of many White Rock members as they fulfilled their God-ordained purposes in life. These members included, among others, Dr. Aaron McDuffie Moore, Dr. James E. Shepard, James Evans, Hattie Shepard, Maude Logan, Annie day Shepard, and Charles Spaulding. These were men and women of faith. They were great examples of how believers must use their God-given talents, skills and passions to give God glory, to fulfill His purpose for their lives, and to expand His Kingdom. In doing so, they learned that the lives of the less fortunate were forever changed for the better. While fighting for the right to worship and to be educated, these men and women also joined others to use their God-given talents to help their race gain economic freedom and political rights.

---

[66]Ibid.

Chapter Eight

Launching "Black Wall Street" and an All-Black Community: White Rock Members Engage in Black Economic Development

"For even when we were with you, we would give you this command: If anyone is not willing to work, let him not eat."
— 2 Thessalonians 3:10 (ESV)

W hile peering out of her kitchen window at 606 Fayetteville Street, in Durham, North Carolina, Sara McCotta "Cottie" Dancy Moore quietly hummed the first verse of the old Negro spiritual, "Swing Low, Sweet Chariot." She smiled as she thought about how the little Black children innocently engaged in play while the world around them was rapidly changing. It was 1898 and the images of slavery, which ended a mere 33 years earlier, were still vivid in her mind. Unlike the parents of many of the children playing a few feet outside of her window, Cottie Moore, as she was fondly called, and many of her family members had

Sara Cottie Dancy Moore, Wife of Dr. Aaron McDuffie Moore, Durham's First African America Doctor, Courtesy of White Rock Baptist Church Archives, Durham, N.C.

been born free, in Tarboro, North Carolina. In fact, her uncle, John Dancy, was a nationally-recognized and respected Republican politician, educator and journalist. She had relocated to Durham after meeting and marrying the city's first African-American doctor, Aaron McDuffie Moore.

Cottie Moore decided to prepare tea for both herself and her husband while they patiently waited for a visit from their good friends, John and Martha Hunter Merrick. While the tea was brewing, Cottie glanced at the clock. "My, I wonder what is keeping them?" she whispered. "I thought they were coming over right after church. Well, maybe they will be here soon. But, then again," she thought, "Pastor Eaton ended services at White Rock today a little earlier than we had anticipated. Since John and Martha are faithful members of St. Joseph's, they would not leave until services had ended. Well," she sighed, "they could arrive at any time." She resumed humming "Swing Low, Sweet Chariot" and then

The home of Dr. Aaron McDuffie Moore and Mrs. Cottie Dancy Moore at 606 Fayetteville Street, Durham, N.C., White Rock Baptist Church is to the right, Courtesy of White Rock Baptist Church Archives, Durham, N.C.

realized that the tea was ready. Just as she opened the cupboard to look for the sugar and honey, someone knocked on the front door. Mrs. Moore headed to the door, quickly examining her appearance in the hall mirror. She opened the door and greeted her friends who immediately apologized for being late. She ushered them into the parlor and then went upstairs to inform her husband that their guests had arrived. Dr. Moore joined them as Mrs. Moore served their guests hors d'oeuvres. After 45-minutes of "small talk," or informal discourse, as was customary, Cottie and Martha left the room so that the men could engage in a more serious conversation about important business matters.

Both Moore and Merrick were among the many African-American men of ability and talent who, with strong desires to improve their economic lot, had migrated to Durham in the late 1800s and early 1900s. Such men believed that power and security lay in property not politics. Dr. Aaron Moore and John Merrick also met a demand in Durham's growing African-American community. For one, the city needed an African-American physician who eventually became Dr. Moore. But, he happened to be more than a mere Doctor of Medicine.

Dr. Moore answered calls from the destitute. He fed the hungry, delivered babies, comforted the bereaved and dashed about on horse and bicycle in the African-American community to visit and bring relief to the miserable whom he loved to call "the least of these, my children." He often treated his patients on the back porch of his house as well. Dr. Moore worked hard at his practice, trying to establish himself as a physician in whom the people could give their trust and as a civic and religious leader. He often spoke of how poor his patients were; he would charge one dollar a visit, when and if he could collect, and would sometimes complain that African Americans regarded him as a horse or witch doctor, or a man of magic.[1] He vowed to change that image, and spent his life doing so. Although he did not become involved in factional politics, Moore did become familiar with the ways and thoughts of the leading White citizens of Durham like the Dukes, the Carrs, the Watts, and others. Also, like Dr. Shepard and Dr. Spaulding, he became adept at interpreting his people's needs to its rich White citizens.

The father of two daughters, Lyda and Mattie, Dr. Moore worked hard so that they would not have to endure the challenges that he confronted. He also trained and educated them in the importance of mercy, education, and "good works" as principles whereby the Christian was to live.

Moore also understood very well the circumstances of the time in which he lived. This awareness provided him with a special talent to lead, teach, and inspire. He spent his life

---

[1]Louis Mitchell, "Aaron McDuffie Moore: He Led His Sheep," *Crisis Magazine* (August-September 1980), 250.

personally seeking the rejected and the needy so that God's mercy could be extended to them. For him, every human need, every unjust conflict became a demanding sacrifice. It was also during these early years in Durham that Dr. Moore met John Merrick, a barber-brickmason and businessman, became lifelong friends. Historical records show that the two of them were associated with everything in Durham pertaining to the African-American community's economic and cultural progress. They were the top wage earners in the community and, therefore, exercised a great deal of influence.

Unlike his friend, Aaron Moore, Mr. Merrick was born a slave near Clinton, North Carolina. At age 12, as a free person of color, he worked at a brickyard in Chapel Hill, North Carolina. He later moved to Raleigh where he worked as a brickmason, and shoe shiner in a barber shop. Eventually, the barber shop owner promoted him to barbering, which allowed him to meet some of Durham's most important Whites on their visits to Raleigh. Durham did not have a barber shop in 1880; therefore, prominent Whites like Washington Duke, Julian Carr and William Blackwell persuaded Merrick, who was in his early twenties, to move to Durham with a fellow barber, John Wright, to open a shop in the

town with a rapidly growing population. Merrick did so and the barber shop, located on Main Street, flourished with a mostly wealthy White clientele. The African-American owned business was considered as a White establishment because African Americans were serving Whites. The barber shop soon became profitable and John Merrick invested his money in property on Fayetteville Street. He eventually bought Wright's share of the barber shop, subsequently making himself the sole owner. Next, he acquired interest in a fraternal order

James Buchanan "Buck" Duke, American Tobacco and Electric Power Industrialist, Courtesy of the Public Domain.

which had the right to sell insurance to its members. Both African Americans and Whites began to make comments about how Merrick had amassed a considerable amount of wealth in a short period of time.

One day, while being shaved, James Buchanan "Buck" Duke, a well-established White American tobacco and electric power industrialist, said to Merrick, "John, you have too much sense to be a mere barber. Why don't you hunt up for a better job?" When John Merrick asked what better job there might be for an African-American person, Duke replied, "Organize an insurance company and make every dinged nigger in the United States pay you twenty-five dollars a year."[2] Merrick, who eventually owned six barber shops and a real estate business in Durham, did not dismiss the idea. Instead, he told "Buck" Duke that he would give it serious consideration.

Exploring the possibility of establishing an insurance company and other African American-owned businesses in Durham was the purpose of the meeting between John Merrick and Aaron Moore on that cool, spring day in 1898. Furthermore, this would be the third meeting that the two men had on this subject. Dr. Moore had called a meeting of the group on two separate occasions. Both meetings, which included Merrick, Moore, Dr. James Shepard, D.T. Watson, P.W. Dawkins, Attorney E.A. Johnson, and William G. Pearson, were held in the basement of White Rock Baptist Church.

After briefly reflecting on their respective experiences, the two men prayed and then began their conversation about the state of African-American life in Durham. Both men expressed surprise at how quickly the African American population in Durham had grown in the last decade. They agreed that the rapid increase was due to three specific factors. First, African Americans had founded two churches in Durham, which attracted a significant number of ex-slaves and free Blacks. In 1866, for example, Margaret Faucette and several other ex-slaves had organized what eventually became known as White Rock Baptist Church. Two years later, in 1868, Edian Markum (also spelled "Markham") arrived in Durham, from Elizabeth City, North Carolina. He

---

[2]Jonathan Daniels, *Tar Heels: A Portrait of North Carolina* (New York, New York: Dodd, Mead and Company, 1947), 127; and William Kennedy Boyd, *The Story of Durham: City of the New South* (Durham, North Carolina: Duke University Press, 1925), 286.

purchased some land, built a cabin for himself and a brush arbor for his ministry. His brush arbor grew into St. Joseph's African Methodist Episcopal Church. These two churches, Moore and Merrick agreed, became the power centers of the African-American community, spiritual home to the movers and shakers, visionaries, and money men who created an African-American enterprise with their wealth.[3] The African-American community's elite, such as Moore and Merrick, resided along the Fayetteville Street ridge, in Durham, looking down upon and in clear view of the neighborhoods and businesses below.

The second reason for the precipitous increase in African Americans in Durham was the development of African-American business groups in the city who built a series of strong companies which commanded respect from African Americans across the country. This phenomenon caused Durham to be called the "Negro Business Center of the South."

The third reason for the rapid growth in the African-American population was the growth of the tobacco and textile industries. People moved to the city to work at Washington Duke and Sons Tobacco Company, Durham Hosiery Mill, and the Durham Cotton Manufacturing Company.

Furthermore, the two men discussed how the increase in the African-American population had also resulted in a higher mortality rate and, therefore, boosted the need for an insurance company to help with funeral costs. While many African Americans, Dr. Moore and Mr. Merrick reasoned, thought of the grave as having its victory, the two men believed that death itself brought a devastating theme—thereby echoing Paul the Apostle's words. The heavy grief coupled with the enormous economic burdens were unmanageable for far too many members of their race. The men talked about how grieving families collected money from neighbors during wakes and funerals to offset the

---

[3]Jim Wise, *Durham: A Bull City Story* (Charleston, South Carolina: Arcadia Publishing, Inc., 2002), 73.

funeral expenses. Moreover, there were only a few insurance companies and, even if African Americans tried to get a policy, they could not afford the costs. Therefore, both men agreed that it was time for them to start an insurance company for African Americans. An idea that "Buck" Duke shared with John Merrick some years ago was now becoming a reality. Both men agreed to hold another meeting with other interested men at White Rock Baptist Church to finalize a plan.

Moore and Merrick concluded their meeting and then joined their wives in the dining room. The couples had a delicious late lunch while enjoying more "small talk." After lunch, the Moores and Merricks exchanged good-byes as the Merricks departed for home.

Establishing a Drug Company for African Americans

When Dr. Moore and John Merrick first met to discuss opening an insurance company, they had already engaged in other joint ventures. They believed that such Black-owned businesses would enable their community to develop its own skilled educated class and provide jobs for them.[4] The first business enterprise undertaken by Dr. Aaron Moore and some of his colleagues was the establishment of the Durham Drug Company in 1895. Dr. Moore was the chief organizer; however, others who assisted him in establishing the city's first drugstore for African Americans were William G. Pearson, J.A. Dodson, Richard B. Fitzgerald and James E. Shepard. Dodson and Shepard were pharmacists at the time.[5] These men used their personal finances as well as funds donated by the Duke and Carr families to finance the company.

---

[4]*Biographical Sketches of E.R. Merrick and Aaron McDuffie Moore* (circa 1967 and undated). North Carolina Mutual Life Insurance Company Archives, ca. 1885-2008 and undated, Box 31, David M. Rubenstein Rare Book and Manuscript Library, Duke University, Durham, N.C.; Louis D. Mitchell, "Aaron McDuffie Moore: He Led His Sheep," *The Crisis* (August 1980): 248-256.

[5]Walter Weare, *African American Business in the New South: A Social History of the North Carolina Mutual Life Insurance Company* (Durham, North Carolina: Duke University Press, 1993), 23.

Once established, the pharmacy gave young African-American pharmacists an opportunity to practice and serve Durham's Black community with dignity and excellence. While the pharmacy never made much of a profit, earning profits was not Dr. Moore's chief goal. Instead, his priority was to provide affordable drugs to the African-American community. He believed that the "Black Business Movement," led by him and several other leaders in the African-American community, was a means to achieve racial self-fulfillment. Moreover, this first venture helped him to establish a strong relationship with John Merrick, with whom he would later establish more African American-owned businesses.

Organizing Durham's First African-American Insurance Company

Seven months after that Sunday afternoon meeting between Dr. Moore and John Merrick, the two men, along with co-organizers D.T. Watson, Dr. James E. Shepard, P.W. Dawkins, Attorney E.A. Johnson and William Pearson as well as incorporators T.O. Fuller and NC. Bruce, held an organizational meeting for an insurance company in the basement of White Rock Baptist Church.[6] They decided that buyers of insurance policies would become part owners of the company and, as such, partly responsible for its success. Further, they felt that the company was greatly needed, since White insurance companies refused to serve African-American customers. The men also discussed how insurance was a necessity. Dr. Moore, in particular, provided examples of well-to-do blacks who, without insurance, lost everything once the major wage earner died. The last action taken by the group that day was the selection of officers. The men agreed that the official staff, appointed for an initial two-year term, would be John Merrick as president; T.O. Fuller, vice-president; D.T. Watson, secretary and general manager; Dr. Aaron

---

[6]The meeting was held on October 20, 1898. North Carolina Life Insurance Company Archives, Records and History Center, James E. Shepard Library, North Carolina Central University, Durham, North Carolina, Box DIG 1, c. 1. Not all available sources agree that the organization meeting for North Carolina Mutual Life Insurance Company occurred in the basement of White Rock Baptist Church.

McDuffie Moore, treasurer and medical director; and E.A. Johnson, attorney.[7] They also agreed that each of them would make an initial investment of $50 and continue to financially support the company until it began to yield a profit.

The company struggled the first year. But, John Merrick and Aaron Moore were not surprised. They both knew that African Americans had short life expectancies, low income and poor health during the late 1880s and early 1900s. Moreover, they realized that it was risky to start a life insurance company for African Americans. Their determination to help their community, however, prompted them to join forces with African American investors like Dr. James E. Shepard, William G. Pearson and Attorney E.A. Johnson to form North Carolina Mutual and Provident Association—the community's first African American insurance company.

Both men also wanted to be more successful than they had been previously with a similar investment. Moore, Merrick and a few other influential African-American businessmen in Durham had purchased the Royal Knights of King David, a semi-religious fraternal and beneficial society for health and life insurance.[8] Although they were not successful, during that transaction, Moore and Merrick learned how insurance worked and how to relate the insurance business to African Americans. They had also witnessed the success and subsequent demise of True Reformers, the first mutual aid and life insurance company in America for African Americans. In their heyday, True Reformers has 100,000 members in 18 states. By 1910, however, the company collapsed.[9] Unfortunately, African Americans could not afford the insurance, which greatly contributed to its downfall. Moore and Merrick knew that in order for them to be successful in providing insurance for Blacks, they needed to be able to sell affordable

---

[7]Ibid.

[8]Jennifer Bihm, "Business in African American History: North Carolina Mutual Life Insurance," *Los Angeles Sentinel* (February 6, 2014), 2.

[9]William Trent, Jr., "Development of Negro Life Insurance Enterprises," (Master's Thesis, University of Pennsylvania, 1932), 21.

policies to their people.

Therefore, having prior experience with insurance, Moore and Merrick were not surprised when the other organizers and incorporators failed to make the initial investment of $50 and subsequently resigned from the group. Yet, they did not quit. Instead, the two men felt it was time for a new direction and a new spark. In other words, a new impetus was decidedly needed. That spark came in the form of Charles C. Spaulding, a nephew of Dr. Aaron McDuffie Moore, from Columbus County, North Carolina. Dr. Moore had sent for Charles Spaulding in order to help him complete his education and further his career. Spaulding finished his high school training in Durham, worked in a White hotel as a busboy, started a grocery store and, finally, jumped at the chance to join Dr. Moore and John Merrick in the insurance business as general manager, bookkeeper and caretaker. Committed to uplifting his race, Dr. Moore was constantly sending to what he referred to as "the country" (meaning Columbus County) to find talent[10] and to help change their lives.

The insurance company was officially organized in 1898 and its founders experienced challenges trying to locate appropriate office space and furniture. A year later, Merrick, Moore and Spaulding decided to use half of Dr. Moore's medical office. Dan White, carpenter and relative of Dr. Moore, built six chairs and table for the office for four dollars. This was the first furniture of the company.

North Carolina Mutual and Provident Association's First Home Office, 1899, White Rock Baptist Church Archives, Durham, N.C.

The charter for North Carolina Mutual and Provident Association was ratified in 1899. Immediately following the ratification of the document, Charles Spaulding made his first sale

---

[10]Louis Mitchell, "Aaron McDuffie Moore: He Led His Sheep," *Crisis Magazine* (August-September 1980), 252.

of a forty-dollar policy and soon after the sale the owner died. According to Asa Spaulding, Charles Spaulding only had "twenty-nine cents that he could contribute to the claim." Therefore, Moore and Merrick had to "make up the difference. Spaulding took the forty dollars, went to the beneficiary, paid the claim, and got a receipt. They [were] determined that they were not going to break the faith with the insured."[11] They knew that the future of the company depended on what happened then. And Moore and Merrick were correct. African Americans began to regard the company as reliable and reputable. Asa Spaulding further added, "The receipt was the thing that turned the tide. If any question arose as to whether or not North Carolina Mutual would be able to pay off, he [Charles Spaulding] would show them that receipt."[12] While progress was slow for North Carolina Mutual and Provident Association, the company stayed the course and eventually became the largest African American-owned insurance business in the United States. In 2016, it was a multimillion dollar firm that serviced millions.

By the time nationally-known race leader, Booker T. Washington, visited Durham, in 1910, North Carolina Mutual and Provident Association had experienced substantial growth. Washington toured the cities and towns of North Carolina, paying tribute to the industrial progress of his race. He spoke to a crowd of eight thousand in Greensboro; elsewhere, churches and halls strained to hold his audiences. Nearly everywhere tobacco warehouses were crowded with African Americans and Whites who competed to hear this popular figure. And at Livingstone College in Salisbury, North Carolina, he shared the rostrum with the vice president of the United States, James Schoolcraft Sherman. Yet, those who hosted Washington, kept telling him, "Wait until you get to Durham, Dr. Washington. Wait until you get to Durham."[13]

---

[11]Ibid., 253.

[12]Ibid.

[13]Undated typescript report of the North Carolina tour, in the Booker T. Washington Papers, Manuscript Division, Library of Congress; Booker T. Washington, "Durham, North

The attraction in Durham that the hosts wanted Washington to see was North Carolina Mutual, which seemed to support his self-help philosophy. A little over a decade later, the insurance company would be able to boast of being the "World's Largest Negro Life Insurance Company," and it would lay claim to having spawned a multitude of lesser African American-owned businesses, including a bank and a cotton mill. Durham's economy so impressed Washington that he ordered Tuskegee Institute's researcher Monroe Work to study the Durham business community. Washington published the findings in an article for a popular White periodical, which praised Durham as "The City of Negro Enterprise."[14]

In the following years, Durham and North Carolina Mutual garnered fame from all sides. In 1912, nationally-renowned Dr. W.E.B. DuBois visited Durham and, like Washington, met with Dr. Moore, John Merrick, Dr. Shepard and Charles Spaulding; also like Washington, he left the city singing its praises.[15] It is amazing how North Carolina Mutual, founded by four White Rock members and a St. Joseph's member about four decades after slavery, formed the hub of a financial empire in the city that the African-American press called the "Capital of the Black Middle Class," "The Magic City," and "The Black Wall Street of America." Clearly this was the work of God. These devout Christians knew the power of prayer and faith in the Lord. And they prayed a lot. They allowed the following words from the Book of James to guide their racial uplift work: "Do not merely listen to the word . . . Do what it says."[16]

Additionally, *Atlanta Independent,* the Black-owned newspaper of Atlanta, which was Black Durham's main competitor at the time, conceded that "Atlanta yielded only to

---

Carolina: A City of Negro Enterprise," *Independent* LXX (March 30, 1911), 642-650.

[14]Washington, "Durham: A City of Negro Enterprise," 642-650; Charles C. Spaulding to Booker T. Washington, November 18, 1910, Booker T. Washington Papers.

[15]W.E.B. DuBois, "The Upholding of Black Durham," *World's Work,* XXIII (January 1912, 334-338.

[16]James 1:22, *Holy Bible,* New International Version.

Durham in economic and industrial progress." The editor further wrote, "The Negroes of Durham are an example for the race . . . There is more grace, grit, and greenback among the Negroes in Durham and more harmony between the races than in any city in America."[17] And in Richmond, Virginia, another city that was considered as a pioneer in Black life insurance, an African-American weekly newspaper urged its elite readers to visit Durham rather than tour Europe. The writer admonished Virginia's African-American citizens:

Go to Durham. . . you need the inspiration. Go to Durham and see the industrious Negro at his best. Go to Durham and see the cooperative spirit among Negroes at its best. Go to Durham and see Negro business with an aggregate capital of millions. Go to Durham and see twenty-two Negro men whose honesty and business sagacity are making modern history. Among your New Year's resolve, resolve to go to Durham![18]

This was the beginning of the New South in Durham, which had been ushered in by several African-American religious, civic and business leaders. The North Carolina Mutual and Provident Association eventually moved to the second floor of a two-story brick structure on Parrish Street, in Durham. In other parts of the building on the same floor were a clothing store, a shoe store, a barbershop, a drug store, and a newspaper — all owned by African Americans.

North Carolina Mutual and Provident Association (later changed name to North Carolina Mutual Life Insurance Company) forever linked together John Merrick, Dr. Aaron Moore, and Dr. Charles C. Spaulding. These men became known as the "Negro Business Triangle." Some of their contemporaries likened them to David, Saul and Samuel. They worked together so much for racial uplift of the African-American community in Durham that sometimes it was difficult to determine which one

---

[17] *Atlanta Independent,* December 22, 1921.

[18] Clipping, *St. Lake Herald,* January 7, 1928, in John Moses Avery Scrapbook in possession of William Jesse Kennedy, Jr., Kennedy Papers, University Archives, James E. Shepard Library, North Carolina Central University, Durham, North Carolina.

was responsible for a new effort.[19] Reverend Dr. James E. Shepard and William G. Pearson, two other influential African Americans in Durham,[20] often invested in many of the businesses that these men started.

North Carolina Mutual anchored the Black middle-class in Durham. It began with three employees—Aaron Moore, John Merrick and Charles Spaulding—and, within a half century, became the largest African American-owned business in the United States. The success of this institution led to the growth of other middle-class and African-American elite enterprises.

North Carolina Mutual and Provident Association Spawns New Black-Owned Companies

The North Carolina Mutual and Provident Association was established to provide benefits to the uninsured African-American community. However, construction was an integral part of the company's success in early years. According to one scholar writing on the subject, "as early as 1903 [North Carolina Mutual] began an investment program in real estate, largely as an outgrowth of John Merrick's efforts, which by this time had made him the owner of more than sixty houses in Durham." He further adds, "By the end of 1907 [sic] real estate holdings accounted for three-fourths of the Mutual's total assets."[21] The majority of those holdings belonged to Aaron Moore, Richard Fitzgerald, John Merrick, Charles Spaulding, and William Pearson.

Moore, Spaulding and Merrick decided that something needed to be done with the holdings, so they formed the Merrick-Moore-Spaulding Real Estate Company and transferred assets from North Carolina Mutual to the new company.[22] The real

---

[19]Walter Weare, *Black Business in the New South: A Social History of the North Carolina Mutual Life Insurance Company*, 6.

[20]William G. Pearson was considered as the wealthiest African American in Durham during this time.

[21]Walter Weare, *Black Business in the New South*, 49-50.

[22]Walter B. Weare, *Black Business in the New South*, 81.

estate company began platting land in the Hayti/Stokesdale neighborhoods.

The economic environment of the 1920s extended to the African-American community and real estate development and building ventures expanded significantly, with North Carolina Mutual and its subsidiaries taking the lead. After John Merrick died in 1919, the firm Merrick-Moore-Spaulding Real Estate Company operated for a while, but by 1922 it became the Merrick (E.R.)-McDougald-Wilson Company, an enterprise that bought and sold real estate and managed Mutual's rental properties. It eventually sold liability insurance, becoming the Union Insurance and Realty Company. The company was managed by John Merrick's oldest son, Ed, and two younger Mutual executives. With collaboration from Moore and Spaulding, the owners of the Merrick-McDougald-Wilson Company found the Mutual Building and Loan Association in 1921.[23]

According to Moore, the purpose of the Mutual Building and Loan Association was to teach African Americans the importance of owning their own homes. This company financed homes and lots that African-American people wanted to purchase from the Merrick-McDougald-Wilson Company. These two companies helped to increase African-American home ownership and led to additional funding sources in the African-American community.

Meeting the Need for a Black-Owned Bank

In 1908, ten years after forming North Carolina Mutual and Provident Association (later renamed North Carolina Mutual Life Insurance Company), Dr. Aaron Moore, Dr. Charles Spaulding and John Merrick joined several other African-American men, namely Richard Fitzgerald, William G. Pearson, J.C. Scarborough, J.A. Dodson and Stanford Warren, to establish a Black-owned bank. It would be housed on the first floor of the North Carolina Mutual building. The bank's name, Mechanics and Farmers,

---

[23]R. McCants Andrews, *John Merrick: A Biographical Sketch* (Durham, North Carolina: Seeman's Printery, 1920), 52-56; *Durham Morning Herald*, 18 November 1924. Walter B. Weare, *Black Business in the New South*, 81-82, 147-151.

reflected the people it hoped to serve—the blue collar workers. The goal of the founders was to teach members of their race how to save and invest their earnings in an effort to improve their lives.

Richard B. Fitzgerald, the First President of Mechanics and Farmers Bank, Courtesy of the Public Domain.

For this particular venture, it was Richard Fitzgerald who took the lead. He was born free in 1843, in New Castle County, Delaware. His father was a mulatto, manumitted from slavery, and his mother was White. In late 1869, after the Civil War, Fitzgerald relocated to Hillsborough, North Carolina, with his family. He and his brothers set up a brick yard on his family's farm. After a few challenges, the Fitzgerald family began to make a considerable amount of money in the brickyard business. He quickly earned the reputation of making "better bricks than any other man in town."[24] Within the next fifteen years, Fitzgerald became Durham's leading brick maker. By 1884, he had a large brickyard on Chapel Hill Road and orders on hand, primarily from Whites, for two million bricks.[25] Fitzgerald, who was involved in many other business ventures, eventually became one of the wealthiest African Americans in Durham.

As one of the original incorporators of Mechanics and Farmers Bank, Fitzgerald became its first president. He and the other eight men who founded the bank had amassed a considerable amount of wealth and used those funds to help start this much needed bank for African Americans. Once the bank was established, members of their race who had begun to make financial progress, would have a place to deposit their funds, thereby creating a culture of saving. Unfortunately, African-American elites, like the founders of the bank, served on its board of directors as well as boards of several other sister African American-owned businesses. These various institutions with their

---

[24]Louis Harlan, Raymond Smock and Geraldine McTigue, eds., *The Booker T. Washington Papers, Volume II, 1911-1912* (Chicago, Illinois: University of Illinois Press, 1981), 58, 63.

[25]Pauli Murray, *Proud Shoes* (New York, New York: Harper and Brothers, 1956), 78.

"overlapping management structures and boards of directors allowed the elite," like Spaulding, Fitzgerald, Shepard, Moore, and Pearson, "to keep the money within their own circle and to reinvest in themselves."[26] While it is not clear what many of the bank's founders did with their massive earnings from the bank and other institutions that they established between the late 1890s and early 1900s, Drs. Aaron Moore and Charles Spaulding invested some of their funds in White Rock Baptist Church. For example, around the same time that the bank's founders were receiving funds from their investments, like the bank, Moore and Spaulding invested in expansion and renovation efforts at White Rock. In 1911, the church completed a renovation, with a new church façade, a library, public baths, an elevated floor in the main sanctuary, and the installation of a pipe organ. In the basement of the church, a kitchen and classrooms were added. Funds for the renovations and expansion were donated by Drs. Moore and Spaulding. This expansion to the church made it one of the most majestic institutions in Durham that was, by now, located in the center of what had become known as "Black Wall Street."

The original incorporators of the bank sometimes relied on the financial institution to support other business investments that they wanted to make. This ultimately led to more wealth for them, thereby creating a new social class in Durham—the African-American elite. This class distinction began to emerge during the latter tenure of Reverend Dr. Augustus Shepard, which was also reflected in the church's demographics as more of these individuals began to join White Rock. From around 1910 to 1932, just before the arrival of the internationally known Reverend Dr. Miles Mark Fisher as pastor of White Rock, the church was comprised of primarily the Black educated elite and a few members of the African-American middle-class who were Baptists. Most of the Black working-class individuals who had

---

[26]Brochures for the Royal Knights of King David, Peoples Building and Loan Association, and the Fraternal Bank and Trust, William G. Pearson Papers, Rare Book Room, Manuscript, and Special Collections Library, Duke University, Durham, North Carolina; Leslie Brown, *Upbuilding Black Durham*, 139.

been attending White Rock began to change their membership to other churches that had been established in Durham, like New Bethel Baptist Church, St. John's Baptist Church and Mount Vernon Baptist Church. This social divide was also evident in the self-contained Black community known as Hayti. This community of ex-slaves and former free Blacks was the result of the entrepreneurship of African-American leaders like Aaron Moore, Charles Spaulding, John Merrick, James Shepard, William Pearson and Richard Fitzgerald.

Creating Durham's First Hospital for African Americans

These men, along with other African Americans in Durham, established numerous African American-owned businesses during the period in America known as the "nadir."[27] Lynching of African Americans substantially increased and vigilante organizations, like the Ku Klux Klan and the "Red Shirts," terrorized Blacks who attempted to make any progress and tried to vote. In many regions of the country, especially in the South, African Americans lost political power. This was a tragic time in race relations across the country, and North Carolina and Durham were by no means immune from this hysteria.

Throughout the late summer and up until election time, the *Durham Daily Sun* vilified African Americans and Republicans without regard to even the most modest journalistic restraints. Passions became so heated that an African-American man rumored to have been living with a White woman (allegedly the wife of a Republican) was lynched and his body left hanging along the roadside between Durham and Chapel Hill to serve as a

---

[27] According to historian Rayford Logan, the nadir of American race relations was the period in the history of the Southern United states from the end of Reconstruction in 1877 through the early twentieth century, when racism in the country was worse than in any other period after the American Civil war. During this period, African Americans lost many civil rights gains made during Reconstruction. Anti-black violence, lynchings, segregation, legal racial discrimination, and expressions of White supremacy increased. Logan coined the phrase in his 1954 book, *The Negro in American Life and Thought: The Nadir, 1877-1901*. He argued that race relations improved after 1901.

ghastly lesson in White supremacy.[28]

Dr. Moore, John Merrick and other Black leaders in Durham closed ranks, and out of their respDr. Charles Shepardonse emerged a multitude of Black-owned businesses and self-help initiatives, many that began in 1899. Not only did this heightened racial strife give rise to the Durham Committee on the Affairs of Negro People but also mutual aid societies, businesses, clubs and organizations exclusively for African Americans. Specific Black-owned businesses include Long's Florist, Dillard's self-Service Grocery, Dillard's Restaurant, Lanier Barbershop, DeShazor Beauty College, Regal Theater, Chamberlain Studio, Ampix Photography, Garrett-Biltmore Drugstore, The Donut Shop, S & W Tailors, Haberdashery, Scarborough Nursery, William D. Hill Play School, Burthey, Ray, Jones Fisher Funeral Home, Speight's Auto Shop, Elvira's Restaurant, Fayetteville Street Gas Station, Pine Street Taxi, J. L. Page and Sons Grocery, and Holt's Barber Shop. The vast majority of these businesses were owned by members of White Rock Baptist Church, like Margaret Shearin, Charles Stanback, Bernice Ingram, James and Pearl Page, George Logan, Sterling Holt, Nathaniel walker, and Wanda Dooms.[29] While various members of the Black community opened businesses in the Hayti community, Dr. Moore and some of the Black leaders continued to aggressively pursue funding for an all-Black hospital.

In 1899, Dr. Aaron McDuffie Moore wrote a letter to James Buchanan Duke requesting a meeting regarding some important benevolent business. He wrote:

October 16, 1899

Dear Sir:

I pray that you grant me a few minutes of your time in the interest of the suffering sick of our city. If possible, please name the hour.

---

[28]*Durham Daily Sun,* October 29, November 5, 7, 1898.

[29]Deaconess Martha Lester-Harris, Interview Mildred Page, July 20, 2017, Durham, North Carolina.

Very respectfully,

Dr. A. M. Moore[30]

Dr. Moore wanted to discuss with Mr. Duke his dream of building a hospital for African Americans in Durham. But, the only way that he could make it a reality was to secure a large amount of money.

The only semblance of a hospital that the African-American community of Durham had was in Dr. Moore's house. According to his daughter, Lyda Moore, "Papa would perform all kinds of things on the back porch, pull teeth, mend broken parts, bandage people up, treat cuts and just about everything else. He took tumors out of people's bodies, sewed up wounds on Saturday nights. In fact, Papa brought contagious diseases into our house. But," she added, "My father was a kind man and could not see such suffering without doing something about it. He even brought scarlet fever and tuberculosis cases from 'down home' into our home and nursed so many people back to health. Papa was always fighting disease to the day he died."[31] This was Dr. Moore. He was a caring, Christian man. Whatever his patients or African-American people in the community needed, he would provide it without saying a word. But, his medical assistance, in particular, was needed.

Second Lincoln Hospital, 1924, 1301 Fayetteville Street, Durham, N.C., Courtesy of White Rock Baptist Church Archives. Durham. N.C.

Four years earlier, in 1895, Washington Duke and George Watts had built a White hospital and given it to the City of Durham. It would not provide medical care to African Americans regardless of the amount of money that they possessed. When Dr.

---

[30]Louis Mitchell, "Aaron McDuffie Moore: He Led His Sheep," *Crisis Magazine* (August-September 1980), 253.

[31]Ibid.

Moore and other African-American leaders began to petition wealthy Whites for funding to build a Black hospital, George Watts announced his intention of adding a "colored ward" to Duke, the hospital for Whites. Dr. Moore responded that such provisions would result in practical difficulties, that Watt's plan "would not give Negro physicians sufficient opportunity to develop," and that such provisions "would prove inadequate with the growing Negro population." Beginning with a plea to his fellow church members, Moore energized them and the larger African-American community to demand health care facilities. He also urged African Americans in his congregation to mobilize other Blacks to act on their own behalf. It finally worked. Moore later said, "Mr. Watts decided that he would not open the ward for colored and the Dukes gave us promise of help."[32]

The Dukes did eventually help by providing funds to help build a hospital in the city for African Americans. Dr. Aaron Moore, Reverend Dr. James Shepard, Dr. Charles Shepard, Dr. Stanford Warren, Charles Spaulding, John Merrick and other African-American leaders in Durham had wanted their own hospital for a while, which became a reality in 1901 when a frame building was constructed on Proctor Street and Cozart Avenue in the city. It became known as Lincoln Hospital and was financed by Washington Duke in exchange for a plaque to be hung in its lobby which read:

MEMORIAM
LINCOLN 1901 HOSPITAL
With grateful appreciation and loving remembrance of the
Fidelity and faithfulness of the Negro slaves to the
Mothers and Daughters of the Confederacy, during the Civil War,
this institution was founded by one of the Fathers and Sons
B.N. Duke J.B. Duke W. Duke
Not one act of disloyalty was recorded against them.
JOHN MERRICK, President
A.M. Moore, Founder and Superintendent

---

[32]Ibid., 255.

The North Carolina General Assembly passed and ratified an act incorporating the trustees of Lincoln Memorial Hospital on February 22, 1901. Duke and his sons gave $8,550. When the hospital burned down in 1922, the Dukes gave $75,000 towards the cost for rebuilding it and the African American community raised $25,000 while the City of Durham donated $50,000. This was a deal that Dr. Moore negotiated with city officials and Washington Duke while on his death bed. Despite his illness, Dr. Moore fundraised and gave generously just as he had given for the construction of the first building in 1901.[33] With the needed funds, the hospital's Black founders—Aaron Moore, Stanford Warren, John Merrick and Dr. Charles Shepard—had Lincoln Memorial Hospital rebuilt in 1924 on Fayetteville Street in Durham.

Lincoln was the fourth hospital for African Americans in North Carolina. It operated as a nonprofit. Many of its first doctors came from the Leonard Medical School at Shaw University in Raleigh, the first four-year medical school for Blacks in the United States. A second ward was added in 1907, and Lincoln Hospital quickly became one of the leading African-American hospitals in North or South Carolina. Once Lincoln Memorial Hospital was fully operational, much of its funding came from African-American churches, like White Rock and St. Joseph's, and more well-to-do African Americans such as Drs. Aaron Moore, Richard Fitzgerald, James Shepard, Charles Shepard, Stanford Warren, John Merrick and William G. Pearson.[34]

Lincoln Memorial Hospital began training nurses as early as 1903. The graduates from the program provided "medical support for Lincoln's staff and public health nurses for the Black community." The medical facility filled a major need in the African-American community because "in return for their training, students filled several roles for the hospital that were

---

[33]Walter B. Weare, *Black Business in the New South,* 81.
[34]Ibid.

necessary to the daily operation."[35] Its program was rigorous, and there was a deep sense of pride for those who were accepted.

Building a African American-Owned Knitting Mill

Durham's African-American leaders continued to build Black-owned establishments wherever they felt that there was a need. A little over three decades out of slavery and living in Jim Crow America, African Americans in Durham continued to believe that if Whites denied them certain economic opportunities, they would create their own.

At the turn of the twentieth century, many African Americans in Durham continued to work in either the fields or as domestic workers for Whites. Many of them wanted to work in the local mills because they could earn more money. The opportunity was made available to African Americans in 1904 when Julian Carr, Jr., a benevolent humanitarian, decided to employ Blacks as machine operators at his factory, the Durham Hosiery Mill No. 2. This was the first time in the history of the country that African Americans were hired to operate machines in a textile mill. Although Young Carr carefully selected African Americans who would work in his factory, he faced much opposition from other Whites for hiring Blacks. They did not care that Carr hand-selected Blacks that he considered as the "more cultured Negroes" in the community. They were still African Americans.

There were various reasons that Whites provided for not supporting African American employment in the hosiery mill. According to Julian Carr, Jr.: "[We were] told that the rhythm of the machines would put the darkies to sleep and thus we could get no work out of them; the white workers said that we were taking bread out of their mouths (although there were not enough whites to go around) and variously threatened to blow up or burn

---

[35]Darlene Clark Hine, *African American Women in White: Racial Conflict and Cooperation in the Nursing Profession, 1890-1950* (Bloomington, Indiana: Indiana University Press, 1989), 12; Lincoln Hospital, *Thirty-eighth Annual Report*; Leslie Brown, *Upbuilding Black Durham*, 159

down the factory. We selected a white man as machine fixer and immediately the girls of the town refused to speak to him. But we went ahead to see the thing through."[36] Because of how Whites felt about hiring Blacks in textile mills, they were never offered the opportunity during this time to work at any mills other than Durham Hosiery Mill No. 2.

Dr. Aaron Moore, Dr. Charles Spaulding and John Merrick did not agree with how Whites felt about African Americans working in mills. Both Moore and Spaulding, active members of White Rock Baptist Church, had many members of their congregation who would have loved to work in Carr's hosiery mill. While a significant number of the church's members had been fortunate enough to be selected to work in Durham Hosiery Mill No. 2, there were a higher number of its members who were not given an opportunity. Yet, Moore and the other two men knew that their church members had the skills to perform well if given the opportunity. Furthermore, Spaulding and Moore reasoned, such an opportunity would help members of their growing population move from working-class to middle-class status. Reverend Dr. Augustus Shepard even encouraged members like Spaulding and Moore, who had already accomplished a great deal, to continue to engage in racial uplift work. Furthermore, all three men—Moore, Spaulding and Merrick—believed that helping members of their race was their purpose in life and, consequently, like Apostle Paul, they could not,[37] allow circumstances to dictate their decisions. For that reason, after witnessing how successful Julian Carr, Jr. had been in hiring African Americans, they became determined to show that similar success could be achieved not only with Black mill workers, but also African American ownership of mills. Therefore, the three men began to plan for such a factory.

---

[36]James G. Leyburn, *The Way We Lived: Durham, 1900-1920* (Elliston, Virginia: Northcross House Publishers, 1989), 77.

[37]2 Corinthians 4:16, NIV, *Bible*.

Eight years later, in 1911, Moore, Spaulding and Merrick established the Durham Knitting Mill (also called the Durham Textile Mill) at the southwest corner of South Elm and Fayetteville streets, in what would become the Hayti community. The mill operated for five years before closing in 1916. World War I effected many communities both in the United States and abroad. In Durham, for example, textile production slowed down during the war, which hurt the Black-owned Durham Knitting Mill.

Interior of African American-Owned Durham Knitting Mill, Durham, N.C., 1911, Courtesy of the Public Domain.

Despite its short existence, Durham Knitting Mill provided employment opportunities for many African Americans in Durham. It provided an opportunity for Drs. Spaulding and Moore, in particular, not only to make paid work available for fellow church members but also to invite non-members who worked at the mill to White Rock. During Reverend Shepard's tenure, the church began to experience an increase in membership. Some of the new members joined after meeting the owners and subsequently being invited to worship.

The Durham Knitting Mill was the first and only hosiery mill owned and operated by African Americans. People came from all around the country to tour the facility. Race leader Booker T. Washington was one such person to visit the Durham mill when he visited Durham in 1911 for another event. He stated:

I was ready to go home, but they wanted to show me one more successful Negro plant. This was the plant known as the Durham Textile Mill, the only hosiery mill in the world entirely owned and operated by Negroes. Regularly incorporated, they operate eighteen knitting machines of the latest pattern, working regularly twelve women and two men and turning out seventy-five dozen pairs of hose each day. The goods so far are standing the test in the market, being equal in every way to other hose of the same price. They are sold mainly by white salesman, who travel mostly in North Carolina, New York, Indiana, Georgia, South Carolina, and Alabama . . .[38]

Two years later, another race leader, Dr. W.E.B. DuBois, visited the mill. He also described what he witnessed. According to DuBois:

. . . we went to the hosiery mill and the planning mill. The hosiery mill was to me of singular interest. Three years ago I met the manager, C.C. Amey. He was then teaching school, but he had much unsatisfied mechanical genius. The white hosiery mills in Durham were succeeding and one of them employed colored hands. Amey asked for permission here to learn to manage the intricate machines, but was refused. Finally, however, the manufacturers of the machines told him that they would teach him if he came to Philadelphia. He went and learned. A company was formed and thirteen knitting and ribbing machines at 70 dollars a piece were installed, with a capacity of sixty dozen men's socks a day. At present the sales are rapid and satisfactory, and already machines are ordered to double the present output; a dyeing department and factory building are planned for the near future.[39]

The Durham Knitting Mill was one of the most important ventures undertaken by Spaulding, Moore and Merrick. It was historically significant because it showed, contrary to White southern myth, that Backs could profitably be employed as textile workers.

Some of the buildings of "African American Wall Street" at turn of the 20th Century, Courtesy of the Public Domain.

Hayti, "Black Wall Street," and White Rock Baptist Church: An Interconnection

In the decades immediately following the Civil War, the major Black-owned institutions in Durham, such as North Carolina Mutual and Provident

[38]Henry Louis Gates and Evelyn Brooks Higginbotham, *African American Lives* (New York: Oxford University Press, 2004), 587.

[39]Ibid.

Association, Lincoln Hospital, Durham Knitting Mill, Mechanics and Farmers Bank and White Rock Baptist Church, served as anchors for a distinct Southern Black community that was disproportionately Baptist and Christian. Most of the founders of the major institutions came out of White Rock Baptist Church. Their prayers (and there were many), hard work and faith helped them to create a community that expressed racial pride through the elites' embrace of capitalism. This approach was unique to Durham. For example, while traveling through Durham in 1913, race leader Booker T. Washington wrote: "Of all the Southern cities I have visited I found here the sanest attitude of the white people toward the African American. . . I never saw in a city of this size so many prosperous carpenters, brickmasons, blacksmiths, wheelwrights, cotton mill operatives, and tobacco workers among the Negroes."[40] Dr. W.E.B. DuBois, militant advocate of radical change in race relations, wrote about Durham during this same time: "There is in this small city a group of five thousand or more colored people, whose social and economic development is perhaps more striking than that of any similar group in the nation."[41]

White Rock Baptist Church, Saint Joseph's African Methodist Episcopal Church, Mechanics and Farmers Bank, North Carolina Mutual and Provident Association and Lincoln Hospital were all located in the southern and southeastern part of Durham in a community that eventually became known as Hayti.[42] The center

---

[40]*Independent*, LXXX, 646; James G. Leyburn, *The Way We Lived: Durham, 1900-1920*, 62.

[41]W. E. B. DuBois, "The Upholding of Black Durham," *World's Work*, xxiii, 334; Leyburn, *The Way We Lived: Durham, 1900-1920*, 62.

[42]No definitive research has yet revealed why the African American community in Durham was given the name of the West Indian republic, with the American spelling and mispronunciation current at the time. Some Durhamites claim that Dr. Aaron Moore named the community Hayti after traveling to Haiti several times and became impressed with a very advanced city being governed by African Americans. If Dr. Moore, or any African Americans for that matter, chose the name, in pride at the first African American republic in the Western Hemisphere and in honor of the achievement of Toussaint L'Ouverture in freeing Haiti from French rule in 1804, they would almost certainly have used the correct spelling, Haiti. For other theorists, it seems much more likely that Whites, aware of the incompetent misrule of the island republic from 1850 onward, used the name, with the current American misspelling, to designate an "island" of African Americans in

of the community was Fayetteville Street. Also, in Hayti were stores, clubs, lodges, Whitted School, Stanford L. Warren Library and the National Religious Training School (eventually became known as North Carolina Central University) — all of the establishments that could be found in White communities at the time. The community's business and civic leaders like Dr. Aaron Moore, Dr. Charles Spaulding, Dr. James E. Shepard, William Pearson, John Merrick and Richard Fitzgerald lived on Fayetteville Street in huge Victorian houses, with spacious porches and situated on large lawns.[43] They were the well-to-do African Americans who, less than a generation out of slavery, lived in a style exactly like that of well-to-do Whites.

Durham Knitting Mill, which employed blue collar or working-class African Americans, was located at a border of the African American community of Hayti known as Smoky Hollow, which had a poor reputation in 1900 because it contained saloons "patronized by many of the worst elements of African Americans." Saturday night brawls were common, and *The Herald Sun* referred to Smoky Hollow as "that dark hole of iniquity and infamy."[44] The mill's owners, on the other hand, lived in in the neighborhoods along Fayetteville Street.

Although African Americans resided in Hayti and it was the center of their business life, one short street in the center of Durham's business district was dominated by Black businesses. It was Parrish Street, which is where Aaron Moore, Charles Spaulding and John Merrick decided to build a brick building to house the offices of their rapidly expanding insurance company and Mechanics and Farmers Bank. Soon after, African American stores, shops, and cafes began to line the north side of Parrish Street.[45] The brick two-story building, also known as the Merrick building, added four more stories, and this portion of Parrish Street came later to be called "the Black Wall Street of America."

Durham.

[43]James G. Leyburn, *The Way We Lived*, 62.

[44]Ibid., 77.

[45]White stores were on the south side of the street.

All the Black-owned stores on this block were equal in appearance to those operated by Whites on the opposite side of Parrish Street.[46]

Furthermore, of all of the African American leaders in Durham during this time, three of them — Dr. Aaron Moore, Dr. Charles Spaulding and John Merrick — set the standard for other African Americans. They made it evident, by their economic success, that African Americans could do just as well as Whites; by their exemplary personal lives they encouraged morality; by their tact and restraint in the touchy and sensitive area of race relations, they were powerful influences for social peace; by their personal achievements they revealed to ambitious young African Americans that, despite all the limitations imposed by law, custom and prejudice, doors to success were open. These three leaders came to Durham as young men: John Merrick, an ex-slave from Clinton, North Carolina, in 1880; Dr. Aaron Moore, the son of a family of free land-owning African Americans in Columbus County, North Carolina, arrived in 1888; and Dr. Charles Spaulding, the nephew of Dr. Moore, in 1895. These men believed that they were successful because of their obedience to God. They always placed their churches first as well as their ministry work. They never started a ministry or business meeting, many which were held in the basement of White Rock, without first praying. They knew the power of prayer. They also believed that God had empowered them to fulfill His purpose through them on earth. Therefore, they always tirelessly worked in the church as deacons, Sunday School superintendents, trustees, and ministry leaders while they tirelessly worked in the community. They glorified God by doing what He told them to do instead of what they may have wanted to do. As they built Durham's African American community after the Civil War and emancipation, these men always first looked to God for guidance. In return, these men

---

[46]It seemed appropriate at the time that, since the Duke family was largely instrumental in stimulating Aaron Moore, John Merrick, Charles Spaulding, William Pearson and their colleagues, to begin their profitable business careers, the impressive skyscraper built in 1966 to house the insurance company should be erected on the site where Benjamin Duke's mansion, Four Acres, had stood.; James Leyburn, *The Way We Lived*, 66.

were blessed.

After the Civil War, practically all of the African Americans in Durham belonged to either Baptist or Methodist churches. Most of Durham's Black leaders at the time were members of the city's oldest and largest African-American church — White Rock Baptist

Some of the Founders of Mechanics and Farmers Bank and "African American Wall Street" were Richard Fitzgerald, William G. Pearson, John Merrick, Dr. Aaron Moore, Dr. Stanford L. Warren, J.A. Dodson, and Charles Spaulding, Courtesy of the Public Domain.

Church. As was customary all over the South during this time, Blacks in Durham had their own churches, with their own ministers serving in their denominations. This certainly was true for White Rock. With its stately architectural style, White Rock was the oldest and most influential church in Hayti. The caliber of the ministers in Hayti churches during the first two decades of the century was high by any standard. Several Black ministers proved their mental acuity and realism in leadership. In the early days of the First World War, for example, White leaders heard that a Baptist minister in Hayti was giving an astute series of lectures on the "complex European political situation, the policies of the Triple Entente and the Triple Alliance, and the relation of American statecraft to European realities."[47] The person that many African Americans and Whites came to see that day was Dr. Edward M. Brawley, pastor of White Rock Baptist Church and noted former college president and prolific author of religious books and tracts.

However, Dr. Brawley was not the only African American minister that Whites held in awe. The Reverend Dr. James Shepard, a member of White Rock who also often delivered

---

[47]Ibid., 76.

sermons when his father died, was regarded by Whites as a remarkable religious leader and educator in the African American community. He was known nationally and internationally as a Christian man who believed in Jesus Christ and, also, started a college to train aspiring African American ministers who he believed had been known to be poorly trained and lacked insight into affairs of wide scope. He was determined to remedy this situation. And he did.

Conclusion

During this era, White Rock flourished because of the work of its members both in the church and in the community. The church and its religious teachings provided a strong foundation for people like the Moores, Spauldings, Evans, and countless others. They always put God and His Kingdom first. They were clear about their purpose in life. Therefore, when challenging circumstances arose, and there were many, they did not allow them to dictate their decisions and subsequent actions.

God revealed His vision for the African-American community to these men and women and, being obedient, they acted on it. In the end, not only were these leaders blessed but so was White Rock Baptist Church, its members and people in the Black community. They had emerged from slavery, many homeless and in virtual poverty with no transferrable skills for the growing industrial economy. Less than a generation later, these same men and women lived in a self-contained all-African American community where they could receive an education at a grade school, high school and Black-owned college, go to an African American-owned hospital when they became ill, work in an African American-owned business, place their hard earned money in an African American-owned bank, purchase a home from an African American-owned real estate company and have it financed by an African American-owned finance company or bank, buy a suit at an African American-owned haberdashery, wear hosiery and socks from an African American-owned mill, have an African American-owned funeral home to bury them, and have an African American-owned insurance company to sell them a policy to help them bury members of their family. The work that Black leaders performed at this time created a unique African-American community in the South—one that attracted presidents, national race leaders and international tourists who were left in awe at what they observed. This all-Black community, formed by Christian men, was an excellent example of what God can do if one only believes and is obedient.

Chapter Nine

A Different Approach to Racial Uplift:
Political Engagement Among White Rock Baptist Church Members

"But avoid foolish questions, . . . and contentions, and strivings about the law; for they are unprofitable and vain." – Titus 3:9 (KJV)

A s Mrs. Elna Bridgeforth Spaulding read the letter of appreciation that she had recently received from the Child Advocacy Commission (CAC) of Durham, North Carolina, she could not help but think about how much progress her race had made since the turn of the twentieth century. At the tender age of 65, she was elected to the Durham County Board of Commissioners. It was 1974 and Durham was finally electing its first Black and first woman to the powerful political entity. When she first arrived in Durham, Blacks, for the most part, were just beginning to become involved in local politics.

Elna Bridgeforth Spaulding, Courtesy of White Rock Baptist Church Archives, Durham, N.C.

Mrs. Spaulding had been in Durham for forty-four years. After graduating from Talledega College, in Talledega, Alabama, she came to the city to teach in the Durham City Schools. After teaching for one year, however, Elna Spaulding accepted a position as chair of the Music Department at Winston Salem Teachers College. Three years after her relocation to Durham, Mrs. Spaulding (nee Bridgeforth) met and married Asa T. Spaulding. At that time, she became actively involved in various religious, civic, educational and political activities.[1]

Of particular interest to Mrs. Spaulding were issues or challenges that women confronted almost on a daily basis ranging from domestic violence to child care. As a member of the Durham County Board of Commissioners, Elna Spaulding gained the reputation of being an advocate for causes effecting women and children. Many people in Durham knew her as founder and first president of Women in Action for the Prevention of Violence and Its Causes.

So, when Mrs. Spaulding read the letter from Norma Van Vleet, President, Child Advocacy Commission of Durham, she felt that it was a thoughtful gesture. Clearly Van Vleet was appreciative of what Mrs. Spaulding had done for the organization. She wrote, "On behalf of the Child Advocacy Commission of Durham I would like to express my personal appreciation to you for the recent approval of our budget (FY 1978-1979). We are keenly aware of the responsibility placed on our elected officials to maintain adequate services for the community while at the same time avoiding excessive taxation. As in the past you may be assured that we will maintain responsible services to Durham in our efforts to improve the lives of our children and youth. If at any time we can be of assistance to you [sic] please feel free to call our office and you may be assured of our complete cooperation."[2] After reading the letter,

---

[1]Andre Vann, *African Americans of Durham County* (Charleston, South Carolina: Arcadia Publishing, Inc., 2017), 68.

[2]Letter from Norma Van Vleet, President, Child Advocacy Commission of Durham, to Elna B. Spaulding, Durham Board County Commission, July 5, 1978. Asa and Elna

Elna Spaulding personally contacted Mrs. Van Vleet to acknowledge receipt of her letter.

Spaulding was also pleasantly surprised when she read another letter that same day. It pertained to funding regarding Lincoln Community Health Center. At the June 1978 Durham County Board of Commissioners' meeting, an official of Lincoln Community Hospital had asked the commissioners for financial support because the medical facility did not receive as much as it had requested from the United States Department of Health, Education, and Welfare (USDHEW). The Commissioners denied the request, which should have not been a surprise. After all, Elna Spaulding was the only Black person on the Durham County Board of Commissioners and many White Commissioners did not support a hospital for Blacks. Although Blacks could not seek medical attention from doctors at Duke Medical Center, many Whites saw Lincoln Community Hospital as a threat.

While the Durham County Commissioners denied Lincoln Hospital's request, Elna Spaulding, unlike her colleagues on the Commission, refused to consider it as an unfortunate loss for Blacks and, therefore, they should just simply move on to the next item on the agenda. She decided, instead, to request assistance from a North Carolina politician who had connections with the appropriate United States Department of Health, Education and Welfare officials. She thought such a politician might be able to persuade his contact with the federal department to reverse the agency's earlier decision. Therefore, on June 15, 1978, she contacted North Carolina's United States Senator Jesse Helms to ask for his help. She also asked other influential Blacks in Durham to make the same request. Upon receiving Mrs. Spaulding's request, Senator Helms sent a letter to Dr. George Reich, Regional Health Administrator, Department of Health, Education and Welfare, located in Atlanta, Georgia, in which he made a special plea for the funding. Senator Helms wrote,

I am writing on behalf of the Lincoln Community Health Center of

---

Spaulding Papers, Special Collections, Duke University, Durham, North Carolina.

Durham, North Carolina [sic] which is in dire need of additional assistance from your agency. The Center has requested $1,994,450 for Fiscal Year 1979, beginning on July 1, 1978, and is slated to receive only $1,557,200 for that period. Their earlier request was the amount necessary to maintain the present level of health services there. For many Durham citizens, the Lincoln Community Health Center is the first opportunity to participate in a system which offers not only standard medical treatment, but also a great degree of preventive and health maintenance care. I am really concerned with cost containment and fiscal responsibility, especially in the health care field; and I feel the additional funds should be provided to the Center for ambulatory care, which is less serious and expensive than regular hospitalization at the later stage of an illness. The Center enjoys a great deal of support from a wide cross section of the Durham community, and I respectfully request your office to do whatever necessary to continue the present level of HEW appropriation for them. The City of Durham and surrounding Durham County have a great need for improved health care, especially in progress which serve the lower income population of the area, as does the Lincoln Community Health Center. I am grateful for your cooperation, and am looking forward to your response.[3]

The second letter that Mrs. Spaulding opened that day was from Senator Helms. She nervously opened the envelope while secretly praying that the senator had honored her request. After opening the envelope and retrieving the letter, Mrs. Spaulding slowly read every word: "I received many letters from a great cross section of people in support of the Lincoln Community Health Center and I was glad to add my support. I know the Center is a great asset to Durham and I commend you for what you are doing on behalf of the community. I am also pleased to inform you that the Center has been approved by the U.S. Department of Health, Education and Welfare for the additional $397,250 requested. If I can assist you in any way, please let me know. Honorable Jesse Helms, U.S. Senator, North Carolina."[4]

---

[3]Letter from Jesse Helms, United States Senator, to Dr. George Reich, Regional Health Administrator, Department of Health, Education and Welfare, July 19, 1978.

[4]Letter from Honorable Jesse Helms, United States Senator, to Elna Spaulding, Member, Durham County Board of Commissioners, August 8, 1978. Asa and Elna Spaulding Papers, Special Collections, Duke University, Durham, North Carolina.

Mrs. Spaulding began praising God and crying tears of joy. She knew without a doubt that God was responsible for this good news, especially coming from Senator Helms. His support again reminded her of how much some things had changed for members of her race despite moments of digression. As a local Black female politician, she had received such a kind and supportive letter from Senator Jesse Helms, once known as America's "last prominent unabashed white racist politician."[5]

Gaining Senator Helms' approval also reminded Mrs. Spaulding of God's power and authority. She perhaps thought about the fact that God was the supreme ruler. She also may have thought about how so much had changed since she first arrived in Durham. Although she was the first Black woman to be elected to the Durham County Commissioners, Black men had been involved in local politics for at least two decades; however, they had not been involved as long as members of their race in other parts of the State and the South. One could say that Durham's Blacks were latecomers to political participation. They essentially shied away from holding political office and believing that a typical politician was the best solution for helping ex-slaves after the Civil War. There is a noticeable shift in the late 1920s and early 1930s as more Blacks, like Elna Spaulding, began to view politics as an effective way to address racial equality. A quick overview bears out this observation.

Black North Carolina's Political Leadership Emerges after Emancipation without Orange County and the Durham Township on Board

During slavery, for the most part, African Americans, whether free or enslaved, did not have political rights. In other words, they did not participate in the political process as voters and office holders. In all states, except Wisconsin, the franchise and office holding were reserved exclusively for Whites.

In fall of 1865, immediately following the end of the Civil War and just before the 13th Amendment was ratified by the needed

---

[5]David S. Broder, "Jesse Helms, White Racist," *Washington Post*, July 7, 2008, p. 1.

number of states, 117 ex-slave and free Black delegates, representing approximately half of the counties of North Carolina, decided to hold a convention in the capital city of Raleigh to demand certain rights as free persons. Some of these so-called delegates were self-educated and most had skilled occupations such as carpenter, teacher, minister, and barber. These individuals had been "elected" by Black North Carolinians to represent their interests. These leaders, such as A.H. Galloway of Fayetteville, one of the organizers, and James Harris of Raleigh,[6] pressed for Black rights and simultaneously appealed for White cooperation.

The African-American delegates, at their hastily called convention, drafted an address and sent it to White politicians who were also hosting their own convention across town. The Black delegates' address was strong and carefully worded. It began with a more conciliatory tone, explaining how they saw the Civil War, the reasons for their perception, and reminding Whites that they had remained obedient during the major conflict between the North and South, although they knew the war was being fought for their freedom. They ended the address by looking to the future. They acknowledged that their conduct would affect their place in society, but they asked the White lawmakers for help. In their address to white political leaders, African-American delegates listed their demands. They said, "We desire education for our children, legal protection for the nigra family, aid for orphans, and support for reunification of families broken up by slavery," they declared before adding, "We most earnestly desire to have the disabilities under which we formerly labored removed, and to have all the oppressive laws which make unjust discriminations on account of race or color wiped from the statutes of the State."[7]

---

[6]Jeffrey Crow, Paul Escott and Flora Hatley, *A History of African Americans in North Carolina* (Raleigh, North Carolina: North Carolina Office of Archives and History, 2002), 77.

[7]Howard Rabinowitz, ed., *Southern Black Leaders of the Reconstruction Era* (Champaign, Illinois: University of Illinois Press, 1982), 46.

The address made it clear that Black North Carolinians wanted justice and equal rights. They did not make a specific reference to holding political office or voting but they believed that both would be necessary if they were going to successfully combat unjust discrimination. A Black man who witnessed the events at the time told Whitlaw Reid, a northern journalist, when asked about it, "We ain't noways safe, 'long as dem people makes de laws we's got to be governed by. We's got to hab a voice in de'pintin' of de lawmakers."[8] Gaining that voice, though, would depend on the course of politics in the South and the nation.

Whites did not respond favorably to Blacks' demands. They had already warned their colleagues at the convention that African Americans would begin making impracticable requests. Then they received the address from Black delegates, which confirmed their fears. The White delegates subsequently ignored the list of ultimatums. They also decided to vehemently resist, even with violence, any demands from African Americans for equality. And that they did.

North Carolina's Blacks were not undeterred by the vigilante violence, a form of White resistance to their demands. They knew that freedom came with a cost; therefore, it would not be easy. Again, they relied on their faith in God to help them claim the true benefits of long awaited freedom. They also protested by marching through the streets of Raleigh with banners that read "Equal Rights Before the Law: The Only Equality We Ask."

First Black Congressmen and U.S. Senator from the South. (left to right: Senator Hiram Revels (R-MS); Representatives Benjamin Turner (R-AL), Robert DeLarge (R-SC), Josiah Walls, R-FL), Jefferson Long (R_GA), Joseph Rainey (R-SC), and Robert Elliott (R-SC), Courtesy of the Public Domain.

For two years after the Civil War and emancipation, African Americans in North Carolina fought for freedom and equality

---

[8]Ibid.

while Whites maintained a death-like grip on Southern state governments. Blacks could not vote nor hold political office. Nor would whites treat them as free persons. This is illustrated by some of the laws that existed. Blacks could not testify in court against Whites, enter into contracts worth ten dollars or more on their own, serve on juries, or even keep a gun without a special license. For the most part, African Americans continued to fight for rights that had been long denied.

Blacks' struggle, however, was not in vain. As the years advanced, their status began to slowly change. Furthermore, as more radical Republicans from both the North and South began to win more seats in the United States House of Representatives and Senate, they passed legislation designed to politically empower African Americans while disempowering Southern Whites. Thus, Blacks, with the majority residing in the South, began to join the Republican Party which had been formed, in March 1854, by Whites opposed to slavery.[9] Also, as they gained the right to vote and their citizenship, African-American men began to run for political office. Blacks gradually began to dominate Southern state legislatures once controlled by White Democrats. Specifically, at the new constitutional convention, assembled in Raleigh, in 1868, the Republican Party, once absent in the South, had both Black and White delegates. The Republican Party delegates won 107 of the 120 seats in the convention; fifteen of the

---

[9]In Ripon, Wisconsin, former members of the Whig Party (one of two major political parties at the time) met to establish a new party to oppose the spread of slavery into the western territories. The Whig Party, which was formed in 1834 to oppose the tyranny of President Andrew Jackson, had proven to be incapable of coping with the national crisis over slavery. The Whig Party disintegrated in early 1854 when Congress decided to allow slave or free status in the territories to be decided by popular sovereignty. By February 1854, anti-slavery Whigs had begun meeting in the upper Midwestern states to discuss the formation of a new party. One such meeting, in Wisconsin on March 20, 1854, is generally remembered as the founding meeting of the Republican Party. The Republican Party opposed the spread of slavery and granted equal rights to all Southern citizens after the Civil War and emancipation Abraham Lincoln became the first candidate of the Republican Party for President. The Democratic Party supported slavery at the time and opposed equal rights for all Southerners. Both political parties held these beliefs until the mid-1930s. By 1936, the Democrats were supporters of equality for all and big government while Republicans believed just the opposite. When this shift occurred, Blacks moved en masse from the Republican Party to the Democratic Party.

delegates were Blacks.[10] The constitution that they drafted was much more democratic than it would have been if Blacks and liberal Whites were not in office.

Shortly after the convention adjourned, Republicans swept to power all over North Carolina in the first election for the new government. They elected a Republican governor and put Republicans in more than two-thirds of the seats in the legislature. Among the legislators were twenty African-American men, which comprised three state senators and seventeen representatives. All of them came from the east, specifically from counties in which Blacks formed the majority. Most had been slaves, the majority were from the eastern region of the state, four were mulattoes, some were Union army veterans, three were ministers, and one was an attorney.[11]

By late 1868, Black and White voters in the Piedmont region of North Carolina began to support the Republican Party, whose political ideology they espoused. After the November elections that year, the majority of the Piedmont counties were governed by Republicans. Between 1868 and 1900, 111 African-American men held political office as either a member of the North Carolina House of Representatives or Senate. While the eastern counties continued to have more Black politicians, counties such as Granville, Wake, Caswell and Vance claimed the majority of African-American male politicians in the Piedmont region.

Noticeably absent from the group of Black legislators were men from Orange and Durham counties. Although Durham County was not organized until 1881, prominent and very vocal African-American men like Dr. Aaron McDuffie Moore, John Merrick, Reverend Dr. Augustus Shepard, and Dr. James Shepard lived in the Durham Township of what was then Orange County.

---

[10]John Hope Franklin and Alfred Moss, Jr., *From Slavery to Freedom: A History of African Americans*, 9th Edition, Volume II (New York City, New York: McGraw Hill, 2010), 83.

[11]Jeffrey Crow, Paul Escott, and Flora Hatley, *A History of African Americans in North Carolina* (Raleigh, North Carolina: North Carolina Office of Archives and History, 2002), 85.

Yet, with the exception of Dr. Moore, none of the men ran for public office on the state level or local level in the first ten years after the Civil War. With the advent of the Republican Party in North Carolina, the political empowerment of Blacks and the popularity of these men, any of them could have easily won an election in Orange County. Instead, most of them chose to take a different approach to racial uplift.

Dr. Moore, on the other hand, expressed some interest in local politics when he was nominated for the Office of the Coroner of Durham County in 1888.[12]   Nonetheless, his campaign was met with much resistance from Whites as shown by coverage in the Durham *Recorder:* "White men of Durham, those who have any respect for the Anglo-Saxon race, will you fail your duty on the 6th of November?   Will you allow Negro rule or a White man's government?"[13] Dr. Moore, the city's first African-American doctor who scored higher than most White physicians on his medical exam, was in a campaign marked by racial discrimination. Dismayed by the antagonism, he withdrew as a nominee. No other Black leaders in Durham stepped forward to participate in politics until the Great Depression. Many of them, however, were qualified to serve in a political role and, therefore, could have easily won an election.   Instead, they chose to approach politics and address racial equality in a different way in the years after the Civil War and emancipation.

A Different Culture in Durham Creates an Emerging Black Leadership with a Different Approach to Politics

After the Civil War and emancipation, the overwhelming majority of Durham's Black leadership were active members of White Rock Baptist Church.   They could also be considered as devout Christians, obedient to God and committed to placing Him first in their lives. These were men who also embraced Christian

---

[12]Jim Wise, *Durham: A Bull City Story* (Charleston, South Carolina: Arcadia Publishing, Inc., 2002), 89.

[13]Jim Wise, *Durham Tales: The Morris Street Maple, the Plastic Cow, the Durham Day That Was and More* (Charleston, South Carolina: The History Press, 2008), 68-69.

principles in their approach to life and had a profound belief that they had to fulfill their God-given purpose in life. Therefore, it is not surprising that they took a different approach to politics than many of their contemporaries in other parts of the State.

In the decades following the Civil War, North Carolina's ex-slaves' overall experiences in the southeastern section of Orange County, which later became Durham County, were radically different than that of ex-slaves and free Blacks in other Piedmont and coastal counties. In the area of race relations, Durham[14] presented a marked contrast to the eastern section of the state. In post-Civil War Durham, African Americans made significant progress due, in large part, to their attitudes toward Whites and the attitudes of White leaders toward them, which were non-antagonistic in both situations. As long as Blacks remained in their communities and did not bother them, Whites did not chastise Blacks, and vice versa.

Compared to slavery and the conditions of Blacks across the state, Durham's African-American population was regarded by many as being fortunate. As previously mentioned, nationally renowned Black leaders Booker T. Washington and W.E.B. DuBois, agreed when they either visited Durham and/or traveled around the country. Washington once wrote: "Of all the Southern cities I have visited I found here the sanest attitude of the white people toward the black. . . I never saw in a city this size so many prosperous carpenters, brickmasons, blacksmiths, wheelwrights, cotton mill operatives, and tobacco workers among the Negroes."[15] DuBois, who was more of a radical than Booker T. Washington, wrote about Durham: "There is in this small

W.E.B. DuBois, Later 19th century Race Leader, Courtesy of the Public Domain.

---

[14]For the sake of clarity, we will use the term "Durham." The section of Orange County referred to in this section eventually became known as Durham County during the period discussed.

[15]W.E.B. DuBois, "Upholding Black Durham *Independent*, LXX, 646.

city a group of five thousand or more colored people, whose social and economic development is perhaps more striking than that of any similar group in the nation."[16] Both Washington and DuBois were good friends of Dr. James Shepard, Dr. Aaron McDuffie Moore, Charles Spaulding, John Merrick and William D. Hill, and had often visited them in Durham.

By and large, Durham's Blacks and Whites also appeared to cope well with one another. While racial tensions were critical in many parts of the South during the post-Civil War and emancipation era, Durham seemed to have fared much better. Although African Americans were lynched in other North Carolina cities and counties, for instance, and subsequently fought against those injustices with a call to hold political office, Durham had no such incidents[17] for many of those years. Several reasons account for the amicability between Blacks and Whites in Durham.

First and foremost, both groups had leaders from the very beginning whose attitudes were ones of peaceful cooperation, with encouragement of African-American achievement by Whites, and with constant emphasis of all leaders on Christian virtues and American ideals of hard work, thrift, individual responsibility, and morality. Blacks saw a definite opportunity for advancement under existing conditions. This was best exemplified when race leader and pastor, Reverend Augustus Shepard, began a campaign to remodel White Rock Baptist Church. Dr. Aaron McDuffie Moore, by then president of the church's Sunday School and a leader in the African-American community, helped raise the huge amount of $26,000 needed to complete the initiative. Dr. Moore was an avid supporter of the project because he strongly believed that "these were lines along which the [Black] race had to improve in order to advance successful participation in the democracy." They did not depend on Whites for funds to make

---

[16]W.E.B. DuBois, "Upholding Black Durham, *World's Work*, xxiii, 334.

[17]For accounts of these lynchings as well as statistical data by each North Carolina county of lynchings, see the following editions of the *Durham Sun:* August 27, 2013; January 28, 2014; and November 17, 2003.

these changes. Instead, they used their personal resources as well as funds from members of the White Rock congregation to complete the project. These leaders fully embraced the racial self-help ideology. They were determined to serve as role models for the community's Black youth and instill in them these same Christian principles and values. Dr. Moore once stated, "Youth must recognize individual responsibility to the race, the nation, and to humanity and prepare themselves to become a working unit in their [*own*] development."[18] After all, this is how Moore lived his life.

Dr. James E. Shepard, Founder and First President, North Carolina College for Negroes, Courtesy of White Rock Baptist Church Archives, Durham, N.C.

Another example is Dr. James E. Shepard, a White Rock Baptist Church member and prominent Black leader in Durham, who took a much more conciliatory and cooperative approach to addressing better race relations. Often compared to Booker T. Washington, Shepard rejected both confrontation and legislation. As a Christian he favored, instead, conciliation at the conference table and argued that "we cannot legislate hate out of the world or love into it." Dr. Shepard articulated these views on racial affairs over the years in speeches, writings, and statewide radio broadcasts. Whites in Durham and North Carolina were some of the major supporters of Dr. Shepard's non-threatening approach. After many years of playing a major role in the struggle for equal rights, the North Carolina General Assembly best summed up how White leaders felt about Dr. Shepard during his funeral services when it stated: "This native born North Carolinian labored . . . with wisdom and foresight for the lasting betterment of his race and his state, not through agitation or ill-conceived demands, but through the advocacy of a practical, well considered

---

[18]Louis Mitchell, "Aaron McDuffie Moore: He Led His Sheep," *Crisis Magazine* (*August*/September 1980), 254-255.

and constant program of racial progress."[19] He was also regarded in the African-American community as a hero and influential leader. Reverend James Shepard's views on race relations were unquestionably influenced by his strong Christian beliefs.

Second, a number of Blacks had proved themselves to be not merely capable business men, but enterprisers of astuteness that approached genius after initial aid and support by important White men. This was not witnessed anywhere else in North Carolina at the time. Not only did they show themselves as being capable of organization and planning, Blacks also successfully calculated risk-taking far in excess of most White businessmen at the time. Even more unusual is that race leaders, like White Rock members Dr. Aaron McDuffie Moore, Dr. James E. Shepard, and James Rufus Evans, were being talked about by both Blacks and Whites in the first decade of the 20th century for the wealth that they had accumulated. The lesson of these African-American men's triumphs and the circumstances under which they achieved them were not lost upon younger Blacks; Whites learned a lesson as well.

Margaret Kennedy Goodwin, Courtesy of Sue Jarmon and White Rock Baptist Church Archives, Durham, N.C.

These Black Durham leaders gave credit to Whites for helping them to become successful. Dr. Moore, one of the major founders of Lincoln Memorial Hospital,[20] secured a considerable amount of assistance from Durham's White millionaires. Spaulding, on the other hand, credited his success to his religious upbringing and White support. As third president of North Carolina Mutual Life Insurance Company,[21] Spaulding once commented that he had grown

---

[19]Charles Eagles, "James Edward Shepard," *Dictionary of North Carolina Biography*, edited by William Powell, Volume 4 (Chapel Hill, North Carolina: University of North Carolina Press, 1994), 63.

[20]The organization and development of Lincoln Memorial Hospital will be discussed in detail in Chapter 5.

[21]North Carolina Mutual Life Insurance Company will also be discussed in greater detail in Chapter 5.

up in the same "puritanical environment of early risers who took immense pride in their crops and land, homes and families, who looked to religion and work as the main stays of life." In the early days of the company he sold policies and collected weekly payments outside the factories on pay-days. He noted that "when [they] started the company, [they] had no money, no knowledge. [They] only had . . . the highest, most respectable whites [they] could find."[22] Even William D. Hill, senior-level executive at North Carolina Mutual Insurance Company and Board member of Mechanics and Farmers Bank, credited his success, in large part, to the monetary and non-monetary support given by Whites.

Hence, African Americans in Durham, were not considered as a threat to Whites in post-Civil War America and, in exchange, Whites did not prevent them, for the most part, from building their communities and wealth. Whites not only provided financial support to the so-called "good" Black but also made it possible for African Americans to accumulate real property. And the "good" Black did not complain because this was part of his strategy to gain access to certain opportunities in America instead of holding political office like many of his African-American contemporaries in other parts of the State. Black leaders in Durham employed a different brand of politics. While ex-slaves in other parts of North Carolina and the South were fighting for the right to hold political office and to vote, Durham's recently freed Blacks negotiated with White leaders for the building of public institutions for the Black community.[23] While this approach limited Blacks' political power in Durham, it provided them with the opportunity to have their own facilities in a legally

---

[22]John B. Flowers III and Margaret Schumann, *Bull Durham and Beyond* (Durham, North Carolina: The Bicentennial Commission, 1976), 28. When Spaulding first came to Durham he took a job as dishwasher at $10 a month. He progressed first to bell-hop, then to waiter. A White man, Dr. Robert A. Winston engaged him as his butler and general utility man. In this job he was free from 9 a.m. to 3 p.m. to go to school. After an unsuccessful try as a grocer, he was taken into the insurance company by his uncle, Dr. Aaron McDuffie Moore.

[23]Dr. Leslie Brown, *Upbuilding Black Durham: Gender, Class and Black Community Development in the Jim Crow South* (Chapel Hill, North Carolina: The University of North Carolina Press, 2008): 151.

segregated society.

As White Rock member Margaret Kennedy Goodwin once said, Durham's Black leaders at the time "already had learned that even with vision and drive you needed some capital."[24] Therefore, the institutions that Dr. Moore, Rufus Evans, Dr. James E. Shepard and many other members of the Black elite in Durham served were sites from which they challenged legalized segregation, or Jim Crowism. The divine connections were oftentimes Whites with both the wealth and means to help them accomplish certain things not only for themselves but for Blacks as a whole. Their goal, then, was to build financial wealth for Blacks in a capitalist society while striking a more conciliatory tone with Whites in order to achieve racial equality. This unusual brand of politics seemed to work. According to Dr. W. K. Boyd, professor and scholar, Black property ownership in Durham, between 1865 and 1923, increased from 1,366 acres valued at $8,696 to 12,612 acres valued at $4,298,067. It was also during this time that Blacks created, among others, their own grade and high schools, colleges, banks, insurance companies, barber shops, doctor's offices, dentist offices and food establishments. Hence, Black Durhamites, in some cases, had amassed a considerable amount of wealth in less than five decades after gaining their freedom.

Third, amicability between Blacks and Whites in Durham resulted from a sense of pride instilled in African Americans by the success of people like Rufus Evans, Dr. James Shepard, William D. Hill, Dr. Aaron Moore, Allen Goodloe, and Dr. James Hubbard. While Blacks in other North Carolina counties were demanding the right to hold public office and to vote, these same African-American leaders in Durham relied on their faith in God to build Black communities and wealth. Durham's African-American elite could boast of having: (1) built the largest Black insurance company in the world; (2) constructed the best educational and hospital facilities in the state; and (3) gained national attention from respected African Americans such as

---

[24]Margaret Kennedy Goodwin, Interview by Dr. Leslie Brown, 22 December 1995, Durham, North Carolina, Tape Recording.

Washington and DuBois. Furthermore, Black ministers, like Reverend Dr. James Shepard and his father, Reverend Dr. Augustus Shepard, were so knowledgeable about world affairs that White men sometimes came to hear them speak.

Leaders of the Black community in Durham set the standard for members of their race not only in North Carolina but also nationally between 1865 and 1930. They demonstrated that if one placed God first in their lives they could become economically successful and use their accomplishments to help the less fortunate African Americans. Their economic success, moreover, made it evident that Blacks could outdo Whites; their exemplary personal lives encouraged morality; their tact and restraint in the sensitive area of race relations were powerful influences for peace; their personal achievements revealed to young African Americans that, despite the limitations imposed by law and custom and prejudice, doors to success were open; their actions allowed Blacks to see another effective option that they could use to fight racial oppression; and their demonstrated faith in God showed that it was best to rely on their understanding of God's will for African Americans in a racially oppressive society.

Based on their religious teachings, Durham's Black leaders believed that God acted in history, which should serve as an example of how they would effectively cope with racial issues when they reared their repulsive heads. As Christians, these men and women must have thought about how God had acted first in creation, then through the sons and daughters of Israel (e.g., Abraham, Moses, Esther) and the prophets, and then through Jesus Christ. Consequently, if this is what they thought, then surely they genuinely believed that God would also act through them, who were disciples of Christ, as they struggled against the forces of racial and other forms of oppression. Based on the actions that they took, one might suggest that Dr. Moore and his contemporaries rationalized that just as God liberated the biblical Israelites from their captivity in Egypt, just as Jesus liberated the poor, oppressed and marginalized from their dehumanization, and just as God delivered Jesus from the despair of death on the cross by resurrection, so too would God be with African

Americans in the struggle against racial, gender and cultural oppression.

For many of Durham's Black leaders, most who were active members of White Rock, their work began and ended with Durham's first Black Baptist church as they allowed their Christian beliefs to inform their activism. These African-American men and women carefully followed the spiritual blueprint that God prepared for them as they tirelessly worked on behalf of the Black community. God's plan for them, they believed, did not mandate that they hold political office. Instead, they were to employ Christian principles and ideals to work effectively with Whites in establishing opportunities for recently freed slaves and other Blacks. Furthermore, God gave these African-American leaders the vision and then strengthened them to walk in it. This was God's unique purpose for them.

Durham's Black Leaders Become Involved in Local Politics

At the turn of the twentieth century, some of Durham's African-American leaders began to develop and use political organizations to achieve goals for the Black community. This was due to several significant changes. First, tensions rose among Durham's Black elite and Black masses at the height of the Great Depression, which occurred in the early 1930s. The African-American masses, which included the middle-class, were adversely impacted by the Depression whereas the Black elite felt little or no effects. As more African Americans lost jobs during the economic recession, they began to challenge the Black elite who appeared to them to continue to gain an enormous amount of wealth. Second, as tensions rose between the Black elite and the Black masses, a new generation of African-American leaders began to emerge that were more radical than their conservative elders. The younger leaders not only publicly challenged racial injustice but also employed tactics through organized political agencies that were not acceptable to older Black, more conservative leaders. Finally, because of economic distress, Whites began to regard African Americans as more of an enemy — somehow responsible for their job loss and, subsequently, loss of income to pay for food, clothing and shelter. Hence, the Great

Depression marked a turning point in race relations in Durham. As Black elites witnessed this change, they did everything within their power to appease White elites who were in power.

The heightened tensions and subsequent changes also led to the emergence of three distinct factions that crossed paths and subsequently sparred with one another. These factions were: first, the older, conservative Black Republican male leaders, like Dr. Charles C. Spaulding, Dr. James E. Shepard and William Pearson, who were founders and leaders of Durham's most important Black institutions; second, middle- and working- class Blacks, such as teachers and mill workers, who were most effected by the Great Depression; and third, a younger generation of emerging radical African-American Democratic male leaders who called themselves the "Radical Young Negroes." The interactions of these groups with one another best demonstrate how race work in the 1930s transformed from a focus on the inner workings of the Black community to a much broader civil rights agenda that "demanded equal protection and fair implementation of government policy at the federal level."[25] This strategy led to a new demand from a different generation of African-American leaders who wanted to share political space with members of the older generation of Black leaders. This new generation, like the older generation, mostly came from two churches in Durham: White Rock Baptist Church and St. Joseph's African Methodist Episcopal Church.

Dr. James Taylor, Trustee, White Rock Baptist Church, Courtesy of White Rock Baptist Church Archives, Durham, N.C.

During the Great Depression, a new generation of African-American leaders led by James Taylor of White Rock and Conrad Pearson of St. Joseph's began to challenge the political ideology and activism of an older generation of Black leaders such as Charles Spaulding and James Shepard of White Rock and William

---

[25]Dr. Leslie Brown, *Upbuilding Black Durham, 289.*

Pearson of St. Joseph's. One significant way in which the challenge was first manifested was in the fight for racial equality. President Franklin Delano Roosevelt's New Deal legislation, designed to bring economic relief to suffering Americans, was often handled by state and local governments, which made it easier for officials to discriminate when deciding who would benefit. The older generation of Black leaders, mainly Charles Spaulding, James Shepard and William Pearson, decided to take advantage of the New deal on behalf of the race, using conservative tactics that would not alienate Whites. They were successful. Whites embraced them and President Roosevelt invited Dr. Spaulding to serve as an advisor to him on his selection of members for his advisory council known as the Black Cabinet. All of these men, already wealthy, benefited financially from the New Deal. Conversely, new generation leaders Joseph Taylor and Conrad Pearson felt that a more radical approach should be taken to address racial inequality. Too many Blacks in Durham were not benefiting from the New Deal initiatives and nor were they allowed to vote. Taylor and Pearson wanted change for their race of people.

As public outrage by African Americans intensified, the old and new generation of Black leaders decided they needed to form a citizens' committee to address the issues. This was the first time since Durham's Blacks were freed from slavery that they politically organized to combat the racial injustices that they were enduring on a daily basis. The citizens' committee called on White registrars to: (1) cease denying Blacks the right to vote; (2) conduct municipal improvements in Hayti and other African-American neighborhoods; (3) allow Blacks to serve on juries; (4) appoint Black patrolmen to work the streets to combat rising crime in African-American communities; (5) employ Black magistrates and justices of the peace; (6) redistrict Hayti into a single voting ward; and (7) allow Blacks to monitor the polls on election day.[26] For the younger generation of African-American

---

[26]*Durham Morning Herald*, 1 April 1932, 12 April 1933; Arthur Vance Coles to Charles D. Wildes, 31 May 1935, Minute Books, Durham County Republican Executive Committee, Campaign 1936, 4 March 1936, Arthur Vance Cole Papers, Rare Book, Manuscript, and

leaders like North Carolina College for Negroes professor Dr. Joseph Taylor, Attorney Conrad Pearson and *Carolina Times* editor Louis Austin, these had long been issues that had not been resolved by their older, more conservative leaders. To Taylor, Pearson, Austin and several other Blacks, racial strife had become more noticeable, targeted and intense, which called for different action from that of their forefathers. Needless to say, the different positions resulted in partisan politics that, for the first time, divided Durham's African-American community.

The competing political ideologies present in Durham's Black community occurred at the same time that the National Association for the Advancement of Colored People (NAACP) launched a civil rights campaign that used the courts to dismantle legalized segregation, or Jim Crowism. The national organization, in reviewing conditions in Durham, such as the new challenges to issues of racial injustice and the different views of the city's new and old African-American leadership, genuinely believed that Durham was an excellent location to test their new strategy. More importantly, the national NAACP had observed Dr. Charles Spaulding's efforts at addressing civil rights for Blacks over the years and was, in awe, at his ability to be able to successfully negotiate some rights for his people while easing the fears of Whites. But, the early 1930s demonstrated a different time and new challenges as Blacks and Whites in Durham and other cities competed for scarce resources. The NAACP wanted to, therefore, test the influence and leadership skills of Dr. Spaulding by employing the new strategy. The civil rights organization's end goal was to rebuild the nation and fashion a participatory democracy, which included African Americans. To effectively do so, the national NAACP had to be able to move the older generation of Black leaders further left. The NAACP, therefore, decided to begin with public education since it was an experience enjoyed by all Americans, both Black and White.

Durham was also an ideal place to launch a campaign against

Special Collections Library, Duke University, Durham, North Carolina; Leslie Brown, *Upbuilding Black Durham*, 307.

racial inequities because African-American leaders were less likely to suffer economic repercussions for their activism. It also helped the NAACP and its proponents that Durham had a reputation for caution and vigilance in racial affairs. Furthermore, the NAACP knew that Durham's new generation of Black leaders had a history, albeit short, of supporting the civil rights organization. Taylor, Austin, Pearson, and even privately Spaulding and Shepard, along with their supporters who were mostly in their respective churches, donated large sums of money to the NAACP. Additionally, it was obvious that older Black leaders in Durham knew how to manipulate the racial status quo to its benefit. Knowing that Durham's Whites would do anything to maintain segregation, the old conservative guard of Black Durham had gotten some of the best public education facilities for their race in the South. Similarly, in Durham, African-American teachers were the strongest supporters of the NAACP. For these reasons, by launching this initiative in Durham, the NAACP would become social engineers in the battle against segregation and discrimination.

Blacks in Durham were divided over the appropriateness of the NAACP lawsuit, which manifested within White Rock Baptist Church as its members either supported Drs. Charles Spaulding and James Shepard who opposed such action or Professor Joseph Taylor who supported the NAACP's test case. Consequently, when White Rock found itself in need of a new pastor in mid-1932, the selection of Reverend Dr. Miles Mark Fisher was an excellent choice. An internationally-recognized clergyman, educator, scholar, and author, Reverend Fisher served as a bridge for the growing chasm that existed between the old and new generation of African-American leaders both within White Rock and in Durham's community-at-large.

Despite how both groups of Blacks felt about the NAACP's strategy, the civil rights group moved forward by using the *Hocutt* case as its test of Durham's public education system. This case placed White Rock in the middle of this strategy. The religious institution had a large teacher membership and at least three of its members were leaders of one of the two factions that the NAACP depended on to assist them. For the national NAACP officers, the outcome of this case would help them to determine whether a more radical approach in dealing with inequities in education, represented by Joseph Taylor, Conrad Pearson and Louis Austin, was more effective and the right strategy to use or the more conservative and White appeasement approach represented by Dr. Charles C. Spaulding, Dr. James Shepard and William Pearson. Tensions between the two groups made it difficult for them to work with one another both in the community and in the church where they often held meetings. Reverend Dr. Miles Mark Fisher who effectively employed both approaches balanced the two groups and, subsequently, was able to ease growing tensions within White Rock.

Dr. Shepard believed that the *Hocutt* case would undermine his power and influence in Durham's Black community. He believed that the case would not be successful and, as a consequence, it would end his "reign and undermine the progressive stance that whites had been willing to take in expanding educational options for the race."[27] Furthermore, he believed that the state would retaliate to the detriment of African-American education, thereby destroying the most powerful Black institution of higher education — North Carolina College for Negroes — of which he was the founder. Dr. Spaulding was also opposed to the case and the NAACP's involvement but responded a little differently than Dr. Shepard. Expressing sentiments similar to those of Dr. Shepard, Dr. Spaulding refused to publicly acknowledge the NAACP or respond to any messages that he received directly from the civil rights group. For example, when Roy Wilkins, then assistant secretary of the NAACP, wrote to Dr. Spaulding . . . in the fall of 1933, "We are counting on you as always, to advise and aid us in this important matter," Spaulding remained silent.[28]   He would not communicate with NAACP

---

[27]Richard Kluger, *Simple Justice: The History of Brown vs. Board of Education and the Black American Struggle for Equality* (New York, New York: First Vintage Book Edition/Random House, 1975), 157; Dr. Leslie Brown, *Upbuilding Black Durham*, 313.

[28]Roy Wilkins to C.C. Spaulding, 18 September 1933, Select Branch Files, box 146, North Carolina Conference, Group 1, pt. 12, series A, Papers of the NAACP (NAACPP),

officials during the entire time that the test case was the main agenda item.[29]

In the end, the *Hocutt* case was not brought forward by the national NAACP. Instead, in February 1933, Conrad Pearson and another local African-American attorney, Cecil McCoy, took up the matter when they challenged the practice of excluding African-American students from the University of North Carolina at Chapel Hill. They filed a lawsuit, *Hocutt v. North Carolina,* despite opposition from more conservative Whites and some conservative Black leaders like Reverend Dr. James E. Shepard and William Pearson.

Although a conservative, the case secretly had Charles Spaulding's blessings. In fact, Spaulding sent a letter to NAACP Executive Secretary Walter White to apprise him of the dramatic plans for the suit and vouched for the local lawyers as "two of [their] active and progressive young attorneys who [were] approaching [White] with a matter that [Spaulding felt was] of vital importance to Negroes."[30] However, when Thomas Hocutt actually tried to enroll at Chapel Hill, the overpowering White reaction brought such pressure on Spaulding that he promptly ran for cover. He was caught in the middle and then tried to extricate himself. The last thing that he wanted to do was to upset the conservative White community, thereby threatening the gains that he and other conservative Blacks had made for their race.

The lawsuit was filed against Thomas Wilson, registrar of the University of North Carolina at Chapel Hill, who had refused admission to Thomas Hocutt, a graduate of the North Carolina

---

1912-1933, microfilm reel 17 (Frederick, Maryland: University Publications of America, 1986).

[29]Rather, their younger assistants, William Kennedy, Jr. and George Cox, of White Rock and the North Carolina Mutual Insurance Company, and Dr. James Taylor, another White Rock member who worked at North Carolina College at Negroes, negotiated with NAACP national chair, Walter White, to move the rally to Raleigh, North Carolina. George Cox to Walter White, 10 October 1933, Branch Files, NAACP, microfilm reel 17; Conrad Odell Pearson, Interview by Walter Weare, 18 April 1979. Interviews H-218 and H-219.

[30]John Hope Franklin and August Meier, eds., *Black Leaders of the Twentieth Century* (Champaign, Illinois: University of Illinois Press, 1982), 184.

College for Negroes, to the university's school of pharmacy. Behind the scenes, African-American leaders and White officials negotiated two possible courses of action: the state would pay the tuition for Hocutt, the plaintiff, and for any other Black American, who desired to attend graduate school outside of the State or they would make provisions at "one of the Negro institutions now operating for the creation of new graduate programs.[31]

The Durham paper preferred the second option, that Hocutt "be educated at home," in North Carolina, a place that the *Durham Morning Herald* considered a more acceptable environment.[32] In that way, Hocutt would remain within the framework of Jim Crow, compliant with segregation and hopefully inclined to serve the population of African Americans in a similar vein.

Although filed locally, the case became nationally significant as the national NAACP launched its attacks against segregated educational facilities for African Americans. Minorities, in most states, and especially in the South, could not attend the schools where programs led to professional fields that required licensing and specialized training. Therefore, according to Attorney Pearson, in order to practice law or pharmacy, which were regulated by the State, students had to be able to train in the State where they intended to practice. None of the North Carolina Black colleges offered law or pharmacy training and, therefore, it did not fulfill the mission of public education. It would be too costly to pay tuition for Black Southern graduate students to attend programs in the North.

Segregated graduate training also required that Black facilities be equal to those offered at White institutions. In pharmacy and law, this would require the enormous expense of building facilities, hiring faculty, and furnishing libraries and laboratories equal to those of the University of North Carolina at Chapel Hill. Either choice, the lawyers argued, would financially break the Jim Crow system by bankrupting the State. The

---

[31]Dr. Leslie Brown, *Upbuilding Black Durham,* 310.
[32]Ibid.

NAACP was excited about the *Hocutt* case because it believed it began the organization's effort to dismantle Jim Crow.

The case divided African Americans in Durham. Black leaders and the NAACP backed a bill to authorize out-of-state tuition as a "cooling off" strategy. Militant Blacks "voted to demand a showdown of the case."[33] Meanwhile, Spaulding quietly advised the state superintendent of education that he was trying to "work quietly on the Hocutt situation, but now the NAACP [had] charge" and he was "afraid [their] good state [was] going to be embarrassed." Hoping that White leaders might rush to negotiate the integration suit for the tuition bill, he sought to convince the state official that he "would stop the case if some arrangements [were] made to take care of the tuition."[34] That did not occur.

In the meantime, the national NAACP sent William Hastie, its premier attorney, to assist Pearson and McCoy. Filed in Durham County Superior Court, the case was moved to Raleigh and into the state judicial system where Wilson, the university registrar, argued that Hocutt lacked sufficient preparation to enter the institution. Although Attorney Hastie made a strong argument, Hocutt's failure to follow all applications procedures doomed his case. Unable to produce a transcript certified by his graduating institution, Hocutt lost on a technicality that was engineered by Reverend James Shepard, President of North Carolina College for Negroes. The College intentionally withheld Hocutt's transcript. Holding this last card, Reverend Shepard acted to protect his institution and reinforce his position; he declared that Hocutt would not graduate in the spring, as the plaintiff had claimed. Reverend Shepard worried, and rightly so, that the state would retaliate, to the detriment of African-American education, potentially cutting funds or denying any future expansion.

In the end, the case highlighted the strength of direct

---

[33]Ibid., 312.

[34]John Hope Franklin and August Meier, eds., *Black Leaders of the Twentieth Century* (Champaign, Illinois: University of Illinois Press, 1982), 185.

challenge and was a win for Dr. Shepard. This case was the forerunner of all civil rights actions brought in the desegregation of state-supported universities throughout the South and, as a result of the actions of its most active members, Professor Taylor invited attorneys and supporters to meet at White Rock to discuss strategies and recruit more support among African Americans.

Meanwhile, Dr. Shepard's political sensitivity paid off. The Hocutt case was appealed and went all the way to the United States Supreme Court which ordered states, in 1938, to either admit African Americans to White universities or provide equivalent professional training at their Black schools. This was what Dr. Shepard wanted to hear. He could now get the law school that he wanted. In order to get a law school specifically for African Americans, Dr. Shepard had to sacrifice a student. He believed that sometimes sacrifice had to be made by a few people on behalf of the many. After all, Jesus died so that men and women might come to repentance.[35] As far as Dr. Shepard was concerned, Hocutt's sacrifice was much less. It was not long after this incident that he was able to get funds and the North Carolina Legislature's approval for a Law School at North Carolina College for Negroes.

Spaulding, on the other hand, emerged from the *Hocutt* case considerably chastened because the tuition bill that he supported failed. But, he was a different man in some significant ways. With a clearer sense of the new politics of the day, Spaulding, a conservative, began to work with national NAACP chair, Walter White, to organize NAACP branches throughout North Carolina in the fight for equal salaries for African-American teachers. He sent Mr. White funds and asked him to use the money to send NAACP organizers to North Carolina. He then employed tactics that he had earlier mastered to maintain White support for his causes. While quietly supporting the NAACP behind the scenes, Spaulding was publicly condemning such "radical" civil rights organizations. He usually went into his "frightening act" and

---

[35]Romans 5:15, 20-21, King James Version, *Bible*.

alerted the state superintendent that "serious threats [were] being made to organize an active branch of the NAACP in North Carolina, which no one wanted!"[36] Spaulding knew what he was doing. He lay in the background, stroking the influential Whites, while his lieutenants marshaled the resources of the North Carolina Mutual Insurance Company on behalf of the NAACP.[37] The vast network of North Carolina Mutual proved to be the perfect instrument for organizing the NAACP.

Durham Committee on Negro Affairs

After working behind the scenes to organize branches of the NAACP in North Carolina, Charles Spaulding had no choice but to recognize the limitations of his political style, especially at the state and federal levels. Therefore, he reluctantly joined his more aggressive colleagues, like Taylor and Pearson, in Durham in the judgment that "a voteless people is a hopeless people." The political ground shifted beneath him during the 1930s when a new group of more radical Black politicians emerged in Durham. Spaulding merely shifted with it, shielded by a growing body of Black radicals and White liberals. One could say that he tried to fit in with the new group and to make sure he did, Spaulding took his place at the head of the most significant political movement in the history of Black Durham that was begun at White Rock Baptist Church: the organization of the Durham Committee on Negro Affairs (DCNA). The accounts vary as to who actually founded the DCNA. However, most scholars of the DCNA agree that it was founded by two most powerful Black leaders in Durham at the time, Charles Spaulding and James Shepard.[38] Their idea about the organization was allegedly first shared with some of their close friends at White Rock. Moreover, the DCNA supplanted the NAACP as the organization charged with working on behalf of the African-American community's issues. Its

---

[36]John Hope Franklin and August Meier, eds., *Black Leaders of the Twentieth Century* (Champaign, Illinois: University of Illinois Press, 1982), 187.

[37]For a more detailed account, see the C.C. Spaulding Papers, 1889-1990, boxes 4 and 5, Rare Book and Manuscript Library, Duke University, Durham, N.C.

[38]Ibid.

executive committee was comprised of only men but there were a few women leaders who headed subcommittees.

The DCNA, organized in 1935, openly asserted that it put political power in the hands of African-American people. In doing so, it marked the beginning of the modern phase of the quest for civil rights in Durham. According to Attorney Conrad Pearson, Durham's Black leaders who attended the meeting decided in advance to make Mr. Spaulding chairperson because of the image and influence that he had in the African-American community.[39] Attorney Pearson said that they really needed Spaulding's support because he had influence in both the Black and White communities.

Reverend Dr. James Shepard also attended the meeting. Attorney Pearson claimed that Dr. Shepard did not care that Mr. Spaulding had been appointed chair because "he figured he was going to control it anyway." He further added, "Both men had a great deal of influence in town but never were interested in politics." Finally, Pearson implied that Shepard and Spaulding were "safe Negroes for Whites" who would not openly "challenge the status quo." To some extent, this may have been true. These two men believed that the best way for African Americans to achieve success in a society controlled by Whites was to adopt a position of appeasement. Interestingly, they also provided the personal transition in this process of political modernization. They also skillfully moved between two environments — cleverly advancing in the new land of direct politics and Black protest, then retreating with grace to the traditional personal politics and White patrons.

During this transition, Mr. Spaulding's function was to exploit the advantages of both, that is, to preserve the benefits of patron-client relationship while at the same time advocating for African Americans to have the right to vote and truly participate

---

[39]Walter Weare Oral History Interview with Conrad Odell Pearson, August 18, 1979. Interview H-0218. Southern Oral History Program Collection, University of North Carolina, Chapel Hill, North Carolina.

in the democracy. Being chairperson of the DCNA, for instance, did not mean that Charles Spaulding gave up his personal pleading with the governor to commute sentences or to hire more token Blacks in the state government. Nor did it mean that he stopped flattering the city manager and police chief whenever a new streetlight appeared in the Black community or whenever a White policeman showed discretion in dealing with African-American citizens; or that he felt it no longer necessary to send turkeys, hams and other personal gifts to city and state officials at Christmas time.

On the contrary, Mr. Spaulding expanded his personal politics, much of it simply to smooth public relations. In this New South, so to speak, he was not a politician promising to deliver the African-American vote indiscriminately to the Democratic or Republican parties like Durham's new class of Black leaders. Rather in his long-standing relationship with the White community, Spaulding promised, at least in the minds of Whites, to deliver something far more important: social control.

Durham Committee on the Affairs of Negro People Meet with Governor Luther Hodges in the 1950s, Courtesy of White Rock Baptist Church Archives, Durham, N.C.

In exchange, he, like other leading African Americans who adopted the same position, was able to secure much needed White support for some race-related initiatives. In doing so, Spaulding gained the trust, support and admiration of many Blacks whom he invited not only to worship at White Rock but also to become a member.

Using this intentional strategy, Charles Spaulding faithfully chaired the DCNA. In its early years, many of the Committee's meetings were held in the basement of White Rock Baptist Church where he was still an active and devoted member.

The DCNA also focused on: (1) registering voters, with the city going from 50 registered African-American voters in 1928 to over 3,000 (68% of eligible Blacks) by 1939; (2) running Black candidates for election to local office for the first time; and (3) getting Blacks into elected and appointed positions traditionally reserved for Whites.[40] Progress was slow but the DCNA soon became nationally recognized as a political powerhouse in Durham's local elections. It began to win positions for African Americans in a few public offices and on commissions and boards.

In its early years, many of these politicians worshipped at White Rock Baptist Church and some became members at the invitation of Spaulding, James Taylor, William Kennedy, Rufus Evans, and others.

Durham County Board of Commissioners

Despite the DCNA's efforts to assist African Americans in getting elected to local governing bodies, such as the Durham Board of Commissioners (name later changed to the Durham County Board of Commissioners), which had been organized in May 1881, the political entity would not accept African Americans until the 1940s. Some years later, Elna Spaulding credited her success in winning a seat on the Durham County Board of Commissioners to the efforts of the Durham Committee on the Affairs of Black People (DCABP, once known as the DCNA).

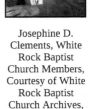

After serving two terms on the Durham County Board of Commissioners, Mrs. Spaulding decided not to seek re-election. The DCABP then asked another White Rock member, Josephine Dobbs Clement, to run for the seat vacated by Mrs. Spaulding.

Josephine D. Clements, White Rock Baptist Church Members, Courtesy of White Rock Baptist Church Archives, Durham, N.C.

At 65 years old, Mrs. Clement had just retired from the Durham City Board of Education where

---

[40]Jim Wise, *Durham: A Bull City Story*, 92.

she had spent the last 10 years. When asked by the Durham Committee to run for the seat, it took Mrs. Clements all of five minutes to agree. She later said, "I wanted to do it [run for the County Commissioners] because I found out maybe I wasn't as old and decrepit as I had thought. So, I filed and ran."[41] Both Mrs. Spaulding's and Mrs. Clement's tenure on the Durham County Board of Commissioners and other organizations will be discussed in greater detail in Volume 2 of *Upon This Rock*.

Conclusion

Whether some of White Rock's most active members in both the church and community were involved in the NAACP, DCNA or the Durham County Board of Commissioners between 1919 and 1932, they did so within the context of the church and their religious training. Oftentimes, as part of the Citizens' Committee, church members Spaulding, Taylor, Shepard and many others hosted planning meetings and strategy sessions at the church, and always began with prayer. Regardless of their level of participation, the majority of White Rock's members who participated in politics had one thing in common: their faith in Jesus Christ and their commitment to the church.

Many of White Rock's early members who became involved in politics, however, did so primarily on a local level. They seemed more concerned with addressing their community's social, cultural, economic and political ills. Unlike African Americans in many other cities and counties in the state, Durham's African-American leaders did not believe that holding political offices on the state and national levels was the key to success for Blacks in the years immediately following the Civil War and Black emancipation. Instead, they focused mainly on African-American religious, economic and educational opportunities, believing those were the keys to success. Once they

---

[41]Kathryn Nasstrom Oral History Interview with Josephine Clement, July 13 and August 3, 1989. Southern Oral History Program Collection, University of North Carolina, Chapel Hill, North Carolina.

became involved in politics at the turn of the twentieth century, they believed that it too often became confrontational, which placed African American leaders, an already vulnerable group, in a weaker position to negotiate certain opportunities for their people with the ruling class.

Unlike many of their contemporaries, White Rock's members who were involved in politics also believed that faith and work along with patience could carry the victory. They protested within the status quo, always believing that America, despite the gravity of its sins, was still capable of redemption. Hence, as devout Christians, they placed their faith in God, profoundly believing that He would help them to develop their own communities.

Chapter Ten

"Lifting as We Climb":
Faith, Benevolence and Self-Help

"But whoso hath this world's good, and seeth his brother have need, and shutteth up his bowels [of compassion] from him, how dwelleth the love of God in him?"–1 John 3:17 (KJV)

W hite Rock Baptist Church's First Lady, Hattie Whitted Shepard, was both excited and nervous. She and her husband, Reverend Augustus Shepard, had been in town for a little over six months and she had already been invited to speak before the local club women about the missionary work that she had been engaged in prior to her arrival and how she might be able to assist the club in fulfilling its goals. Not only did Durham's Black club women invite her to serve as their keynote speaker but they also wanted her to become a member.

Hattie E. Shepard, First Lady, White Rock Baptist Church from 1901-1911, Courtesy of White Rock Baptist Church Archives, Durham, N.C.

Mrs. Shepard was extremely familiar with the various local women's clubs as well as their parent group, the

National Association of Colored Women (NACW), which had been organized by some of the most renowned African-American women educators, community leaders, and civil rights activists in the United States. She was proud to be affiliated with an organization that was founded by notable African-American women like Harriet Tubman, Frances Harper, Josephine St. Pierre Ruffin, Margaret Murray Washington, Ida B. Wells-Barnett, and Mary Church Terrell. The organization was founded in response to a vicious attack on the character of African-American women by a Southern journalist, combined with the spread of disfranchisement, and the desire to "uplift" the race. The NACW wanted to improve the lives of impoverished African Americans. Mrs. Shepard then smiled as she thought about the address given by the NACW's first president, Mary Church Terrell. She was among the members of the audience in 1897 when Terrell, the daughter of African-American millionaire parents, and the wife of a presidential-appointed municipal court justice in Washington, D.C., delivered her first presidential address.[1]

Mrs. Shepard vividly recalled Terrell's leading statement, "The work which we hope to accomplish can be done better, we believe, by the mothers, wives, daughters, and sisters of our race than by the fathers, husbands, brothers, and sons."[2] She remembered leaving the meeting feeling energized and ready to help the less fortunate of her race. After all, this was what Jesus Christ would expect her and other club women to do — work to meet the needs of their respective communities.

She was proud to be among club women who were known to help women and children suffering from poor health, lack of education, decent clothing, and housing. They raised funds for kindergartens, vocational schools, and the elderly. But, she noted,

---

[1]"Robert H. Terrell (1857-1925): Lawyer, Judge, Chronology," encyclopedia.jrank.org. Retrieved 2018-07-20; Robert Terrell, "Judge Terrell," *The Crisis: A Record of the Darker Races* (June1918): 66-76.

[2]Beverly Washington Jones, *Quest for Equality: The Life and Writings of Mary Eliza Church Terrell, 1863-1954* (Brooklyn, New York: Carlson Publishing, 1990), 32.

club women also proudly adopted an elitist attitude saying that it was the responsibility of the "privileged" to help those who were "socially inferior"; some elites felt that the habits of poor African Americans gave the race a bad name. This attitude, however, did not prevent them from doing a lot of good. Shepard thought about how club women supported the right of African-American men and women to vote and, therefore, helped mobilize voter registration drives for Blacks on a local level. Moreover, as role models for acceptable behavior among African Americans, club women also promoted cultural events, including music concerts and poetry reading. They were regarded by Whites as the more cultured group of Blacks.

With that thought in mind, Hattie Shepard returned to practicing her speech, which would focus on how she believed the club women could work within their respective churches to improve the lives of poorer African Americans. She was the president of the Senior Missionary Society at White Rock Baptist Church and, therefore, often witnessed firsthand the suffering, poverty, illiteracy and homelessness in Durham's Black community. Much work still needed to be done to help elevate members of her race who were less than a generation from slavery. Perhaps Hattie Shepard could help make a difference.

***

After Slavery: The Need in the African-American Community for Racial Uplift Activities

After slavery ended, as previously noted, African Americans in Durham turned more and more to each other for support and encouragement. An elite African-American class of leaders slowly emerged, building a wide range of institutions, including churches, schools, colleges, hospitals, drug stores, mills, banks, and insurance companies. These establishments provided opportunities that Whites intentionally and legally denied Blacks in Jim Crow America. The money earned from these institutions created a privileged class of African Americans in Durham, thereby widening the gap between the well-to-do, also known as the Black aristocrats, and the poorer African Americans.

Regardless of their socioeconomic status, these men and women had one thing in common — they were Christians who were active in their churches and believed that they had been ordained by God to help those in need. This ideology was further enforced by Whites in Durham who encouraged African-American achievement and emphasized that African-American leaders should focus on "Christian virtues" and the "American ideals of hard work, thrift, morality, and financial reward for achievement."[3] The Black elite also felt that this was the yardstick used by Whites to measure whether or not they met Whites' defined cultural standard of acceptance. Therefore, they tried extremely hard to meet this goal because the Black elite still wanted and needed White approval. Meeting this goal also meant that privileged African Americans had to more aggressively engage in providing certain religious, economic, educational and political opportunities for members of the Black race while also instilling in them middle-class morals and values.

In Durham, as was customary all over the South after the Civil War and emancipation, virtually all African Americans belonged to either Baptist or Methodist churches. Most of Durham's African-American elite were Baptists and members of White Rock Baptist Church.[4] Consequently, the church produced a disproportionate number of the Black elite and Black leadership, in the city of Durham after the Civil War and emancipation and, subsequently, had more influence than any other church in institution building and racial uplift in the local community. As Christian men and women, Durham's African-American elite felt a need to serve their community's needs and contribute to the cultural development of their race.

***

---

[3]William K. Boyd, *The Story of Durham: City of the New South* (Durham, North Carolina: Duke University Press, 1925), 284; James G. Leyburn, *The Way We Lived: Durham, 1920-1920* (Elliston, Virginia: Northcross House Publishers, 1989), 64.

[4]James G. Leyburn, *The Way We Lived*, 75.

White Rock Baptist Church, the African-American Elite and Racial Uplift: Modeling Middle-Class and/or Elite White Society's Cultural and Social Standards

White Rock Baptist Church played a vital role in African-American life in Durham. In the late nineteenth and early twentieth centuries, especially, it was the center of African-American life and the institution that was not only the most representative of Blacks but had the strongest hold upon them. E. Franklin Frazier, a sociologist best summed up the role that White Rock and other churches played in the African-American community during this period, when he said, "It [was] a multifunctional institution that served as an agency of social control, education, and economic cooperation; it also provided Blacks with both an arena of political life and a refuge from a hostile environment."[5]

The church's pastors, from Reverend Zuck Horton to Reverend Dr. William Ransome (1866-1932), enjoyed great prestige and often occupied positions of leadership in the community. In the first few years, nonetheless, the church's preachers were uneducated. Reverend Dr. Augustus Shepard was the church's first formally educated pastor and the first pastor to have among his ranks more educated individuals and members who were considered as erudite theologians.[6] This shift in demographics also brought a discernible change in how the members of the congregation worshiped. Specifically, worship services became less informal, otherworldly and participatory to more like worship in White churches—that is, formal, unemotional, undemonstrative and temporal.[7]

---

[5]See E. Franklin Frazier, *The Negro Church in America* (New York, New York: Schocken Books, 1974).

[6]White Rock Baptist Church Papers, 1880-1920, North Carolina Collection, University of North Carolina, Chapel Hill, N.C.; Norval Glenn, "Negro Religion and Negro Status on the United States," in *Religion, Culture and Society*, edited by Louis Schneider (New York, New York: John Wiley, 1964), 623, 639; see also Joseph Washington, *Black Religion: The Negro and Christianity in the United States* (Boston, Massachusetts: Beacon Press, 1964, Chapters 2 and 3.

[7]Norval Glenn, "Negro Religion and Negro Status in the United States," 637-638.

Another critical change in African-American churches at the turn-of-the twentieth century was the status of the pastor. Writing in 1908, Monroe Work, an African-American scholar and observer of African-American society, reported a change in the status of the Black minister: "The tendency is for the Negro minister to assume a position in the community similar to that of the white minister; that is, to become the spiritual leader of the people and leave the guidance of social and economic matters to other persons."[8] The primary cause for this change, according to Work, was the emergence of a better educated laity and the prominence in African-American congregations of doctors, lawyers, teachers, and other professionals who were competent to assume direction of nonreligious activities.

White Rock Baptist Church in 1922, Fayetteville Street, Durham, N.C., Courtesy of the White Rock Baptist Church Archives, Durham, N.C.

But African American preachers still occupied more conspicuous roles in the general life of the Black community than did White pastors in their community. This certainly holds true for White Rock's pastors and congregation, beginning with the tenure of Reverend Dr. Augustus Shepard in 1901. Members of the church's congregation became more educated and congregants, like Dr. Aaron Moore, Dr. Charles C. Spaulding, James Rufus Evans, Tempie Whitted, Minerva Womack, Cottie Dancy Moore, Allen Goodloe, William Kennedy, Jr., J. M. Whitted, Burnice Ray, Nancy Cooper, Dr. James Hubbard and countless others, became engaged in institution-building in Durham's African-American community. Meanwhile, White Rock pastors, like Reverend Shepard, Dr. Edward Brawley, Dr. James Kirkland,

---

[8]Monroe N. Work, "The Negro Church in the Negro Community, *Southern Workman*, XXXVII (August 1908), 428-433.

Dr. S. L. McDowell, and Dr. William Ransome, continued to preside over what had become a middle-to-upper-class African-American congregation; yet, they were also well-educated, sophisticated pastors whose influence extended far beyond the church.

Besides, for African-American Baptists in Durham, around the turn of the twentieth century, the church in which they were a member was more important than anything else. White Rock, by this time, had gained the reputation of being the most prestigious African-American Baptist church in the city. Therefore, it was the church that most privileged Blacks wanted to join because the style of worship, education of the pastor, and the collective social standing of the member combined to confer middle-to-upper-class status on him or her. To many, this was an honor. By 1932, White Rock, therefore, counted among its lay leaders some of the most prominent African-American families in the city, including those by the name of Moore, Spaulding, Kennedy, Whitted, Shepard, Womack, Norfleet, Hubbard, Evans, Ray, Stewart, Schooler, and Carr. When Reverend Dr. Miles Mark Fisher arrived in 1933, White Rock was considered a "high tone"[9] church with little resemblance to lower-class Baptist congregations scattered throughout Durham.

Editors in Durham expressed admiration for what they perceived as the "progress from rude to civilized worship" in some of the high tone churches.[10] Like newspapers across the country, they were highly critical of the emotionalism evident in a vast majority of the Black churches in the city and, in doing so, convinced the Black elite that they did not belong in such churches. Many of these newspapers made scathing critiques of the pulpit antics of African-American preachers. For example, a Black resident of Durham observed: "Making noise in the pulpit

---

[9]A high tone church is one that aspired to high standards or refinement, its congregants were considered a part of a genteel society and regarded as being dignified. Its members were also considered to be intellectually, morally and socially superior.

[10]Durham *Sun*, January 9, 1900; Washington *People's Advocate*, May 26, 1883.

is not preaching."[11]   Other papers characterized shouting and noise-making during worship services, as well as the tendency to "beat and lacerate themselves to appease the supposed wrath of God," as painful reminders of slavery. Such behavior in churches, others argued, ought to be put aside, since it was inconsistent with the "growing intelligence" and sophistication of African Americans. They also believed that, along with gyrations, Blacks should abandon "their hankering for plantation melodies" and sing decorous sacred music. For many upper-class and middle-class African-Americans the "moaning and shouting" preacher was a major obstacle to the progress of civilization among members of the race; he symbolized ignorance and thwarted enlightenment among his followers.[12] So, privileged African-Americans at White Rock and other "high tone" churches across the country exhibited a certain type of behavior while worshipping in an effort to gain White acceptance. They embraced an intellectual form of worship that had no room for ardor and emotion. They modeled, therefore, their behavior in church and in the community after that of the White elite.

Hence, members of White Rock were, like other Blacks in other high tone churches, both socially-conscious and class-conscious. Distinguished from African-American congregants in Baptist churches in Durham by their education and wealth, as well as by the erudition of their pastor and the sedateness of their services, some members of White Rock displayed an attitude of condescension toward the African-American masses. Like the Black elite elsewhere in the country, they avoided fellow congregants that engaged in emotional religion and "heathenish" behavior and, instead, gravitated towards those fellow worshippers who emphasized ritual. They felt that the way in which they worshipped and with whom they worshipped

---

[11]Durham *Sun*, March 29, 1902.

[12]Washington *People's Advocate*, May26, 1883; Francis L. Broderick, *W.E.B. DuBois: Negro Leader in a Time of Crisis* (Palo Alto, California: Stanford University Press, 1959), 33; Indianapolis *Freeman*, June 9, 1894, August 12, 1904; *Seattle Republican*, October 19, 1900; Kansas City *American Citizen*, May 31, 1901; Chicago *Broad Ax*, March 26, 1910; *Washington Bee*, July 26, 1884.

determined opportunities for identity and association with the White elite, which conferred status as well as power. This type of thinking may not be too far from the truth. Clearly Dr. Aaron Moore, Dr. Charles Spaulding, and other leading African American, formally educated men in both the church and community, for the most part, had the respect of Durham's White elite like Washington Duke and Julian Carr. They were also empowered by these prominent White industrialists and philanthropists. This, however, was not unusual behavior for the Black elite class.

On the other hand, these same African Americans trusted `that as believers of Jesus Christ, they had a responsibility to take care of the less fortunate of their race. They alleged that the masses were a reflection upon the Black race as a whole. If the poor Black masses were uneducated and engaged in immoral behavior, Whites would not embrace the African-American elite. Therefore, to ensure that they were not dragged down by lower-class African Americans, the same Black elites who did not want to worship with them believed that they must help elevate to a level of civility the least fortunate of their race. The last thing that the Black elite wanted was for Whites to confuse them with the less civilized of their race.

Not All Negroes Are Alike: The Life and Culture of White Rock's Middle- and Upper- Class Members

Like the Black aristocrats in other parts of the South, White Rock Baptist Church's Black elite had a difficult time convincing Whites that they were different from the African-American masses. The idea of an African-American aristocracy, or "upper-class African-American" was extremely alien to most Whites in Durham and other cities. There is documented evidence that the concept was so foreign to Whites in some cities that they engaged in ridicule and scorn of the Black elite. In 1873, for example, in a satire on "Negro society," *Harper's Weekly* printed a cartoon grotesquely caricaturing an upper-class African-American wedding. The caption read: "Mr. Leon de Sooty, the distinguished Society Man, will to-day lead to the altar Miss Dinah Black, the beautiful heiress . . . ."[13]

Since most Whites in the late nineteenth and early twentieth centuries viewed African-Americans as a homogeneous mass of degraded people, they were rarely inclined to think in terms of a stratified African-American society. Rather, the tendency was to classify Blacks as "good Negroes" and "bad Negroes" or to designate certain African-American individuals or families, for one reason or another, as exceptional. But even exceptional African-Americans were considered inferior to Whites. Dr. Charles Spaulding, for instance, realized this fact during the *Hocutt* case when he was spat on by a White man while visiting a store in Raleigh, North Carolina. Those Whites who decided to move beyond vague generalities in dealing with social gradations among African-Americans invariably were surprised to discover the existence of a well-defined social hierarchy within the Black community. They were not surprised that the mass of African-Americans in Durham belonged at the bottom of the social class structure; however, they were surprised to discover a small, growing, upwardly mobile, middle- to –upper class which, in the phrase of the day, had struggled "out of the depths" of bondage. This group appeared to Whites, like the Dukes and Carrs, to be an example of the rewards of hard work, thrift, and "righteous conduct" that awaited even those among a proscribed race.

It was the small group of African-Americans at the top of the pyramid, like the Moores, Merricks and Fitzgeralds – the colored aristocracy – that aroused the greatest curiosity and posed the greatest difficulties for curious Whites. They concluded that there existed an African-American elite (e.g., John and Cottie Moore, Richard and Sarah Fitzgerald), small in number and usually light in complexion, whose culture and style of living more closely resembled that of the "better class of whites" than that of the masses of their darker brothers. The discovery of the upper-class Blacks prompted some Whites to question the validity of the

---

[13]*Harper's Weekly*, XVII (September 20, 1873), 840.

common notion that all African Americans were "upon an equal plane."[14]

Charles Spaulding's Home, around 1910, 1006 Fayetteville Street, Courtesy of White Rock Baptist Church Archives, Durham, N.C.

John Merrick's Home, 506 Fayetteville Street, around 1910, Courtesy of White Rock Baptist Church Archives, Durham, N.C.

Regardless of their privileged position in the African-American community, what the Black elite wanted most was White acceptance, the ability to assimilate into White society. But, they were convinced that the Black masses were unlikely to be incorporated into the larger society within the foreseeable future. Therefore, as previously noted, middle- and upper-class African-Americans, many who were in White Rock Baptist Church, placed greater social distance between themselves and the masses in hopes of gaining individual acceptance by Whites. These African Americans attempted to convince Whites that they were different from other African Americans in education, refinement, manners, morals, wealth and, in some instances, complexion.[15]

The homes of most of White Rock's African-American elite were concentrated in the southern and southeastern portion of the community known as Hayti. Fayetteville Street was considered as the main avenue for Durham's upper- and middle- class African Americans, and in some of the area around North Carolina College for Negroes. A typical upper- class and middle- class residence in Hayti, according to surveys, was a two-story house of seven or eight rooms, with tiled hearths in spacious parlors and a bathroom. The architecture of the houses was Victorian, with spacious porches and set in large lawns. The African-American

---

[14]For a discussion of social distinctions among African Americans during this era, see *New York Times*, August 1, 1906, 7; also see James G. Leyburn, *The Way We Lived*, 61-84.

[15]J.C. Price, "Does the Negro Seek Social Equality?" *The Forum*, X (January1891), 563.

residents took considerable pride in the looks and well-being of their community. They lived in a style exactly like that of well-to-do Whites.[16] The owners of the large, impressive homes were, for the most part, physicians, businessmen, attorneys, merchants, dentists, and teachers. They also regularly traveled and entertained.

The Black elite's homes were removed, culturally and often spatially, from those of the African-American masses. They resided at the top of Fayetteville Street where they could look at the Black masses down below on other streets. The homes of upper- and middle- class residents often had "excellent libraries, beautiful pictures, and musical instruments" that served as an "outward expression of the culture of the masters and mistresses" that once presided over them.[17] Their choice of pictures and the number of books on display gave an air of refinement and culture.

This same group of privileged African Americans also belonged to certain clubs and societies. Hence, many of White Rock's members, at the turn of the twentieth century, were members of a variety of clubs, societies and associations. Some clubs and societies were restricted to male members, others to females, and many others embraced members of both sexes. Because those of the upper-class, like the Moores and Spauldings, tended to be assimilationists or integrationists, they sometimes held membership in predominantly White organizations.

Establishments identified with the middle- and upper- class tended to be restrictive in membership and to include only those whose behavior and lifestyle conformed to the genteel performance. They sponsored balls, cotillions, and dances; however, they never hosted or sponsored "hops," which were common among lower class Blacks. White Rock's Black elite also belonged to two types of clubs and organizations: religious and irreligious.

---

[16]James G. Leyburn, *The Way We Lived*, 62; White Rock Baptist Church Records, 1880s-1980s, #4926, Southern Historical Collection, University of North Carolina, box 9.

[17]Ibid.

Church-based, or religious, organizations included, among others, the Senior Missionary Circle, which extended its reach into the Durham community during this era under the leadership of First Lady Hattie Whitted Shepard, Tempie Whitted, and Minerva Womack; the Volkamenia Literary Club, which brought Durham's "coterie of educated young adults together for cultural and social interaction;"[18] Order of the Eastern Star, which was open to both men and women of all religious beliefs and based on teachings from the Bible; the Royal Knights of King David, a fraternal and social group with religious overtones that provided insurance for its members; and the Lady Knights of King David, a byproduct of the Royal Knights of King David, which was formed to unite fraternally all acceptable African-American women of any reputable profession, business or organization to assist one another. Contrariwise, secular organizations and clubs of which many White Rock congregants were members were, among others, the Twentieth Century Club, a literary society; the Schubert Shakespeare Club, with an emphasis on the arts; North Carolina Federation of Garden Clubs; Algonquin Tennis Club, which served as a "social center for the children of employees of North Carolina Mutual Insurance Company;" and the Gourmet Bridge Club for women.[19] In addition to these clubs and organizations, Durham's African-American elite joined Elks, Colored Knights of Pythias, and other relatively large and well-known national societies.

The oldest and most respected secret fraternal societies, which members of White Rock joined, was Prince Hall Freemasonry. It was composed primarily of men of "education, prosperity and personal culture." It was also elitist and selective but provided its members with a close-knit environment and a national network that supported the values and lifestyle that they represented. It also provided its members with ideological and institutional ties with middle- and upper- class Whites. For many

[18]Leslie Brown, *Upbuilding Black Durham*, 105.

[19]Leslie Brown, *Upbuilding Black Durham*, 105; Also see: Beverly Washington Jones and Andre Vann, *Durham's Hayti* (Charleston, South Carolina: Arcadia Publishing, Inc., 1999).

African Americans in Durham, freemasonry was a means of enhancing or perpetuating their social standing in the community.[20] Also during this period, local chapters of sororities and fraternities, for college-educated men and women, were formed by members of the elite and many White Rock members were quick to join. Finally, some White Rock members joined cultural and intellectual clubs, which included, among others, literary societies, music organizations, and reading clubs. Such clubs and organizations were designed to make the Black aristocrats more refined.

The African-American elite would often hold club meetings in each other's homes. These social non-secular and secular club business gatherings provided the Black middle- and upper- class with an opportunity to socialize and work on projects that had a goal of improving the lives of members of their community. Moreover, these same clubs and organizations pointed to class differences among the middle- and upper- class African-Americans and the masses. Despite their cultural, social and economic differences, the African-American elite, especially women, were determined to engage in activities that would lift the Black masses; hence, which was often the purpose of these club meetings. If they did not, these men and women feared the risk of being dragged backwards into the lower-class ranks. The African-American elite also believed that it was the responsibility of the "few competent coloreds to assist the many incompetent."[21] In other words, they had a responsibility to "lift others as they climbed."

---

[20]See Loretta Williams, *Black Freemasonry and Middle-Class Realities* (Columbia, Missouri: University of Missouri Press, 1980; William H. Grimshaw, *Official History of Freemasonry Among Colored People in North America* (New York: Broadway Publishing Company, 1902). The best single work on the subject is William Muraskin, *Middle Class Blacks in a White Society: Prince Hall Masonry in America* (Berkeley, California: University of California Press, 1975), see especially pages 32-41, 292.

[21]Fannie Barrier Williams, "The Club Movement Among Negro Women," in *The Colored American, From Slavery to Honorable Citizenship* (Atlanta, Georgia: Hertel, Jenkins and Company, 1905), edited by J.W. Gibson, Booker T. Washington, and W.H. Crogman, 101.

"Lifting as we Climb": The African-American Elite Attempts to Uplift the African-American Masses

Although the African-American middle- and upper- class efforts to establish class lines prompted members of the Black masses to accuse them of being cheap imitations of Whites, few of them abandoned concern for the less fortunate of their race. Theirs was an attitude of having an obligation to lift the entire race so that they would all win White acceptance. The Black elite considered themselves as the exemplary practitioners of how African Americans should behave. After all, they exercised the prime attributes of what it was like to be refined, or even cultured.[22] To White Rock's growing genteel[23] middle- and upper-class African-American congregants, they had to teach the poor Black masses how to behave, among other things.

Between 1900 and 1930, there were a number of conferences, workshops and seminars on morals and manners sponsored by the African-American community for its elite. Some of White Rock's members, like Sara Cottie Moore, Hattie Shepard, Tempie Whitted, Susie Norfleet, and Margaret Kennedy, attended some of these workshops.[24] One conference of particular interest to some of White Rock's women was the 1912 Atlanta University Conference, on the topic, "Morals and Manners Among Negro Americans." Participants at this conference found a close correlation between manners and social class. The results of a nationwide survey regarding manners and deportment among African Americans indicated that the higher one's social status the better one's manners. A high social status implied more education and culture, which were closely linked to proper conduct. It was generally agreed, at the time, that the lower strata were "vulgar

---

[22]See Joyce Blackwell, *No Peace Without Freedom: Race and the International League for Peace and Freedom, 1915-1975* (Carbondale, Illinois: Southern Illinois University Press, 2004), especially Chapter 4.

[23]Genteel relates to the middle- and upper- class culture and is defined as being elegant or graceful in manner, appearance, or shape; maintaining or striving to maintaining the appearance of superior or middle-class social status or respectability.

[24]White Rock Baptist Church Records, 1880s-1980s, #4926, Southern Historical Collection, University of North Carolina, box 6.

and loud and sometimes annoying," especially in public places.[25] Once again, this conference reinforced the notion that the Black elite had a responsibility to teach the poorer Blacks how to properly behave in public.

This same group of women also read books on appropriate etiquette for African-Americans. One such book, *The Negro in Etiquette: A Novelty*, written by E. M. Woods, was extremely popular among the Black elite. This study addressed a wide range of topics pertaining to the attributes of polite society and what members of the lower strata should and should not do. For example, on his discourse of proper etiquette in church, Woods counseled against spitting on the floor and moving around during worship services. He denounced the use of too much cologne, the cakewalk and ragtime, the chewing of gum, and maintained that unrefined parents were incapable of rearing refined children. Woods further added that the "colored man [was] . . . the white man's pupil," and Blacks as grateful students should respect and honor their instructors.[26]

The African-American elite also read books on how to be a good conversationalist. Persons needed to have a command of the English language and an ample vocabulary to be considered as having culture. They also needed to be good listeners during the conversation. Blacks had to learn how to use restraint in all matters from emotion and expression to dress. Therefore, throughout the late nineteenth century and early twentieth century, White Rock's elite, like those around the country, not only built institutions in the African-American community for both the upper- and lower- classes, but also assumed the obligation of instructing the lower- classes in the essentials of appropriate genteel behavior. This was done in several ways.

Although racial uplift in Durham took on a variety of forms,

---

[25]W.E.B. DuBois, ed., *Morals and Manners Among Negro Americans* (Atlanta, Georgia: Atlanta University Press, 1914), 17-24.

[26]E. M. Wood, *The Negro in Etiquette: A Novelty* (St. Louis, Missouri: Baxton and Skinner, 1899), especially pages 9-11, 21-24, 34-36, 73-75, 137-139.

through church work or religion, it was mainly done by women, like Hattie Whitted, Susan Norfleet and Tempie Whitted. According to Dr. Leslie Brown, "the church [was] an extension of the home" and, therefore "provided Durham's African-American women a place to set their agenda and direct their initiatives. The church . . . afforded a readymade pulpit from which they could articulate and act on urgent concerns." She added, "Church work . . . brought together diverse sets of hands and accomplished more than any secular organization because the church dominated African-American institutional life in Durham."[27]

Hattie Shepard, Tempie Whitted, Susie Norfleet and several other White Rock women worked with uplifting the Black masses through the church's Senior Missionary Society. Concerned primarily about their needs, these women strategically established auxiliaries of the Senior Missionary Society in various communities around the city of Durham. The auxiliaries were placed in poor neighborhoods. First and foremost, these women believed that the poor needed to first know God's Word. Therefore, they focused on preaching the gospel of salvation as well as the gospel of cooperation.[28]

Moreover, these women also made civic work central to missionary work. In doing so, they created a strategy for resisting Jim Crowism. White Rock Baptist Church and the Women's Home and Foreign Mission Convention provided a safe space for its missionaries to address political issues like racial inequality. Through the Senior Missionary Society of White Rock and other religious organizations, Shepard, Whitted, Womack and other women were able to address these and other racial injustices issues at seminars and conferences that they hosted at the church. These women also enlightened African Americans, both in the

---

[27]Leslie Brown, *Upbuilding African-American Durham*, 100; Charles Wesley, *History of the National Association of Colored Women's Clubs: A Legacy of Service* (Washington, D.C.: National Association of Colored Women's Clubs, 1984), 311-327; Glenda Gilmore, *Gender and Jim Crow: Women and Politics of White Supremacy in North Carolina, 1896-1920* (Chapel Hill, North Carolina: University of North Carolina Press, 1996), 177-202.

[28]Reverend Dr. Miles Mark Fisher, *Friends: Pictorial Report of Ten Years Pastorate, 1933-1943* (Durham, North Carolina: Service Printing Company, 1943), 12, 19.

church and the community, on the link between the political position of Blacks in Hayti and other all-Black communities, and Black morality. They effectively argued that the major issue for Blacks, as far as Whites and the Black elite were concerned, was its "standards of morality." These women believed, just like other missionaries across the state, that issues of morality among Blacks were "destroying [them] as a race."[29]

Whitted, Norfleet and the other women wanted to do more than just talk about principles of morality and respectability among the African-American masses. They also wanted to take some type of action to try to change the behavior of working class Blacks. The best way to address these issues and take action, they believed, was at annual meetings of the Women's Home and Foreign Mission Convention and the Interdenominational Sunday School Convention. These two forums were attended by men and women from all socioeconomic tiers and denominations. For example, at the 1905 annual Interdenominational Sunday School Convention held in Durham, women like White Rock's own Annie Day Shepard, the wife of Dr. James E. Shepard, presented a paper in which she urged men and women to focus on "moral beauty."[30] They also used the Bible to teach morality and literacy, since the Black elite believed that there was a direct correlation between education and morality.

On a more local level, White Rock's members of the Senior Missionary Society made home visitations, provided Bible instruction, and donated clothing, funds and other necessities needed by the Black masses. With auxiliaries strategically placed in Durham's African-American communities, the church's

[29]Charles C. Spaulding to Fannie Rosser, 17 April 1914, Charles C. Spaulding, Rare Book Manuscript, and Special Collections Library, Duke University, Durham, North Carolina; Dolores Janiewski, *Sisterhood Denied: Race, Gender and Class in a New South Community* (Philadelphia, Pennsylvania: Temple University Press, 1985), 110-113; Thornhill Mercantile to Fannie Rosser, 3 December 1922, FRP; James E. Shepard to Fannie Rosser, 21 December 1926, FRP; Virginia Randolph to Fannie Rosser, 11 October 1929, FRP.

[30]*Durham Morning Herald,* 4 August 1905, clipping, Scrapbooks, box 14, Charles N. Hunter Papers, Rare Book, Manuscript, and Special Collections Library, Duke University, Durham, North Carolina.

missionaries were able to engage in race uplift activities that effected a wider range of people. These women also supported the Colored Orphan Asylum by making annual monetary donations. They also worked with families of displaced youth and the orphanage by seeking a placement for the children. According to author and church member, J. A. Whitted, these women also sponsored tutorials for children in various disciplines, both at the church and in their homes because they believed that education provided future opportunities for voting, college entrance and property ownership. Both the Senior Missionary Society at White Rock and the Women's Convention, of which the church's missionaries were extremely active, engaged in "home training and guiding and instructing family members on values, mores, and behavior." They felt that so much needed to be done for the poor of their race. Finally, J.A. Whitted contended, both the Women's Convention and White Rock's Senior Missionary Society, applied a "biblical interpretation of Negro women's place in communities that rid them of the negative stains of slavery." Hence, "Negro Baptist Women as soon as they were free to work and earn wages for themselves followed the example of the women Jesus had trained for the first Missionary Society."

The African-American middle- and upper- class women always believed that not only did they have a responsibility to improve the image of the Black masses but also how African-American women, regardless of socioeconomic status, were negatively perceived by White America. They embarked, therefore, on a two-fold mission: one, to have women uplift themselves through their employment and church work; and two, have missionaries to engage in uplift work of other women, and men, among the African-American masses, by focusing on "good moral character."[31]

---

[31]J.A. Whitted, *A History of the Negro Baptists of North Carolina* (Raleigh, North Carolina: Edwards and Broughton, 1908), *113-114; Proceedings of the Forty-Fourth Annual Session of the Women's Home and Foreign Mission Convention, 11; Proceedings of the Fortieth Annual session of the Women's Home and Foreign Mission Convention, 26-27.*

An example of a club organized that existed in 1911. The Just for Us Girls (JUG) was a group of single, educated, middle class women who were involved in a number of community-based activities. The club members are, from left to right, as follows: (first row, seated) Gazelle Poole, Eula Ruffin, Martha Merrick, Sarah Amey, and Fannie Poole; (second row, standing) Minnie Whitted, Ora Sneed, Henrietta Christmas, and Beatrice Bynum; and (third row, standing) Theresa Shepard, Mittie Ray, Senena Shepard, and Mattie Moore. Courtesy of White Rock Baptist Church Archives, Durham, N.C.

For men and women of White Rock who were not actively involved in missionary or Sunday School work, they still contributed to racial uplift work through the various secular, or irreligious, clubs and organizations in which they were actively involved. For instance, The Volkamenia Club provided scholarships for African-American youth who could not afford to pay for college. For working-class adults, the Club initiated voter education and literacy programs.[32] Moreover, musical organizations in Black Durham offered free piano lessons to poor children. Additionally, local fraternities like Alpha Phi Alpha and Omega Psi Phi as well as sororities such as Delta Sigma Theta and Alpha Kappa Alpha provided scholarships for needy students interested in attending college as well as tutorial and mentoring programs. These fraternities and sororities were identified with civic and racial uplift enterprises. Even some of the Black-owned businesses like North Carolina Mutual and Provident Association, provided programs that specifically targeted the African-American masses in their racial uplift efforts. For example, North Carolina Mutual, especially during the tenure of White Rock member William D. Hill, hosted a variety of activities for Durham's Black youth.

Finally, the club activities of upper- and middle- class Black women focused primarily on civic reform and racial uplift efforts. African-American clubwomen, in Durham and other cities, had

---

[32]Leslie Brown, *Upbuilding Black Durham*, 105.

become convinced that they "owed something to those outside the home nest and themselves." For upper-class Black women, like White Rock Baptist Church First Ladies, Hattie Whitted Shepard and Sophronia Dickerson Brawley, attention to public issues emphasized by the National Association of Colored Women brought a new found pleasure in doing something worthwhile and demonstrating that their labors were of utilitarian value to the entire race. According to Ms. Shepard, the purpose of the women's club was to "cultivate among the people a finer sensitiveness as to rights and wrongs, the proprieties and improprieties that enter into—or may regulate—the social status of the race."[33] They saw the Black club movement as women's organized effort for humanity.

The popular National Association of Colored Women adopted as its motto, "Lifting as we Climb," which meant that they would lift those beneath them—that is, the Black masses. Their goals included, among others, working for the economic, moral, religious and social welfare of women and children, raising the standard and quality of life in home and family, promoting the education of women and children, and obtaining for all Black families the opportunity of reaching the highest levels of human endeavor. Many of the clubwomen, in Durham, tirelessly worked to achieve these goals. They lectured on topics of morality and manners, served on boards of organizations with a focus on education and charity, hosted book clubs and tutorial programs, and always served as role models for masses who needed to see women of culture, refinement and financial independence.[34]

Conclusion

Late nineteenth and early twentieth century middle- and

---

[33]White Rock Baptist Church Records, 1880s-1980s, #4926, Southern Historical Collection, University of North Carolina, box 3.

[34]Fannie Barrier Williams, "Club Movement Among Negro Women," in William Crogman, *Progress of a Race: Or the Remarkable Advancement of the American Negro from the Bondage of Slavery, Ignorance and Poverty to the Freedom of Citizenship, Intelligence, Affluence, Honor and Trust* (Whitefish, Montana: Kessinger Publishing, 2007), 207.

upper- class African-American men and women performed a large amount of socially useful work. While some of them had concerns about being associated with the "less cultured" of their race whom Whites found objectionable, it did not mean that they despised lower-class Blacks. Rather they conceived of themselves as the civic mothers and fathers of the Black race. In fact, they emphasized race pride and race progress at the same time that they embraced assimilationist or integrationist ideology. Notwithstanding their elitism, African-American men and women—especially the latter—were more successful than their White counterparts in bridging class barriers and in addressing the issues of importance to the poor and illiterate women and men of their race.

Between 1900 and 1930, the majority of the African-American elite in Durham, were Baptists and attended White Rock Baptist Church. They were considered as the colored or Black aristocracy. They created a culture similar to that of the White elites. Upper- and middle- class African Americans were well-educated, refined, cultured and had amassed a considerable amount of wealth from the African-American institutions that they built after the Civil War and emancipation. This wealth afforded them many opportunities that the Black masses lacked. Moreover, despite the fact that their lifestyles rivaled those of the White elite, they were still regarded as just another Negro because Whites initially could not comprehend social class stratification within the African-American community. Once Whites realized that there were at least three social classes within the African-American community, they began to recognize differences in behavior. But, they could not fully embrace the most elite of the African-American race as long as there were among them those who lacked a certain level of sophistication. Consequently, the African-American elite, who longed for White acceptance, realized that the only way for the entire race to advance was to engage in racial uplift activities. To ensure that they were teaching the least desirable of their race proper behavior, the more privileged Blacks attended conferences and seminars and read books and articles on appropriate morals and manners. The more they learned, the more privileged African-Americans changed their lifestyles so that they would be good examples to poor Blacks of how they should behave in their homes, church and community.

The African-American elite in Durham began uplift activities in the church. Therefore, leading African-Americans in Durham's community who were active in missionary and Sunday School work at both White Rock and the annual Baptist conventions used those safe spaces to sponsor racial uplift activities for the less fortunate in Durham. While doing so, they continued to model genteel behavior, which was best reflected in their church affiliation, educational level, homes, and social, intellectual and cultural activities. Further, for the African American elite in Durham, church preference often served as a means to cultivate group consciousness and exclusivity and to preserve their privileged heritage. These men and women felt that it was an honor to be a part of a "high tone" church like White Rock—a church where education, culture and gentility were evident in the practice of religion.

The Black masses, who were not always willing students, benefited from the race uplift work conducted by the Black elite. As a consequence, many poorer Blacks were able to earn a college degree or a trade that allowed them to get a higher paying job and move to a better neighborhood. This upward mobility almost guaranteed a better life for the next generation of Blacks. Many members of the Black elite, especially those in White Rock, regarded their race uplift work as a way in which they interpreted their Christian faith.

PART 4

Unsung Heroes and Heroines of White Rock Baptist Church

Chapter Eleven

Other Unsung Heroes and Heroines:
Ten Men and Women Who Interpreted Their Christian
Faith by Quietly Serving the Black Community's Needs,
1866-1932

*"Do not do this while you are being watched in order to please men, but
be like slaves of the Messiah, who are determined to obey God's will."–*
Ephesians 6:6 (ISV)

A strikingly handsome couple, William J. Kennedy, Jr. and Margaret Lillian Spaulding Kennedy exemplified the culture, behavior, and life style of Durham's Black aristocrats. Exhibiting the

William
Kennedy, Jr.,
Courtesy of
White Rock
Baptist Church
Archives,
Durham. N.C.

Margaret
Kennedy,
Courtesy of
White Rock
Baptist Church
Archives,
Durham, N.C.

decorum, dignity, and restraint characteristic of the polite society of which they were a part, they abided by the prevailing canons of proper etiquette and avoided ostentatious display. They held membership in a variety of high-status social clubs and racial uplift organizations, were affiliated with White Rock Baptist Church, which some called at the time a "high tone" church, and were sufficiently affluent to enjoy the amenities of life denied most African Americans. They were both committed to the Christian values derived from the teachings of Jesus Christ and, regardless of the challenges that they faced on a daily basis, the Kennedys remained committed to the twin concepts of Black equality and racial uplift.

After having served years in executive-level positions at North Carolina Mutual and Provident Association, William Kennedy, Jr., was now president of the largest Black-owned insurance company in the United States and the first Black-owned insurance company in Durham. Given his many achievements, Mr. Kennedy was obviously considered an ideal husband by the Spaulding family. Margaret, the sister of a member of one of Durham's African-American elite, Charles C. Spaulding, subscribed to the same social clubs as did her husband. Both William and Margaret were from two of the most prominent Black families in Durham. As members of the genteel culture, they were concerned about proprieties and decorum, which were important if they were to gain White acceptance. They were somewhat disdainful of the materialism that they believed to be rampant among Blacks and Whites. Nor did the Kennedys approve of people who made an ostentatious display of their wealth. Such behavior automatically placed such persons among the uncultured, the vulgar of society. From clothing and jewelry to behavior both in the community and church, William and Margaret Kennedy preferred simple but elegant things in life and believed that people needed to exercise restraint in all that they do. Therefore, although they were members of Durham's Black

elite, they did not display their wealth. Active in their church and community, the Kennedys quietly worked in the background as they helped the less fortunate.

Tempie Whitted, Courtesy of White Rock Baptist Church Archives, Durham, N.C.

The Kennedys were not the only White Rock Baptist Church members of Durham's upper- and middle- class that contributed significantly both to their church and the African-American community. So did Hattie Shepard, Minerva Womack, Sylvia Williams, Tempie Whitted,

William D. Hill, Dr. James Hubbard, Sr., Sarah "Cottie" Moore, and James R. Evans. These men and women quietly and effectively worked in their church while serving the Black community's needs at a time when both were very much needed.

Hattie Whitted Shepard, Minerva Womack, Sylvia Williams and Tempie Whitted: The Missionaries

Hattie Shepard, Courtesy of White Rock Baptist Church Archives, Durham, N.C.

Hattie Whitted Shepard was born just outside of Durham, in Hillsborough, North Carolina, in 1858. She met her husband, Reverend Augustus Shepard in the early 1870s while he served as pastor of a Baptist church in her hometown. They were married in 1875.

Mrs. Shepard was known in her community as a devout Christian woman; therefore, it was no surprise to anyone that she would marry the town's handsome, bachelor pastor. The townspeople loved the couple and enjoyed visiting their home. One of Mrs. Shepard's relatives observed, "Everyone who came into [their] home felt at once its benign influences; aglow as it was with 'sunshine and song,' and with mottoes here and there upon the walls bearing scriptural texts, which were unmistakable evidence that the Word of God had a constant place in their lives and practices. Everyone who entered [their] home was deeply impressed at the scriptural rule, and that was the rule and guide of this home. No day had duties too numerous, or tasks too arduous, for family devotion."[1]   Both Mrs. Shepard and her husband, Reverend Shepard, were seemingly devoted to a life of faithful service and prayer.

Minerva Womack, Courtesy of White Rock Baptist Church Archives, Durham, N.C.

Hattie Shepard and her spouse eventually had twelve children. Four of them died very young. Of the eight remaining children, there were five

---

[1]J.A. Whitted, *Biographical Sketch of the Life and Work of the Late Rev. Augustus Shepard, D.D.* (Raleigh, North Carolina: Edwards and Broughton Printing Company, 1912), 15.

daughters and three sons. As soon as the children were old enough to read and understand the Scriptures, their parents presented them with a Bible and constantly compelled them to read so many Scriptures each day. This clearly had a positive influence on the couple's children. The oldest son, Dr. James E. Shepard, for instance, eventually became an ordained preacher, around the same time that he found the National Religious Training School, in Durham, North Carolina, primarily to train ministers. He was also one of the first Black pharmacists in North Carolina and, later, was appointed as Field Superintendent of the International Sunday School Association. The second oldest son, Charles, became a physician and subsequently opened one of the largest practices in Durham. He was also the first Black physician in North Carolina to successfully perform abdominal operations. He was also an active member of White Rock Baptist Church until his death. Both children were examples of not only the Christian influences of not only their father but also their mother.

While their children were growing up, Reverend Augustus Shepard received an appointment as pastor of White Rock Baptist Church. Therefore, in 1901, he, Mrs. Shepard and their children relocated to Durham. This new location was great for Hattie Shepard because she was now closer to Raleigh where she had long been involved with the Baptist Woman's Home and Foreign Missionary Convention (formerly known as the Woman's Convention).   The Convention was one of the South's most influential associations of churchwomen. Its purpose was to bring ideas developed by one group of women to a "broader constituency." It was this body that called on all Baptist Churches to establish mission circles.[2]

When Mrs. Shepard arrived at White Rock as its First Lady, she was still involved with the Baptist Woman's Home and Foreign Missionary Convention. She had also previously served as secretary to the Women's Baptist Missionary Circle in Raleigh that founded the statewide convention. Therefore, she had a great

[2]Leslie Brown, *Upbuilding Black Durham*, 34.

deal of missionary experience and a strong desire to help Black Baptist churches build strong missionary departments. This is precisely what she did at White Rock. Working with some of the church's leading missionaries, Minerva Womack, Essie Trice, Sylvia Williams and others, Mrs. Shepard helped to establish one of the best missionary societies in the State of North Carolina.

When First Lady Shepard arrived at White Rock, she was impressed with the missionary work performed by Trice, Womack, Williams and Whitted. Therefore, they agreed to build upon what had already been established. Despite limited resources, these women established a very impressive Senior Missionary Society. It consisted of auxiliaries that would provide mission help to the African-American community well beyond the boundaries of the church. The auxiliaries were strategically placed in two locations in Durham's East End and a third location to serve all citizens of Durham. One of the East End auxiliaries was under the leadership of Mrs. Mollie Crews and another auxiliary, located on Grant Street, was under the leadership of Mrs. Minerva Womack, president. Mrs. Sylvia Williams presided over White Rock's City Missionary Society where Tempie Whitted was also one of the leaders.[3] Whitted was also one of the church's major missionaries until her death. She donated not only her time but funds to ensure that the Senior Missionary Society's goals were met. Furthermore, Whitted was involved in missionary work on the state level, and a regular attendee and session leader of the annual Baptist Woman's Home and Foreign Mission Convention and the Lott Carey Convention.

The Senior Missionary Society and its auxiliaries promoted Christian fellowship. They also cooked and delivered meals to people across the city, prayed and offered Christian devotion with individuals, and even supported the North Carolina Colored Orphan Asylum.[4] She and other prominent Baptist missionaries used these forums to continue to engage in racial uplift work— using their skills, knowledge and resources to improve the lives of

---

[3] Reverend Dr. Miles Mark Fisher, *Friends*, 12.

[4] Minerva Fields, Notes, November 6, 2017.

poorer Blacks. In addition, these missionaries were active in other ministries within their church. Before long, the Senior Missionary Society was recognized as a model for other missionary circles not only in the City of Durham but across the State of North Carolina. As a consequence of her ministry work, Mrs. Whitted had the Tempie Whitted Classroom named after her at White Rock Baptist Church.

Eventually, the auxiliaries began to lose members. As a result, the three groups' leaders decided to combine the auxiliaries with the Senior Missionary Society, thereby becoming known as the White Rock Baptist Church Shepard, Womack, Williams (SWW) Missionary Circle.[5] These women are great examples of White Rock members who quietly made a major impact on the community through their ministry work.

Today, the descendants of Minerva Womack — Paulette Singletary and Minerva Fields — have taken leadership of the SWW Missionary Circle. The SWW Circle continues to support the mission efforts of the church as well as those of the Woman's Baptist Home and Missionary Convention of North Carolina. They also worship, have devotions, and pray together. Additionally, they assist, the Global Missions Ministry, from time to time, in its work with food distribution to members of the community, international missions and initiatives on human trafficking. Because of the efforts of women in these mission ministries, White Rock Baptist Church is still noted for its work in these areas.

William Daniel Hill: The "Energetic Trustee"

William Daniel "W.D." Hill was born in Richmond, Virginia, in 1890. After graduating from high school, Hill enrolled in Virginia Union College. After completing his studies at Virginia Union, he attended Columbia University, in New York. He left Columbia to join the U.S. Army. Just as America entered World

---

[5]See White Rock Baptist Church website's Shepard-Womack-Williams Missionary Circle History.

War I in 1917, Hill, who had served two years and earned an honorable discharge, relocated to Durham, North Carolina, to accept a position as field agent with North Carolina Mutual Life Insurance Company.

As soon as Hill arrived in Durham, he joined White Rock Baptist Church and immediately began to become active in its ministries. While a comptroller at North Carolina Mutual, he also used his mathematical and business acumen to serve as one of the church's finance officers. Hill, also known in both the church and community as W.D. Hill, was eventually appointed to White Rock's Trustee Board. He became one of the most "energetic trustees" at the church. He was also the church's representative for Shaw University and helped to raise funds for the beleaguered institution. During his tenure, White Rock became Shaw's largest church donor.[6]

William D. Hill, Courtesy of White Rock Baptist Church Archives, Durham, N.C.

A devoted and busy leader in the church, W.D. Hill learned how to interpret his Christian faith by serving the needs of African-American people in the community. He spent twenty-eight years at North Carolina Mutual, moving from one executive position to another. His biggest accomplishment at the insurance company was advancing the firm's projects to serve the city's Black youth. In an effort to find some meaningful and productive events for young people, he successfully spearheaded several types of recreational, cultural and educational activities. Before his death, Hill also created the John Avery Boys Club with North Carolina's first female judge, Jamie Dowd Walker, in 1939. It still exist today as the Boys and Girls Club.[7] Furthermore, he became the namesake of W.D. Hill Recreation Center, on Fayetteville Street, in Durham, North Carolina, because of his extensive work

---

[6] Reverend Dr. Miles Mark Fisher, *Friends*, 27.

[7] White Rock Baptist Church Records, 1880s-1930s, Southern Historical Collection, University of North Carolina at Chapel Hill, box 11.

with the city's Black youth.

While busy working at White Rock and North Carolina Mutual, Hill found time to join some of the clubs formed by the city's African-American elite and to serve on various boards of Black-owned businesses. He was a member of the Algonquin Tennis Club and The Volkamenia Literary Club. Hill also served as a board member of Mechanics and Farmers Bank. While on the board, he worked with John Wheeler to lobby for and win a USO club for Black GIs in Durham. The club was one of four USOs in Durham opened to serve soldiers stationed at the 30,000-person Camp Butner training and medical post near Durham. After World War II, the club was reorganized in Hill's memory as the W.D. Hill Community Center.[8] Hence, Hill was another White Rock member who interpreted his Christian faith by quietly serving the needs of the African-American community.

Dr. James Hubbard, Sr.: Another Exceptional Leader of White Rock's "Great Sunday School"

Dr. James Madison Hubbard, Sr., was born in Clinton, North Carolina, on November 26, 1892. An ambitious young man, he left home at the tender age of sixteen to enroll in the Joseph K.

Brick School, in Enfield, North Carolina. After graduating from the vocational program at Joseph K. Brick, Hubbard enrolled in the National Religious Training School and Chautauqua, in Durham, in 1912. He immediately established a friendship with the school's founder, Dr. James E. Shepard, which would last a lifetime.

James Hubbard, Courtesy of White Rock Baptist Church Archives, Durham, N.C.

While a student at Dr. Shepard's school, Hubbard attended White Rock Baptist Church but did not join. Instead, he soon left the city to assume a teaching position in Burgaw, North Carolina. After

---

[8] Ibid.

teaching for a short time, Hubbard resigned and enrolled in Howard University's School of Dentistry. After graduating from Dentistry School, in 1922, he returned to Durham to begin his dentistry practice. A year later, Dr. Hubbard married Ethel Grissell and decided to join White Rock Baptist Church, where his wife was already a member. He immediately became involved in a number of ministries and continued to faithfully serve the church for the next fifty years. He spent several years as a Sunday School teacher; he served during Dr. Aaron Moore's tenure as Sunday School Superintendent. In 1930, Dr. Hubbard became White Rock's Superintendent of Sunday School and remained in the position for twenty-one years, or virtually the entire time that Reverend Dr. Miles Mark Fisher was pastor. The Sunday School continued to thrive under his leadership. Dr. Hubbard also joined the church's Trustee Board and served as its assistant chair for several years.

Like William D. Hill, William Kennedy, Jr., First Lady Hattie Shepard, and a host of other White Rock members, Dr. Hubbard devoted a considerable amount of time and energy to ministries within the church but also found time to work in the African-American community. Like his friends at White Rock, he interpreted his Christian faith as being able to help serve members of his community. He was appointed to the North Carolina College for Negroes Board of Trustees, thereby becoming the second Black to serve on the prestigious Board. While serving on the Board, he was responsible for the inauguration of Founders Day at the College. He also spent eleven years serving as, first, Secretary of the Board of Trustees and, later, Vice Chairperson. Moreover, as chair of the College's Board of Trustee's Building Committee, Dr. Hubbard spearheaded implementation of plans for the schools most extensive physical expansion. To show its appreciation for Dr. Hubbard's work, North Carolina College for Negroes awarded him the degree of Doctor of Humanities and, afterwards, named the school's new James Madison Hubbard Chemistry Building in his honor. Among his other work with the college, Dr. Hubbard organized the James E. Shepard Memorial

Foundation, which helped many students to obtain a college education.[9] Like his good friend, William Kennedy, Jr., Dr. Hubbard was another Christian whose faith led him to use his energy and time to work not only in his church but also in his community so that he could improve the lives of others.

Sara "Cottie" Dancy Moore: A Leader in Religious and Civic Engagement

Sara "Cottie" Dancy Moore was born in 1866, a year after slavery ended in the United States. She was the sister of John C. Dancy, a nationally-known African Methodist Episcopal Zion churchman and Black Republican leader in the eastern part of North Carolina.[10] After graduating from the Tarboro Public School System and Saint Augustine's College, "Cottie" relocated to Durham, in 1889, where she met and married Dr. Aaron McDuffie Moore, the city's first Black physician. She then joined White Rock Baptist Church where her husband was a member.

Sarah "Cottie" Moore, Courtesy of White Rock Baptist Church Archives, Durham, N.C.

The mother of two daughters, Mattie and Lyda, Mrs. Moore found time to become actively involved in White Rock Baptist Church, the local Black community and the state Woman's Convention. For several years, she either chaired or worked with several church ministries, including teaching Sunday School on a regular basis, serving as a missionary with the Senior Missionary Society, and helping with Communion services.[11] A devout Christian and member of the Black elite, Mrs. Moore felt that she had a responsibility, based on her Biblical teachings, to help the less fortunate in the community. Therefore, she became a resource to her community, feeding the hungry and clothing those who needed such. When her husband's patients came to their home

---

[9]The information about Dr. James M. Hubbard, Sr., was an excerpt from his Obituary, dated February 15, 1972.

[10]Leslie Brown, *Upbuilding Black Durham*, 35.

[11]Reverend Dr. Miles Mark Fisher, *Friends*, 10.

for medical care, she, too, provided additional assistance that they may have needed. Furthermore, people in the community would often call on her for advice and counsel.[12]

Mrs. Moore also joined several clubs, which provided her with an opportunity to interact and socialize with other members of Durham's African-American elite. These clubs included the North Carolina Federation of Negro Women Clubs, the Daughters of Dorcas Club (formerly known as the Busy Women's Club), the Volkamenia Literary Club, and the Order of the Eastern Star. Her membership in the Order of the Eastern Star drew another set of important connections. As a member, she worked closely with Minnie Sumner Pearson, the wife of one of Durham's wealthiest African-American men, William Pearson; Hattie Shepard, the wife of Reverend Dr. James E. Shepard; and Mary Pauline Fitzgerald, the daughter of prominent businessman, Robert Fitzgerald.[13] These couples often joined "Cottie" and her husband in Black institutional building in the city.

She also helped to found the Negro Civic League that addressed issues of home ownership, better education and public health in the Black community. The League hosted several activities, including clean up days and health campaigns that focused on homes and neighborhood in the poverty-stricken areas of the city. Moreover, the League was one of the few organizations that consisted of African American and White women working together. As part of the League's work, "Cottie" was extremely interested in tackling the tuberculosis epidemic, which seemed to disproportionately affect Black families. Therefore, she appealed to Brodie Duke, the son of Washington Duke, for a tuberculosis hospital to be built on a site that she had secured. She was not

---

[12]John C. Dancy, *Sands against the Wind: The Memoirs of John C. Dancy* (Detroit, Michigan: Wayne State University Press, 1966), 70; Leslie Brown, *Upbuilding Black Durham*, 35.

[13]R. McCants Andrews, *John Merrick: A Biographical Sketch* (Durham, North Carolina: Seeman's Printery, 1920), 26; Albon Holsey, "Pearson—The Brown Duke of Durham," *Opportunity 6* (April 1928): 116-117; Walter Weare, *Black Business in the New South: A Social History of the North Carolina Mutual Life Insurance Company* (Urbana, Illinois: University of Illinois Press, 1972, 59.

successful; but, with financial contributions from the White women's civic league, Lincoln Hospital was able to add a wing for tuberculosis patients. The women who founded the Negro Civic League were indirectly thanked by the city's mayor for their work on helping to secure "and equip a tubercular annex," which he believed was a "blessing to the entire community."[14]

Finally, after Mrs. Moore's husband died, she assumed positions that he had held on numerous trustee boards of religious and civic institutions. She represented Dr. Moore extraordinarily well until her tenure officially ended.[15] A Christian woman and avid Bible reader, she, too, interpreted her Christian faith as that of helping those in need. And, Sarah "Cottie" Dancy Moore indeed did so.

James Rufus Evans: The Deacon, Trustee, Barber, Business Owner and Executive Who Quietly Worked for the Good of the Black Community

James Rufus Evans was born in 1865, the same year that the Civil War ended and the remaining twenty-five percent of slaves, who were not freed by the Emancipation Proclamation, gained their hard-fought freedom. Fifteen years later, he had earned a degree from Shaw University. After graduating from Shaw, Evans became a teacher. He also learned how to cut hair and eventually became one of the first African-American barbers in Durham.

Evans joined White Rock Baptist Church while a student at Shaw University. Not long after graduating from college, he met and married Effie Sellers and they had nine children; the five

---

[14]Jean Anderson, *Durham County: A History of Durham County, North Carolina* (Durham, North Carolina: Duke University Press and the Historic Preservation Society of Durham, 1990), 255; Glenda Gilmore, *Gender and Jim Crow: Women and the Politics of White Supremacy in North Carolina, 1896-1920* (Chapel Hill, North Carolina: University of North Carolina Press, 1996), 170-172; *Durham Morning Herald*, 5 February 1981; Leslie Brown, *Upbuilding Black Durham*, 162. The mayor specifically thanked the Durham Civic League, which was a White-only organization. Therefore, some people do not believe that he was really thanking the Black women.

[15]"Last Tribute to Mrs. Cottie S. Moore," *Whetstone*, n.d., ca. 1950, clipping, box 5, Charles C. Spaulding Papers, Rare Book, Manuscript, and Special Collections Library, Duke University, Durham, North Carolina.

daughters who survived infancy joined and grew up in White Rock.

Evans worked in many ministries while at the church. However, his longest tenure was serving as chair of the Deacon Board. His second oldest daughter, Ruby, served as the Church Secretary. While serving as chair of the Deacon Board, Mr. Evans also served on the Trustee Board.[16] Both of these positions kept him very busy at the church.

However, despite the amount of time and energy that he devoted to White Rock, Evans found time to work in the African-American community because he, too, interpreted his Christian faith as helping others. For instance, earlier in his career, he served as treasurer at North Carolina Mutual Life Insurance Company. Later, he became vice-president of Mechanics and Farmers Bank. Evans also served as president and manager of Community Damp Wash Laundry.[17] He was indeed a busy man—a Christian and great humanitarian. Despite the many roles that he held, Evans still had time for his church and his family.

James R. Evans, Courtesy of Janet Young-Peeler and White Rock Baptist Church Archives, Durham, N.C.

A Return to William Kennedy, Jr. and Margaret Spaulding Kennedy

The eight men and women described in this chapter were, in many ways, mirror images of William and Margaret Kennedy. They were Christian members of the upper- and middle- class in Durham, refined, cultured, and committed to racial uplift. They used their talents and skills to help those who could not help themselves. Like these men and women, William and Margaret Kennedy were also active members of White Rock Baptist Church,

---

[16]Reverend Dr. Miles Mark Fisher, *Friends*, 10.

[17]White Rock Baptist Church Records, 1880s-1930s, Southern Historical Collections, Manuscript Department, Wilson Library, University of North Carolina at Chapel Hill, box 7.

and held leadership positions in their communities and, if they worked, on their jobs.

Margaret Kennedy spent most of her time at White Rock involved in the Sunday School program. When the Sunday School was departmentalized, she became superintendent of departments, reporting to Dr. James Hubbard, the overall superintendent. She also assisted with the missionary circle and other ministries while raising small children.

Margaret Kennedy also joined several clubs, including the Volkemenia Literary Club, National Federation of Women's Clubs and the Order of Eastern Star. She was also quick to help others of her social circle who were engaged in racial uplift work.

William Kennedy, Jr., on the other hand, was also an active member of White Rock Baptist Church. He was a trustee and treasurer and, for more than fifty years, he taught the Aaron Moore Bible Class, which was renamed the Moore-Kennedy Bible Class, partly in his honor in 1975.[18] Yet, Mr. Kennedy still had time to work for the good of his race.

He was very active in the business and civic affairs of Durham for many years, but, he was humble and practiced restraint. As a consequence, many people were not aware of the many roles that he played in the community. Kennedy, for instance, served as chair of the Board of Mechanics and Farmers Bank and of the Mutual and Savings Loan Association while working as president of North Carolina Mutual Life Insurance Company. He served on the North Carolina State Board of Higher Education and the Selective Service Board of Durham County. Equally important, Kennedy founded the Durham branch of the National Association for the Advancement of Colored People.[19] Each of these positions allowed him to work to bring positive change in Durham's African-American community.

---

[18]William Jesse Kennedy, Jr. Papers, Southern Historical Collection, Manuscript Department, Wilson Library, University of North Carolina at Chapel Hill, box 5.

[19]Ibid.

In addition to serving on local and state levels, William Kennedy served as a member of the Board of Trustees for Howard University. He also served on the boards of the Boys Club of America, the James E. Shepard Foundation, the National Council of the United Negro College Fund and the Durham Business and Professional Chain, the latter being the minority counterpart to the Durham Chamber of Commerce.[20] Although Kennedy relinquished some of his positions on boards after he retired, he continued to tirelessly work for his church until his death.

Conclusion

The men and women highlighted in this chapter were some of the most faithful and active members of White Rock Baptist Church. They believed that their Christian faith required that they work for the good of the church and the community. As Christians, they had a responsibility, they believed, to help uplift the Black masses. And, that is precisely what they attempted to do each and every day.

---

[20]William Jesse Kennedy, Jr. Papers, Southern Historical Collection, Manuscript Department, Wilson Library, University of North Carolina at Chapel Hill, box 5.

Conclusion

"'For I know the plans that I have for you,' declares the Lord, 'plans to
prosper you and not to harm you, plans to give you hope and a future."
Jeremiah 29:11 (NIV)

When Margaret Faucette, Reverend Zuck Horton, Reverend Samuel "Daddy" Hunt, Melissa Lee, Gos Lee and other newly-freed slaves organized prayer meetings beneath brush arbors and in their crowded living quarters, they had no clue that their actions would eventually lead to an organized, structured house of worship. The church, inspired through prayer and built primarily around the Word of God was made significant through its members who interpreted their Christian faith by serving the African-American community's needs. White Rock Baptist Church, organized in 1866, in Durham, North Carolina, served as a context in which members, like Margaret Faucette, Minerva Womack, Tempie Whitted, J. M. Schooler, Rufus Evans, William Kennedy, Jr., Maude Logan, Dr. Aaron Moore, Susie Norfleet, Reverend Augustus Shepard, Reverend Zuck Horton, Reverend Dr. Edward Brawley, and Dr. Charles C. Spaulding, made plans to rebuild their lives as free men and women while they continued to be obedient to Jesus Christ. As a result of their work in Durham's first African-American church, a unique culture and community developed among Blacks.

As a Christian people, White Rock's pastors and members were not concerned only about their own lives but the lives of others, especially in the African-American community. Reverend Zuck Horton along with thirteen other preachers from across North Carolina began planning a convention as early as 1867 to help newly-freed African Americans organize Baptist churches, train Black preachers, and provide religious instruction for members of Black churches. They were barely educated themselves but, as Christian men, Reverend Horton and his colleagues believed that they were fulfilling their God-given purpose. Therefore, they allowed God to use them to build His Kingdom. As a consequence of their efforts and the divine connections that God provided, thousands of newly-freed men and women across the State became Christian disciples and glorified God through Kingdom building.

Over the next sixty years, these men and women joined with countless others to not only continue their work in church ministries but also engage in building a strong African-American community. They used their God-given talents to do so.

White Rock's members, for example, took the lead in developing grade schools for Black students in rural areas of the State. Dr. Aaron Moore, White Rock's superintendent of Sunday School was so instrumental in improving educational opportunities for African Americans in the state that he was given the title, "Father of the Rural School Movement for Negroes in North Carolina." He is an excellent example of a church member who allowed God to use his talents to help with building His Kingdom. Moore tirelessly worked to help take care of the less fortunate Blacks whether it was in the area of education or in medicine.

Even after White Rock's members became educated and amassed a considerable amount of wealth, they continued to demonstrate their Christian faith by reaching back and helping their less fortunate brothers and sisters. The insurance companies, banks, stores, pharmacies, hospitals, haberdasheries, mills, schools, colleges, clubs, associations, organizations, libraries, clothing stores, theaters, and mutual ad societies that they used their skills, talents and connections with the White community to build were for the entire African-American community. Their work in the various ministries and in the community, cloaked in Christian love, gave poorer African Americans hope at a time when they needed it most.

Many in White Rock also used their ministries to impart knowledge to African Americans about Jesus Christ and his goodness. They felt that it was equally important that all Blacks understood that God had a purpose for their lives. These men and women served as examples by using their God-given skills and talents to fulfill their purpose or destiny in life. They were often guided by Jeremiah 29:11, which states: "'I know the plans that I have for you,' declares the Lord, 'plans for welfare and not for calamity to give you a future and a hope.'" That, they genuinely believed, was God's promise for them and others.

These men and women also believed that God revealed His vision to them for the Black community. Therefore, they were obedient as they fulfilled God's purpose for their lives. In the end, not only were they blessed but so was White Rock Baptist Church and people in the Black community. Faucette and the others who followed her had emerged from slavery, many homeless and in poverty with no transferable skills for the growing industrial economy; yet, less than a generation later, these same men and women lived in a self-contained African-American community with many educational, political, economic, social and religious opportunities. Look at how God works!

There is a valuable lesson to be learned from this story. God wants each of us to live out our destiny and/or purpose in life. While living out one's destiny involves his or her family and church, it also involves helping others to live out their God-given purpose. That is what the many men and women in this book attempted to do each and every day.

They realized that their destiny was about much more than them. It also included others living out their destinies too. Therefore, living up to one's destiny is a God-given responsibility that includes one's talents, skills, passion, experiences and so much more. God links all of these together as His gift to each of us so that we may live our lives as a gift to Him and others.

Therefore, we all have a destiny and purpose in life. We must seize it and go forth. We must do as Jesus would want us to do. We must make a difference in the lives of others. Like the Faucettes, Goodloes, Logans, Evans, Spauldings, Moores, Hills, Shepards, Hortons, Hunts, Brawleys and countless other White Rock members, we must make a positive difference in the lives of others.

Bibliography

Primary Sources

Manuscript Collections

Chapel Hill, N.C. Southern Historical Collection, Wilson Library, University of North Carolina, Chapel Hill, N.C.
    White Rock Baptist Church Records, 1870s-1980s,
Durham, North Carolina. Rare Book Room, Manuscript and Special Collections Library,
    Duke University, Durham, N.C.
    Arthur Vance Cole Papers
    Asa and Elna Spaulding Papers
    Benjamin Newton Duke Papers
    Charles C. Spaulding Papers
    Charles N. Hunter Papers
    Washington Duke Papers
    William J. Kennedy, Jr. Papers
    William G. Pearson Papers
Durham, N.C. North Carolina Central University, University Archives, Records and   History Center, James E. Shepard Memorial Library.
    James E. Shepard Papers
    White Rock Baptist Church Papers
Durham, N.C. North Carolina Mutual Insurance Company Archives.
    North Carolina Mutual Life Insurance Company Papers
Raleigh, N.C. Historical Archives, Shaw University.
    Henry Tupper Papers
    Leonard Medical Center Papers
Washington, D.C. Library of Congress
    NAACP Papers

Interviews

Clement, Joseph. Interview by Kathryn Naastrom, 13 July and 3 August 1989, Chapel Hill, N.C.

Goodwin, Margaret. Interview by Leslie Brown, 22 December 1995, Transcript, Durham, N.C.

Fields, Minerva. Interview by Saundra Hartsfield, 17 November 2017, Durham, N.C.

Page, Mildred. Interview by Martha Lester-Harris, 17 November 2017, Durham, N.C.

Parker, Debra. Interview by A. Leanne Simon, 8 August 2013, _Upbuilding Whitted School_ Video, Durham, N.C.

Pearson, Conrad. Interview by Walter Weare, 18 April 1979, Transcript, in the Southern Oral History Program Collection, University of North Carolina, Chapel Hill, N.C.

Smith, Mary Hester. Interview by A. Leanne Simon, 8 August 2013, _Upbuilding Whitted School_ Video, Durham, N.C.

Welch, Eileen Watts. Interview by A. Leanne Simon, 8 August 2013, _Upbuilding Whitted School_ Video, Durham, N.C.

Newspapers

American Citizen
Durham _Herald_
Durham _Sun_
Chicago _Broadax_
Indianapolis _Freeman_
Seattle Republican

Secondary Sources

Bible

1 Corinthians 5, New International Version
2 Corinthians, New International Version
Ephesians 6: 5, 9, New International Version
Ephesians 6:6, International standard Version
Exodus 3, New International Version
Ezekiel 18:4, English Standard Version
Galatians 3: 26-29, New International Version
James 1:22, New International Version
1 John 3:17, King James Version

Mark 16: 15, English Standard Version
Matthew 18:10, King James Version
Proverbs 18:15, King James Version
Romans 5:15, 20-21, King James Version
Romans 12: 4-5, New American Standard Bible
2 Thessalonians 3:10, English Standard Version
Titus 3:9, King James Version

Books

Anderson, Jean. *Durham County: A History of Durham County, North Carolina.* Durham, North Carolina: Duke University Press, 1990.

Andrews, R. McCants. *John Merrick: A Biographical Sketch.* Durham, North Carolina: Seeman's Printery, 1920.

Ballard, Allen. *One More Day's Journey: The Story of a Family and a People.* New York, New York: McGraw-Hill, 1984.

Bibb, Henry. *Narrative of the Life and Adventures of Henry Bibb, An American Slave.* North Charleston, South Carolina: CreateSpace Independent Publishing Platform, 1849.

Blackwell, Joyce. *No Peace Without Freedom: Race and the Women's International League for Peace and Freedom, 1915-1975.* Carbondale, Illinois: Southern Illinois University Press, 2004.

Boyd, William. *The Story of Durham: City of the New South.* Durham, North Carolina: Duke University Press, 1925.

Broderick, Francis. *W.E.B. DuBois: Negro Leader in a Time of Crisis.* Palo Alto, California: Stanford University Press, 1959.

Brown, Leslie. *Upbuilding Black Durham: Gender, Class and Black Community Development in the Jim Crow South.* Chapel Hill, North Carolina: University of North Carolina Press, 2008.

Caldwell, Arthur, ed. *History of the American Negro.* Atlanta, Georgia: A.B. Caldwell Publishing Company, 1921.

Cone, James. *For My People.* New York, New York: Orbis Press, 1984.

Crow, Jeffrey, Escott Paul, and Hatley, Flora. *A History of African Americans in North Carolina.* Raleigh, North Carolina: North Carolina Department of Cultural Resources, 2002.

Culp, Daniel. *Twentieth Century Negro Literature: Or a Cyclopedia of Thought on the Vital Topics Relating to the American Negro.* Atlanta, Georgia: J.L. Nichols and Company, 1902.

Dancy, John. Sands Against the Wind: The Memoirs of John C. Dancy. Detroit, Michigan: Wayne State University Press, 1966.

Daniels, Jonathan. *Tar Heels: A Portrait of North Carolina.* New York, New York: Dodd, Mead and Company, 1947.

Davis, Lenwood. *Selected Writings and Speeches of James E. Shepard, 1896-1946: Founder of North Carolina Central University.* Madison, Wisconsin: Fairleigh Dickerson University Press, 2013.

DuBois, W.E.B., ed. *Morals and Manners Among Negro Americans.* Atlanta, Georgia: Atlanta University Press, 1914.

Fallin, Wilson. *Uplifting the People: Three Centuries of Black Baptists in Alabama.* Tuscaloosa, Alabama: University of Alabama Press, 2007.

Felder, Cain. *Stony the Road We Trod: African American Biblical Interpretation.* Minneapolis, Minnesota: Fortress Press, 1991.

_____. *Troubling Biblical Waters: Race, Class and Family.* Maryknoll, New York: Orbis Books, 1990.

Fisher, Miles Mark. *Friends: Pictorial Report of Ten Years Pastorate, 1933-1943.* Durham, North Carolina: Service Printing Company, 1943.

Fisher, Miles Mark. *Negro Slave Songs in the United States.* Ithaca, New York: Cornell University Press, 1953.

Franklin, John Hope and Moss, Jr., Alfred. *From Slavery to Freedom: A History of African Americans.* New York, New York: McGraw Hill, 2010.

Franklin, John Hope and Meier, August, eds. *Black Leaders of the Twentieth Century.* Champaign, Illinois: University of Illinois Press, 1982.

Frazier, E. Franklin. *The Negro Church in America.* New York, New York: Shocken Books, 1974.

Gaines, Kevin. *Uplifting the Race: Black Leadership, Politics, and Culture During the Twentieth Century.* Chapel Hill, North Carolina: University of North Carolina Press, 1996.

Gates, Henry Louis and Higginbotham, Evelyn. *African American Lives.* New York, New York: Oxford University Press, 2004.

Gilmore, Glenda. *Gender and Jim Crow: Women and the Politics of White Supremacy in North Carolina, 1896-1920.* Chapel Hill, North Carolina: University of North Carolina Press, 1996.

Greeley, Horace. *The American Conflict: A History of the Great Rebellion in the United States of America, 1860-1864.* Chicago, Illinois: O.D. Case and Company, 1866.

Grimshaw, William. *Official History of Freemasonry among Colored People in North America.* New York, New York: Broadway Publishing Company, 1902.

Harding, Vincent. *The Other American Revolution.* Los Angeles, California: University of California Press, 1980.

Harlan, Louis, Smock, Raymond and McTigue, Geraldine, eds. *The Booker T. Washington Papers, Volume II.* Chicago, Illinois: University of Illinois Press, 1981.

Higginbotham, Evelyn Brooks. *Righteous Discontent: The Women's*

Movement in the African American Baptist Church, 1880-1920. Cambridge, Massachusetts: Harvard University Press, 1993.

Hill, Ruth., ed. *The Black Woman Oral History Project.* Berlin, Germany: Walter de Gruyter, 2013.

Hine, Darlene. *African American Women in White: Racial Conflict and Cooperation in the Nursing Profession, 1890-1950.* Bloomington, Indiana: Indiana University Press, 1989.

Hoffschwelle, Mary. *Preserving Rosenwald Schools.* Washington, D.C.: National Trust for Historic Preservation, 2003.

Johnson, Guion. *Antebellum North Carolina: A Social History.* Chapel Hill, North Carolina: University of North Carolina Press, 1937.

Johnson, F. Roy. *The Nat Turner Slave Insurrection.* Mufreesboro, North Carolina: Johnson Publishing Company, 1966.

Jones, Beverly. *Stanford L. Warren, 77 Years of Public Service: A Phoenix in the Durham Community.* Durham, North Carolina: Durham County Library, 1970.

_____. *Quest for Equality: The Life and Writings of Mary Eliza Church Terrell, 1863- 1954.* Brooklyn, New York: Carlson Publishing, 1990.

Kealey, John and Shenk, David. *The Early Church and Africa.* New York, New York: Oxford University Press, 1975.

Kennedy, Jr., William. *The North Carolina Mutual Story: A Symbol of Progress, 1898-1970.* Durham, North Carolina: North Carolina Mutual Life Insurance Company, 1973.

Kluger, Richard. *Simple Justice: The History of Brown vs. Board of Education and the Black American Struggle for Equality.* New York, New York: Random House, 1975.

Leiter, Andrew and Smith, Natalia. *Colored Orphan Asylum of North Carolina.* Oxford, North Carolina: Public Ledger Print, 1900.

Leyburn, James. *The Way We Lived: Durham, 1900-1920.* Ellingston, Virginia: Northcross House Publishers, 1989.

Logan, Rayford. *The Betrayal of the Negro: From Rutherford B. Hayes to Woodrow Wilson.* Cambridge, Massachusetts: DeCapo Press, 1997.

Logan, Shirley. *We are Coming: The Persuasive Discourse of Nineteenth-Century Black Women.* Carbondale, Illinois: Southern Illinois University Press, 1999.

Mbiti, John. *African Religions and Philosophy.* London, United Kingdom of Great Britain: Heinemann Publishers, 1969.

McLester, Johnnie. *A Brief History of the Women's Auxiliary to the Lott-Carey Baptist Foreign Mission Convention,* Place of Publication Unknown: Publishing Company Unknown.

McPherson, James. *Battle Cry of Freedom: The Civil War Era.* Oxford, United Kingdom of Great Britain: Oxford University Press, 1988.

Montgomery, William. *Under Their Own Vine and Fig Tree: The African-American Church in the South, 1865-1900.* Baton Rouge, Louisiana: Louisiana State University Press, 1995.

Morgan, Philip. *Slave Counterpoint: African American Culture in the Eighteenth-Century Chesapeake and Lowcountry.* Chapel Hill, North Carolina: University of North Carolina Press, 1998.

Moyd, Olin. *Redemption in Black Theology.* Valley Forge, Pennsylvania: Judson Press, 1979.

Muraskin, William. *Middle Class Blacks in a White Society: Prince Hall Masonry in America.* Berkeley, California: University of California Press, 1975.

Murray, Pauli. *Proud Shoes.* New York, New York: Harper and Brothers, 1956.

Prather, Sr., H. Leon. *Resurgent Politics and Educational Progressivism in the South: North Carolina, 1890-1913.* Rutherford, New Jersey: Fairleigh Dickinson University Press, 1997.

Rabinowitz, Howard, ed. *Southern Black Leaders of the Reconstruction Era.* Champaign, Illinois: University of Illinois Press, 1982.

Reid, Ira. *The Urban Negro Worker in the United States, 1925-1936.* New York, New York: Alexander Press, 1930.

Sears, Stephen. *Landscape Turned Red: The Battle of Antietam.* New York, New York: Houghton Mifflin Company, 2003.

Shaw, Arnold. *"Honkers and Shouters": The Golden Years of Rhythm and Blues.* New York, New York: Crowell-Collier Press, 1978.

Simmons, Martha. *Preaching with Sacred Fire: An Anthology of African-American Sermons, 1750 to the Present.* New York, New York: W.W. Norton and Company, 2010.

Simmons, William and Turner, Henry. *Men of Mark: Eminent, Progressive and Rising.* Cleveland, Ohio: G.M. Rewell and Company, 1887.

Smith, Jessie. *Black First: 2000 Years of Extraordinary Achievements.* Detroit, Michigan: Visible Link, 1994.

Smith, Timothy. *Revivalism and Social Reform: American Protestantism on the Eve of the Civil War.* Eugene, Oregon: WIPF and Stock Publishers, 2004.

Starks, Glenn. *Historically Black Colleges and Universities: An Encyclopedia.* Santa Barbara, California: ABC-CLIO, 2011.

Taylor, Marian. *Harriet Tubman: Antislavery Activist.* Langhorne, Pennsylvania: Chelsea House Publishers, 2004.

Thompson, Douglas. *Richmond's Priests and Prophets: Race, Religion and Social Change in the Civil Rights Era.* Tuscaloosa, Alabama: The University of Alabama Press, 2017.

Vann, Andre. *African Americans of Durham County.* Charleston, South Carolina: Arcadia Publishing, Inc., 2017.

Vann, Andre and Jones, Beverly. *Durham's Hayti: An African American*

History. Charleston, South Carolina: Arcadia Press, 1998.

Washington, Booker T. *Up From Slavery: An Autobiography.* Garden City, New York: Doubleday and Company, Inc., 1901.

Washington, Joseph. *Black Religion: The Negro and Christianity in the United States.* Boston, Massachusetts: Beacon Press, 1964.

Weare, Walter. *Black Businesses in the New South: A Social History of the North Carolina Mutual Life Insurance Company.* Durham, North Carolina: Duke University Press, 1993.

Wesley, Charles. *History of the National Association of Colored Women's Clubs: A Legacy of Service.* Washington, D.C.: National Association of Colored Women's Clubs, 1984.

Whitted, J.A., *Biographical Sketch of the Life and Work of the Late Reverend Augustus Shepard, D.D.* Raleigh, North Carolina: Edwards and Broughton Printing Company, 1912.

_____. *History of Negro Baptists in North Carolina.* Raleigh, North Carolina: Presses of Edwards and Broughton Printing Company, 1908.

Williams, Loretta. *Black Freemasonry and Middle-Class Realities.* Columbia, Missouri: University of Missouri Press, 1980.

Williams, M.W. and Watkins, George. *Who's Who Among North Carolina Negro Baptists: With a Brief History of Negro Baptist Associations.* Place of Publication Unknown: Publishing Company Unknown, 1940.

Wilmore, Gayraud and Cone, James. *Black Theology: A Documentary History, 1966-1979.* New York, New York: Orbis Press, 1979.

Wise, Jim. *Durham: A Bull City Story.* Charleston, South Carolina: Arcadia Publishing, 2002.

_____. *Durham Tales: The Morris Street Maple, the Plastic Cow, the Durham Day That Was and More.* Charleston, South Carolina: The History Press, 2008.

Woloch, Nancy. *Women and the American Experience.* New York, New York: The McGraw-Hill Companies, Inc., 2002.

Wood, E.M. *The Negro in Etiquette: A Novelty.* St. Louis, Missouri: Baxton and Skinner, 1899.

Articles

Author Unknown. "Race Riots his Theme." *Evening Star Newspaper,* 20 October 1899, 16.

Bihm, Jennifer. "Business in African American History: North Carolina Mutual Life Insurance Company." *Los Angeles Sentinel* (February 6, 2014): 2-5.

Broder, David. "Jesse Helms, White Racist. *Washington Post* (July 7,

2008): 1.

Brooks, Walter. "The Evolution of the Negro Baptist Church." *Journal of Negro History* 7 (1922): 51-55.

DuBois, W.E.B. "The Upholding of Black Durham." *World's Work* XIII (January 1912): 334-338.

Eagles, Charles. "James Edward Shepard." *Dictionary of North Carolina Biography*, ed. By William Powell (Chapel Hill, N.C.: University of North Carolina Press, 1994.

Fleming, John. "Black Theology." *The Black Christian Experience*, ed. Emmanuel McCall (Nashville, Tennessee: Broadman Press, 1972.

Harper, Matthew. "The End of Days: African American Religion and Politics in the Age of Emancipation." *North Carolina Historical Review* (April 2003), Volume 80, No. 2.

Holsey, Albon. "Pearson—The Brown Duke of Durham." *Opportunity* 6 (April 1928): 116-122.

Jackson, Wayne. "A Troubled Church." *Christian Courier* (November 11, 2011): 13-15.

Lougee, George. "Merchant Almost Reached His Goal—100th Birthday." *Durham Morning Herald,* 30 January 1977, 5.

Mitchell, Louis. "Aron McDuffie Moore: He Led His Sheep." *Crisis Magazine* 81, 7 (August/September 1980): 251-253.

Terrell, Robert. "Judge Terrell." *The Crisis: A Record of the darker Races* (June 1918): 66-76.

Vaughan, Dawn. "He Co-founded N.C. Mutual and a Library in the Jim Crow South. Now a Biography is in the Works." *The Herald Sun,* 12 June 2017.

Washington, Booker T. "Durham, North Carolina: A City of Negro Enterprises." In the
_____. *Booker T. Washington Papers* 2, by Louis Harlan and Raymond Smock, eds., 56-64. Urban, Illinois: University of Illinois Press, 1981.

Williams, Fannie Barrier. "The Club Movement Among Negro Women." In the *Colored American, from Slavery to Honorable Citizenship* (Atlanta, Georgia: Hertel, Jenkins and Company, 1905), eds., J.W. Gibson, Booker T. Washington and W. H. Crogman.

Work, Monroe. "The Negro Church in the Negro Community." *Southern Workman* XXXVII (August 1908): 428-433.

Booklets, Programs, Reports

Bryant, Kelly. "A Historical Sketch of White Rock, September 7, 1999.
"Colored Orphan Asylum of North Carolina," Oxford, N.C., Pamphlet, 1900.

Faucette Family Reunion Program Booklet, July 11-13, 2008.

Fields, Minerva. Notes. November 6, 2017.

James Hubbard, Sr. Obituary, February 15, 1972.

Lipscomb, Gazella and Bryant, R.K., Jr. "A Directory of White Rock Baptist Church and Its Members." Looseleaf Handout, September 7, 1999.

"Report to the Board of Directors of the Colored Orphanage of North Carolina," 1963.

Shaw University Bulletin, Diamond Jubilee Souvenir, Raleigh, N.C., 1940

Smith, Natalia. "Colored Orphan Asylum." Pamphlet, 1909

Correspondence

Coles, Arthur Van to Charles D. Wildes, 31 May 1935, Transcript in the Arthur Vance Cole Papers.

Helms, Jesse Honorable to Dr. George Reich, 19 July 1978, Transcript in the Asa and Elna Spaulding Papers.

Helms, Jesse Honorable to Elna Spaulding, 8, August 1978, Transcript in the Asa and ElnaSpaulding Papers.

Spaulding, Charles C., to Booker T. Washington, 18 November 1910, Transcript in the Booker T. Washington Papers.

Van Vleet, Norma to Elna Spaulding, 5 July 1978, Transcript, Asa and Elna Spaulding Papers.

Thesis

Blackwell, Joyce. "The Control of Blacks in North Carolina, 1829-1840." M.A. Thesis, North Carolina Central University, 1977.

Seay, Irene. "A History of North Carolina for Negroes." M.A. Thesis, Duke University, 1941.

Trent, William, Jr. "Development of Negro Life Insurance Enterprises." M.A. Thesis, University of Pennsylvania, 1932.

Index

A

Abraham Lincoln, 29, 30, 205
Algonquin Tennis Club, 244, 255
Allen Goodloe, 4, 127, 213, 237
Alpha Kappa Alpha, 251
American Baptist Home Mission
    Society, ix, 70, 73, 78
American Baptist Publication
Society, ix, 56, 57, 75, 77
Ampix Photography, 182
Anna Jeanes, 4, 131
Annie Day Shepard, 4, 97, 140, 249
Antebellum, 7, 8, 14, 15, 17, 20, 29,
    67, 125
Asa T. Spaulding, 198

B

B.N. Duke, 185
Baptist Educational and Missionary
    Society, ix
Baptist State Sunday School
    Convention, ix, 134
Baraca Class, 53
Bennett College, 104
Bible, 6, 7, 8, 10, 14, 16, 17, 18, 20,
34, 36, 39, 50, 53, 59, 64, 67, 68, 69,
    74, 83, 90, 91, 93, 104, 123, 134,
    148, 150, 152, 175, 188, 224, 243,
    249, 251, 260, 262, 270, 271
Black aristocracy, 253
Black Codes, 34
Black rural schools, 137
Black Sunday School Movement,
    75, 78

C

Chamberlain Studio, 182
Charles C. Spaulding, 4, 103, 118,
    119, 172, 175, 176, 216, 220, 237,
    248, 249, 260, 266, 269
Charles Stanback, 183
Child Advocacy Commission, ix,
    197, 198, 199
Child Advocacy Commission of
    Durham, 198, 199
Christian education, 123, 130, 141,
    149
Christian virtues, 209, 234
City of Negro Enterprise, 174, 175
Civil War, 8, 11, 15, 17, 30, 31, 32,
36, 41, 55, 65, 67, 70, 83, 100, 127,
    128, 150, 161, 179, 185, 190, 194,
    201, 202, 204, 205, 206, 207, 208,
    212, 230, 234, 253, 260, 274, 275
Colored Baptist Orphan
    Association of North Carolina,
    104, 105
Colored Knights of Pythias, 244
Colportage, 75
Conrad Pearson, 216, 217, 219, 221,
    226
Cornelius Jordan, 42
Cottie Dancy Moore, 82, 94, 96, 123,
    163, 164, 237, 241, 246, 250, 257,
    258, 259, 260

D

David Walker, 22